Virtual and Collaborative Teams:
Process, Technologies and Practice

Susan H. Godar
William Paterson University, USA

Sharmila Pixy Ferris
William Paterson University, USA

IDEA GROUP PUBLISHING
Hershey • London • Melbourne • Singapore

Acquisitions Editor: Mehdi Khosrow-Pour
Senior Managing Editor: Jan Travers
Managing Editor: Amanda Appicello
Development Editor: Michele Rossi
Copy Editor: Lori Eby
Typesetter: Sara Reed
Cover Design: Lisa Tosheff
Printed at: Yurchak Printing Inc.

Published in the United States of America by
        Idea Group Publishing (an imprint of Idea Group Inc.)
        701 E. Chocolate Avenue, Suite 200
        Hershey PA 17033
        Tel: 717-533-8845
        Fax: 717-533-8661
        E-mail: cust@idea-group.com
        Web site: http://www.idea-group.com

and in the United Kingdom by
        Idea Group Publishing (an imprint of Idea Group Inc.)
        3 Henrietta Street
        Covent Garden
        London WC2E 8LU
        Tel: 44 20 7240 0856
        Fax: 44 20 7379 3313
        Web site: http://www.eurospan.co.uk

Library of Congress Cataloging-in-Publication Data

Virtual and collaborative teams : process, technologies, and practice /
Susan Godar, editor, Sharmila Pixy Ferris, editor.
        p. cm.
Includes bibliographical references.
  ISBN 1-59140-204-2 (hardcover) -- ISBN 1-59140-268-9 (pbk.) -- ISBN
1-59140-205-0 (ebook)
  1. Virtual work teams. 2. Teams in the workplace--Computer networks.
3. Communication in organizations. I. Godar, Susan, 1948- II. Ferris,
Sharmila Pixy.
  HD66.V555 2004
  658.4'036--dc22
                        2003022607

British Cataloguing in Publication Data
A Cataloguing in Publication record for this book is available from the British Library.

All work contributed to this book is new, previously-unpublished material. The views
expressed in this book are those of the authors, but not necessarily of the publisher.

Virtual and Collaborative Teams:
Process, Technologies and Practice

Table of Contents

Preface

Teams are integral elements in today's corporate and industrial worlds, considered by some to be the fundamental units of organizations, and technology has become essential to teamwork. In fact, technology enabled the creation of a new type of work team: virtual teams. These are proliferating exponentially. Organizations assemble and support them for a variety of activities, such as new product development, knowledge sharing, and education. The advantages of such teams are obvious: people no longer must work in the same physical location to work "together"; participants can contribute from any part of the world, at any time of the day (or night). By breaking down the barriers of space and time, a virtual team fully utilizes the expertise of the members of an organization—or of several organizations—without pulling them from other projects or incurring relocation expenses. Hence, at least notionally, such teams have immense potential for improving organizational effectiveness.

This book began as a cross-disciplinary conversation about whether, why, and how virtual teams either do or do not fulfill that potential. As organizations implement more virtual teams, it becomes increasingly important to know how best to structure and manage such teams. There are, of course, research-based strategies for managing traditional work groups, and over two decades of research on the benefits and perils of computer- or technology-mediated communication on individuals. We suspected that the compounding of these two elements—working in a group and using primarily or exclusively technology to do that work—would engender new challenges for participants as well as for those who manage virtual teams.

That suspicion led us to ask academics in a number of disciplines to explore the functioning of virtual teams. The result is this book, in which researchers in Business, Communications, Psychology, Sociology, and Information Technology highlight some of the challenges for virtual teams and offer research-based recommendations to maximize their effectiveness. We believe that managers who want to use virtual teams more effectively will find the book useful, and the research articles will also interest academics, as they continue investigating these teams.

DEFINING VIRTUAL TEAMS

We use the term *team* in this book in the commonly accepted sense. That is, the term refers to a collection of four to 12 individuals collaboratively working on a common and interdependent task or goal. The goal is often one requiring a decision or a solution to some problem. The elements of common tasks/goals and interdependence are integral to our definition of a team, at least in respect to an imposed need to arrive at a collective position on a matter under consideration. In addition, the teams we discuss here are distinguished by one additional factor: the dimension of virtuality.

A group of organizationally or geographically dispersed workers brought together to work on a common project through communication and information technologies is a virtual team (Townsend, DeMarie, & Hendrickson, 1998). Such a team conducts all or most of its interactions via electronic means (Grosse, 2002). It holds few, if any, face-to-face (F2F) meetings, because its members are not proximate in physical space. In fact, the team members may be widely geographically dispersed—in different countries or on different continents. They may be members of different organizations, brought together due to their expertise or interests, to find a common solution to a problem.

Virtual teams, then, are teams that meet either partially or exclusively in techno-space. Initially, their team meetings would have been conducted exclusively via communication both *to* and *through* a mainframe computer, primarily through e-mail, the Internet, and groupware. Increasingly, however, computer technology is supplemented by telecommunication: cell phones and videophones.

Technology and virtuality arguably change work groups in three important ways: they introduce new dimensions of communication among members by breaking down traditional barriers of space and time; they modify traditional group processes; and they enormously enhance the group's capacity to access, share, manipulate, retrieve, and store information. While there is a substantial amount of research findings on each of these three effects of technology, the preponderance of it focused on individuals rather than on groups. Over two decades of research has found, for example, that technologically mediated or computer-mediated communication between individuals promotes equality and flexibility of roles but is less "rich" than traditional F2F communication and often leads to feelings of isolation and de-individuation (see, for example, Kraut et al., 1998). This and other research on individuals can certainly contribute to our understanding of teams. Yet, as the chapters in this book show, more deliberate and focused research into virtual teams uncovers information of use to academics and to managers.

ORGANIZATION OF THE BOOK

This book is organized into four sections and has 15 chapters. A brief description of each section and chapter follows.

Section I: Make-Up of Virtual Teams

In these chapters, various ways that a virtual team can exist, and issues around how teams should be composed are discussed.

Chapter 1: Within virtual teams, according to "Virtual Teams as Sociotechnical Systems," by Cuevas, Fiore, Salas, and Bowers, there is much ambiguity and artificiality, a concept that they call "team opacity." Because the team members are in an environment of an increased level of abstraction due to their technology-mediated communication, and because of the influence of the external environment on their work, they run the risk of having lower cohesion and trust than in teams who communicate F2F. Building on the organizational psychology literature, the authors advance relevant ideas for managers to consider when creating a virtual team. While other researchers focused on in-process interventions to keep a virtual team functioning at a high level, this article adds to the literature by suggesting pre- and postprocess interventions that an organization could utilize to get the most out of the virtual team process.

Chapter 2: Unlike traditional teams, virtual teams often do not have stability, regular interaction, and team member proximity. Rather, they exist primarily in the minds of the members and the organizations that support them. In "Effective Virtual Teamwork: A Sociocognitive and Motivational Model," Kyriakidou and Millward offer insights gleaned from interviews with 40 team-building experts and two focus groups on the creation of intelligent virtual teams. These intelligent teams share common goals, manage their own processes, and self-regulate. By actively engineering and managing team focus and team competence, the team leader will create a more effective group. According to their research, it is important for teams to keep a shared mental model of their potency, and of the fact that they are really a team.

Chapter 3: Who should an organization put on virtual teams? Is it better to have complementary expertise or to have people who will interact well? Potter and Balthazard explain, in their chapter "Understanding Composition and Conflict in Virtual Teams," that it is much better to have good interaction styles if the organization wants a high-level performing team. Based on multiple studies, they contend that a constructive communication style is critical to team success. In particular, a team should have some extroverts to spur conversation, but having too many will lead other team members to be passive. In addition, the authors offer a discussion of the diagnostic tools that practitioners can use to identify the communication styles of potential team members, and interventions that can be undertaken if the team does not appear to be living up to its potential.

Section II: Leading Virtual Teams

The chapters in this section cover leadership issues for teams.

Chapter 4: Based on their interviews with 21 leaders of global teams from a variety of industries, Connaughton and Daly advanced propositions on how successful team leaders approach the challenges of virtual teams in their article "Leading from Afar: Strategies for Effectively Leading Virtual Teams." In this informative chapter, they discuss the importance of the leader's communication skills, cultural nuances, media choice, and the leader's awareness of the challenges. As more organizations adopt virtual teams, it is critical that they understand and adopt the strategies that will work and avoid the ones that will not. With its effective interweaving of "tales from the trenches" with theory building, the information in this chapter will help the reader identify a number of successful and ineffective strategies. The cautionary tales of strategies that did not work will be useful to virtual team leaders.

Chapter 5: Interviewing 39 participants from six teams in three industries allowed Staples and Cameron to test the factors and processes affecting attitudinal outcome variables in their chapter, "Creating Positive Attitudes in Virtual Team Members." One of their interesting findings was that "team spirit" can exist in virtual teams, as it does in F2F teams. By setting aside specific blocks within a team's interaction times for social chitchat, managers may find that team members are more satisfied with the team and with their jobs, and have more motivation and organizational commitment. When viewed in light of prior studies on team effectiveness, the support of this type of attitudinal outcome is productive for the team and for the organization. The results of this study add to our understanding of how to make teams more effective.

Chapter 6: In their chapter, "Trust in Virtual Teams," Bradley and Vozikis contend that virtual team members rely heavily on their prior experiences in setting their expectations for trust within their team context. As they point out, the socialization process that occurs in F2F teams is not usually available to virtual teams. Most members of a virtual group, however, start with the belief that they will be able to trust the other members. Because trust is an important foundation for the success of teams and because the swift trust necessary for virtual interactions is fragile, they contend that it is imperative that each team have a designated leader from the start. Without such a facilitator, a self-organized group may soon deteriorate, as the expectations of the group members are not met. By setting the norms of behavior within a virtual team, a good facilitator can keep the level of trust high. As managers establish these teams, they should be aware of the importance of a good facilitator.

Section III: Communication in Virtual Teams

In this section, the chapter topics range from the socialization of new team members to the types of technologies that can be used by virtual teams.

Chapter 7: When a person joins a new organization, he or she goes through a socialization process, learning about the norms, tasks, and roles in the group. As Picherit-Duthler, Long, and Kohut point out in their chapter "Newcomer Assimilation in Virtual Team Socialization," computer-mediated communication changes the manner in which a new person becomes a real member of the group. After reviewing the literature from communications and management perspectives, this cross-disciplinary team of researchers offers interesting insights for supervisors of virtual teams. One of those insights is that supervisors should not try to manage teams, but rather should act as facilitators of the team. Encouraging "small talk" among members achieves better assimilation and, thus, better outcomes for the group.

Chapter 8: Emphasizing the importance of "small talk" in the creation of teams is the basis of the chapter "Negotiating Meaning in Virtual Teams: Context, Roles, and Computer-Mediated Communication in College Classrooms," by Crider and Ganesh. The authors analyzed the conversation streams across student teams with members from three universities (two in the United States and one in the Philippines), working on a common project. Based on this research, they were able to identify the conversational themes that led to a shared group identity and performance on task. Using typical conversation topics like movies, music, etc., the students were able to develop a shared context in which to work. While this chapter is based on students, the lessons learned are also important to team leaders in other organizational settings: for people to work together, they must exchange information through informal communication so that they can develop a shared work context.

Chapter 9: The focus of much research on virtual teams looked at how to manage members of a team, where the members are physically located away from the organization. In this interesting chapter by Leonardi, Jackson, and Marsh, the reverse is explored: how the virtual team member can manage the distance. In "The Strategic Use of 'Distance' Among Virtual Team Members: A Multidimensional Communication Model," the authors suggest that team members will sometimes manipulate the fact that they are located at a distance to meet their individual needs. Lengthy interviews were conducted with 46 virtual team participants in a variety of industries, and the results are presented here. The authors found that distance is not perceived in the same way by all participants. By looking at the impact of distance on worker's emotions, identity, and communication strategies, this research team adds a new dimension to the study of virtual teams.

Chapter 10: Face-to-face (F2F) meetings may also occur between team members on teams that operate in a virtual environment. Some managers believe that they are critical to the success of projects and are willing to invest significant amounts of travel money to facilitate them. Johnson's chapter, "How Hard Can It Be to Communicate? Communication Mode and Performance in Collaborative R&D Projects," may give those managers cause to rethink that belief. Based on an analysis of 25 projects sponsored by a consortium funding technology research, the author found that hard modes of communication work equally well, if not better, when the innovation is incremental, and the goals are clear. Only when the innovation is radical and the goals are not agreed upon are soft modes of communication, like F2F meetings, necessary. This finding should be useful to managers, as they evaluate the best allocations of project funds.

Chapter 11: A wide variety of software and technology aids is discussed in the bibliographic essay, "Technology and Virtual Teams," by Ferris and Minielli. Group support systems such as asynchronous and synchronous messaging systems, data management technologies, and proprietary groupware packages are covered. A brief discussion of technologies used as course management systems in education is also found here. To provide assistance to managers interested in exploring the use of this technology, the URLs for the software products highlighted in the chapter are included.

Section IV: Effective Uses of Virtual Teams

In this final section of the book, ways in which teams may be used and ways to measure their effectiveness are given.

Chapter 12: How can teams use creative techniques to improve their performance? Gascó-Hernández and Torres-Coronas outline some helpful ideas in their chapter "Virtual Teams and their Search for Creativity." These authors identify techniques that are particularly suitable for a virtual environment. Their recommendations for divergent techniques—ones that generate a number of ideas—are electronic brainwriting, synectics, and attribute listing. They then consider the pros and cons of each in a virtual setting. According to them, convergent techniques—ones that select the best idea for further study—need more work to improve their utility for a virtual environment due to their time-consuming nature. Provided in this chapter are good ideas for fostering creativity, and highlighted are some areas in which more work should be done by researchers interested in virtual group creativity.

Chapter 13: In their chapter, "Virtual Teams in an Executive Education Training Program," Reeves and Furst tell of their work with teams from two industries, as those teams worked on projects and learned how to function as teams. While the teams had different characteristics, they had a common genesis: their organizations identified the respective team members as having potential for promotion. But, the ways in which the teams were set up, the tasks that the teams were given, and the support they received from top management led to different outcomes. In addition to offering substantial insights into how top management can help a team perform better, this interesting chapter highlights some things that management should not do in setting up teams, unless they want to set up the team for failure.

Chapter 14: Unlike other chapters in this book, which presume that people are placed on virtual teams to accomplish some organizationally defined goal, this one considers voluntary group membership. It answers the question: why do people join virtual groups and then become a "community"? This question is particularly significant for marketers, because, as Dholakia and Bagozzi point out in "Motivational Antecedents, Constituents, and Consequents of Virtual Community Identity," group members often look to one another for information in buying situations. By identifying the salient characteristics of a virtual group and motives for membership in a group that cause participants to identify more strongly with the group, these authors offer advice of particular interest and use to marketers seeking to organize a virtual group of customers who would then influence other purchasers.

Chapter 15: In "A Model for the Analysis of Virtual Teams," Andriessen and Verburg adapted Andriessen's Dynamic Group Interaction (DGIn) model to the new team environment. Their important contribution is the reminder that teams will vary by degree of "virtuality." All virtual teams are not created equal: they may differ greatly on dimensions of geographic distribution, time frame for the work, and organizational or cultural constraints. They contend that team-building exercises, training in cultural diversity, structuring of communication, and use of groupware tools must be adjusted for these varying levels of virtualness. The information in this chapter serves as a reminder to managers and to researchers that they must be cognizant of such differences as they assemble and research such teams.

THE FUTURE

We believe that the use of virtual teams will continue to grow. People currently entering the workforce after college have been immersed in the use of virtual teams in their classes. They are used to working on projects that involve the coordination and even holding of meetings via technology. They will bring those experiences into the workplace, and it is anticipated that they will continue to use this type of teamwork.

So, too, will organizations expect that virtual teamwork will grow. As organizations worry about their bottom lines and reduce travel, they will more strongly support the existence of virtual teams. They will focus, too, on increasing the productivity of those teams.

This book, then, is but a start. It lays out some of the issues of virtual teamwork and offers suggestions for practitioners to utilize. It also offers some direction to future researchers as they explore this type of collaborative work. We hope that practitioners and academic researchers will find it useful, as they attempt to realize all the promise that these teams hold.

REFERENCES

Grosse, C. U. (2002). Managing communication within virtual intercultural teams. *Business Communication Quarterly, 65*(4), 22–39.

Kraut, R., Kiesler, S., Mukhopadhyay, T., Scherlis, W., & Patterson, M. (1998). Social impact of the Internet: What does it mean? *Association for Computing Machinery: Communications of the ACM, 41*(12), 21–23.

Townsend, A., DeMarie, S., & Hendrickson, A. (1998). Virtual teams: Technology and the workplace of the future. *Academy of Management Executive, 12*(3), 17–29.

ACKNOWLEDGMENTS

The editors would like to acknowledge the help of all involved in the collation and review process of the book, without whose support this project could not have been satisfactorily completed. Many of the authors of chapters included in the book also served as referees for articles written by other authors. In addition, our colleagues at William Paterson University—Bob Lawson, Steve Betts, and Fuan Li—provided insightful and constructive reviews. Patricia O'Connor provided special assistance in the final editing of the book. Thanks go to all of you.

The support of the departments of Communication and Marketing and Management Sciences at William Paterson University is acknowledged for use of office computers and copiers. The University, too, receives our thanks for creating an atmosphere that encourages cross-disciplinary collaborations.

In closing, we wish to thank all of the authors for their insights and excellent contributions to this book.

Sue Godar
Pixy Ferris
October 2003

Section I:

Make-up of
Virtual Teams

Chapter I

Virtual Teams as Sociotechnical Systems

Haydee M. Cuevas, University of Central Florida, USA

Stephen M. Fiore, University of Central Florida, USA

Eduardo Salas, University of Central Florida, USA

Clint A. Bowers,University of Central Florida, USA

ABSTRACT

In this chapter, we adopt a sociotechnical systems approach to understand the challenges faced by members of an organizational unit that is not constrained by geographical, temporal, organizational, or national boundaries. Specifically, we examine virtual team performance within the context of an open sociotechnical system, highlighting the effects that the technological subsystem (e.g., collaborative information technology) and external environmental factors (e.g., lack of colocation) have on the personnel subsystem (i.e., virtual team members) within the organization. The organizational psychology literature on group productivity, motivation, and shared mental models is reviewed to, first, better understand team performance within the context of distributed environments, and second, offer guidelines and interventions for organizational practice.

VIRTUAL TEAMS AS SOCIOTECHNICAL SYSTEMS

Despite their rising popularity, a number of issues exist surrounding how it is that virtual teams can productively coordinate their resources, activities, and information, often in dynamic and uncertain task environments (Fiore, Salas, Cuevas, & Bowers, 2003; Townsend, DeMarie, & Hendrickson, 1998). With the structure of teams in organizations increasing in complexity to include both colocated and virtual team members, explicit linkages between theory and practice are critically needed to mitigate the negative effects that technology-mediated interaction may have on virtual team productivity. In this chapter, we attempt to integrate theories and principles from organizational psychology (e.g., Steiner, 1972) with the sociotechnical systems approach (e.g., Hendrick, 1997) to explore the unique challenges faced by this small, but growing, subset of teams.

A Sociotechnical Systems Approach to Virtual Team Performance

The radical change in organizational structure brought about through advances in technology represents a critical challenge for the appropriate application of organizational psychology principles in system design. Researchers and practitioners need to focus on system design issues not only at the individual or task level, but also at the team, and quite possibly, at the organizational levels. This involves conducting a system-level analysis of the sociotechnical factors that interact to shape organizational outcomes and may hinder the attainment of organizational goals (Hendrick, 1997). These sociotechnical factors include the following: (a) the personnel subsystem, comprised of the organizational unit's members; (b) the technological subsystem, which represents the technology available to the organizational unit; and (c) the relevant external environmental variables that act upon the organizational unit (Hendrick, 1997). The technological component, in particular, plays a key mediating role by setting limits upon the system's actions as well as by creating new demands that must reflect in the internal structure and goals of the organizational unit (Emery & Trist, 1960). Taken as a whole, these subsystems collectively represent the organizational unit as a *sociotechnical system*. In addition, because this organizational unit acts on and is acted upon by external forces, it should more appropriately be referred to as an *open* sociotechnical system (Emery & Trist, 1960; Katz & Kahn, 1966). The organizational unit, therefore, can be viewed as a complex set of dynamically intertwined and interconnected elements, including inputs, processes (throughputs), outputs, feedback loops, and the environment in which it operates and interacts (Emery & Trist, 1960; Katz & Kahn, 1966).

In distributed environments, the technological subsystem may potentially have a greater effect on team member interactions than would be expected in traditional colocated task environments. For the most part, virtual teams rely primarily on electronic communication processes to work together both synchronously (e.g., videoconferencing, Internet chat rooms) and asynchronously (e.g., e-mail, bulletin boards) to accomplish their tasks (Avolio, Kahai, Dumdum, & Sivasubramanium, 2001). Such technology-mediated interactions may potentially alter team processes and performance. For example, research in computer-supported collaborative work emphasizes the importance of team members' abilities to monitor and track individual member's actions and team members' interactions, referred to as *workspace awareness* (Gutwin & Greenberg, 1998; in press). Similarly, research on performance in virtual environments highlights the need for *telepresence* (the degree to which contextual factors typically present in colocated groups, such as voice, gesture, and body language, are found with distributed groups) and *teledata* (the team and task artifacts, such as shared workspaces, that require effective collaboration) (e.g., Anderson, Smallwood, MacDonald, Mullin, Fleming, & O'Malley, 2000; Draper, Kaber, & Usher, 1998; Greenberg, 1991). Lately, the term *social presence* (de Greef & Ijsselsteijn, 2000) has been used to describe how collaboration technology can adequately capture a sense of social interaction.

We argue that technology-mediated interactions increase the level of abstraction forced upon teams — a phenomenon referred to as *team opacity* (for a detailed discussion, see Fiore et al., 2003). Essentially, team opacity describes the experience of increased ambiguity and artificiality (i.e., the unnatural quality) associated with interaction in distributed environments. This decreased awareness of team members' actions, resulting from the distributed organizational structure, creates an environment lacking in the rich visual, auditory, and social array of cues normally experienced in colocated team member interaction, potentially altering the team processes that lead to workspace awareness, social presence, and other related constructs. Moreover, by limiting the use of implicit coordination and communication strategies, team opacity may further negatively alter team member interactions and impede the development of positive team attitudes (e.g., cohesion, trust) that are integral to successful team evolution and performance (e.g., Morgan, Salas, & Glickman, 1993).

Fiore et al. (2003) explored these factors within the context of a sociotechnological framework they labeled a *distributed coordination space*. The primary components of this framework are composed of the attitudes, behaviors, and cognitions of virtual teams that may emerge at various phases of interaction among team members. In particular, Fiore et al. (2003) suggested that these factors occur not only during *in-process* interaction but also during *pre-* and *post-process* interactions. Specifically, whereas in-process interaction occurs during actual task execution, pre-process interaction involves preparatory pre-task behaviors (e.g., project planning session), where initial shared expectations are created in anticipation of team interaction (Fiore, Salas, & Cannon-Bowers, 2001; Wittenbaum, Vaughan, & Stasser, 1998). Similarly, post-process interactions would include post-task reflection on performance (e.g., after-action review, see Smith-Jentsch, Zeisig, Acton, & McPherson, 1998). Such antecedent or consequent behaviors may be critical to team development and the successful execution of team processes.

Here, following a sociotechnical systems approach, we expand on two subcomponents of the distributed coordination space framework, specifically, *team attitudes* and *behaviors*. We examine virtual team performance within the context of an open sociotechnical system, analyzing the effects that the technological subsystem (e.g., collaborative information technology) and external environmental factors (e.g., lack of colocation) have on the personnel subsystem (i.e., virtual team members) within the organization. The organizational psychology literature on group productivity, motivation, and shared mental models is reviewed in order for us to better understand performance within distributed environments, highlighting how these theories can be applied to overcome the difficulties that may arise from this increasingly important organizational structure. We conclude with guidelines and interventions for organizational practice.

GROUP PRODUCTIVITY IN VIRTUAL TEAMS

Several models and theories have been proposed over the last few decades to describe the underlying mechanisms for effective team performance. For example, the Team Effectiveness Model (TEM), proposed by Tannenbaum, Beard, and Salas (1992), is an input–throughput–output feedback model that specifies the variables that may potentially impact team effectiveness in organizations (e.g., team and task characteristics). Similarly, we contend that virtual teams function as open sociotechnical systems, comprised of complex sets of interconnected input, throughput, and output variables, influenced by external environmental factors (Emery & Trist, 1960). These input and throughput variables, in particular, can be synthesized using Steiner's (1972) theory of group productivity that specifies three critical components to successful task performance: the resources available to the group, the task demands, and the combination processes enacted by the group that dictate how these resources are used to meet the task demands. In the next section, we describe the components of our conceptual framework, focusing primarily on the throughput variables (refer to Figure 1), in an attempt to better understand virtual team productivity.

Figure 1: Conceptual framework of group productivity in distributed environments.

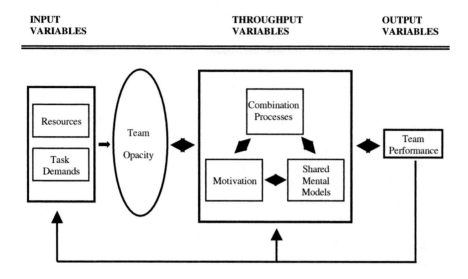

Resources: Personnel Subsystem

Resources would include the input variables found in the personnel subsystem, such as individual member attributes (e.g., knowledge, skills, and attitudes) and team characteristics (e.g., group size, group composition) that are critical for competent team performance (e.g., Becker & Dwyer, 1998; Forsyth, 1999; Steiner, 1972) and that may be particularly influential in multinational teams interacting in distributed environments (e.g., Van Ryssen & Godar, 2000). To illustrate the importance of these factors, consider that member interactions in distributed environments occur primarily electronically, with limited opportunities for face-to-face (F-T-F) interactions. Consequently, interactions and subsequent performance may be influenced by the level of media richness associated with the technological subsystem available to virtual team members (Avolio et al., 2001; Kock, 1998). On the one hand, to the extent that media richness is low, team opacity may filter out critical paralinguistic cues and delay the establishment of perceptions of competence and positive interpersonal orientation, hindering the development of mutual trust (Avolio et al., 2001; Fiore et al., 2001). On the other hand, this lack of visual cues may lead team members to focus more on task-relevant member attributes (e.g., skills, abilities) and to rely less on the task-irrelevant attributes (e.g., gender, race) that promote stereotypes (McKenna & Green, 2002). Furthermore, because factors such as physical appearance and degree of interpersonal dominance are less influential in distributed environments, the emergence of team leaders would be more dependent on how closely the individual embodies the values, ideals, and goals of the group, and less on stereotypical factors, such as age, gender, or race (McKenna & Green, 2002). Illustrated in this example is how the personnel subsystem may be differentially affected by the limitations associated with the technological subsystem found in distributed environments. In the next section, we discuss how task factors may interact with team opacity to negatively impact team processes and performance.

Task Demands: Technological Subsystem and External Environment Constraints

Task demands would be determined by input variables, such as the nature of the task (e.g., task complexity) and work structure factors (e.g., communication channels) that form the technological subsystem and external environment, each of which may impose unique demands on the personnel subsystem, that is, virtual team members (e.g., Fussell et al., 1998; Straus & McGrath, 1994). Specifically, Fiore et al. (2003) argued that the team opacity emerging within distributed environments may limit the use of implicit communication (e.g., paralinguistic cues) when conveying information crucial to the coordination and the completion of complex tasks. Consequently, over-reliance on explicit communication strategies may result in poor task performance, most notably when faced with conditions of high task complexity, high workload, time pressure, and environmental uncertainty (Entin & Serfaty, 1999). As such, researchers need to determine how the technological subsystem's level of media richness interacts with personnel subsystem characteristics (e.g., group composition) and task characteristics (e.g., task complexity) to influence the team's attitudes and behaviors, and subsequent task performance (e.g., Avolio et al., 2001; Bos, Olson, Gergle, Olson, & Wright, 2002; Carey & Kacmar, 1997). As will be discussed next, these technological and environmental characteristics may dramatically impact the efficacious execution of team processes in distributed environments.

Combination Processes: Process Loss in Virtual Teams

Combination processes are represented as throughput variables, specifically, the processes by which resources (i.e., individual and team characteristics) are used to meet the task demands. Throughput variables in distributed environments call attention to the various implicit and explicit team processes and behaviors necessary to accomplish the team's goals and task objectives. Previous work by Tang (1991) exemplified the importance of such combination processes, particularly with regard to implicit team behaviors. In his observations of small collaborative work groups engaged in an human–machine interface design task, Tang (1991) found that team members used hand gestures to uniquely communicate important information. He also found that the process of creating drawings (i.e., the integrated interaction of the team members as they performed the design task) provided much information not contained in the resulting drawings.

Yet, the technological subsystem available to virtual teams, particularly if characterized by low media richness (e.g., e-mail), may limit or altogether eliminate the use of such crucial nonverbal, paralinguistic cues, and thus, may inadequately support the use of implicit communication and coordination in the collaborative work process. Team opacity, therefore, potentially alters team-work to a degree sufficient that some form of pre- or in-process intervention is needed to enhance these combination processes. This could include incorporating training targeted at maximizing pre-process interactions or utilizing technology designed to support in-process interactions. Indeed, recent efforts by computer scientists in the area of computer-supported collaborative work (see Gutwin & Greenberg, in press) addressed how systems can be designed to scaffold "consequential communication" in areas such as distributed collaborative design (see also Segal, 1994).

Furthermore, as will be discussed later in this chapter, the degree to which these combination processes (e.g., coordination, communication, and decision making) are effectively executed is especially dependent upon the team members' motivation and their development of a shared mental model. These two factors may also impact the development of positive attitudes among team members, such as mutual trust, collective efficacy, and team cohesion. But first, we describe another factor that may diminish group productivity, what Steiner (1972) conceptualized as *process loss*.

One phenomenon of group productivity that may be acutely susceptible to the negative effects of team opacity in distributed environments involves a problem inherent in the dynamics of being part of a team, namely, the occurrence of *process losses* when individuals perform as a group (Steiner, 1972). Basically, as one moves from the individual level to the group level, performance may suffer due to process losses resulting from poor coordination among team members (i.e., lack of simultaneity of effort) or decreased social motivation (Steiner, 1972). As stated earlier, a problematic consequence of the lack of nonverbal cues and the ambiguous nature of distributed interaction is over-reliance on explicit strategies that may hinder the team's ability to execute the combination processes needed to attain desired outcomes (Fiore et al., 2003). Essentially, because team opacity limits the use of implicit communication and coordination strategies, process losses may be intensified in virtual teams (Fiore et al., 2003).

Process losses can also arise from poorly developed team attitudes and decreased social motivation. For example, the Team Evolution and Maturation Model (TEAM), proposed by Morgan, Glickman, Woodward, Blaiwes, and Salas (1986), illustrates the dynamic nature of teams, that is, the notion that teams develop over time (McIntyre & Salas, 1995). The TEAM emphasizes the importance of realizing that a group of individuals brought together as a team will develop the skills needed in task performance over the course of training; that is, skilled performance will evolve over time as team members learn to resourcefully coordinate their efforts (Morgan et al., 1993). Additionally, the team members' attitudes will mature as activities strengthen the quality of their interactions (e.g., coordination, communication) and their relationships (e.g., trust, cohesiveness) (McIntyre & Salas, 1995). While normally transparent in colocated teams, in virtual teams, these activities become opaque (Fiore et al., 2003); thus, team opacity may impede the evolution of mutual trust, collective efficacy, and group cohesion among virtual team members. Fitting the notion of team opacity with the TEAM approach, we argue that these obstacles to team development must be overcome via pre-, in-, and post-process training interventions. These would be intended to support the evolution and maturation cycle as well as increase social motivation (discussed next) but would be designed specifically to do so for virtual teams.

Motivation in Virtual Teams

Motivation theories, such as goal-setting and self-regulation, focus on the underlying behaviors necessary to accomplish set goals (Kanfer, 1992). According to goal-setting theory, the goals set by an individual or team affect task-oriented behavior via four mechanisms: (a) goals serve a directive function, by directing attention and effort toward goal-relevant activities; (b) goals serve an energizing function, by mobilizing increased effort on the task; (c) goals promote task persistence, particularly for difficult tasks; and (d) goals indirectly affect task performance by guiding strategy development (Locke, 1968; Locke & Latham, 2002). Two principle characteristics of goals are *intensity* (i.e., the perceived importance of the goal and commitment to the goal) and *content* (i.e., difficulty, specificity, complexity, and goal conflict) (Locke, 1968; Locke & Latham, 2002). Maintaining the intensity of the team's goals becomes increasingly more difficult in distributed environments because of the impoverished nature of the interactions among team members, a significant consequence of team opacity. Specifically, virtual teams may lack the motivating influence of paralinguistic cues inherent in F-T-F interactions (e.g., Teasley, Covi, Krishnan, & Olson, 2000). Communication in distributed environments may also be impacted by the nature of the information flow utilized (i.e., synchronous or asynchronous) (e.g., Fussell et al., 1998). Such complex technology-mediated interactions imposed by the technological subsystem may impede the development of a common and engaging direction for the team, resulting in poor motivation to meet training and performance objectives. This problem is exacerbated when teams of teams interact, as is often found in military command and control operations (e.g., Klein & Miller, 1999; Kleinman & Serfaty, 1989).

Related to the goal-setting approach, social cognitive theory also views behavior as goal directed, focusing on the cognitive processes that facilitate regulation of thoughts and actions to achieve set goals (Kanfer, 1992). Bandura (1986) identified three principal components of self-regulation: self-observation (i.e., monitoring one's own behavior), self-evaluation (i.e., comparing one's performance with the goal standard), and self-reaction (i.e., one's internal response to the self-evaluation judgment). This self-regulation process and feedback on performance has a direct effect on the individual's level of self-efficacy (i.e., the individual's perceived ability to attain a specific goal) (Bandura, 1986). One's level of self-efficacy, in turn, influences behaviors related to future goal setting and to attempts at attaining new goals. At the group level, this self-regulation process and feedback may have a direct effect on the team's collective efficacy (i.e., the members' belief in their team's ability or competence to attain desired outcomes) (e.g., Fiore et al., 2001). Thus, team or collective efficacy (Gibson, 2001) may be a more complex phenomenon and one exacerbated by distributed interaction. In particular, by decreasing awareness of team members' actions, distributed environments may hinder the development of a positive collective efficacy due to limited opportunities for monitoring and evaluating other members' performances (Fiore et al., 2003).

Furthermore, such decreased awareness of team members' actions arising from the team opacity found in distributed environments may also lead to *deindividuation*, where the reduction in an individual's self-awareness produces feelings of anonymity (for a more detailed discussion, see McKenna & Green, 2002). On the one hand, deindividuation may attenuate team members' motivation by decreasing their sense of responsibility as well as their conformity to the group norms that may be viewed as important by other team members. On the other hand, the effect that deindividuation will have on team members may be dependent upon the social context of members' interactions (McKenna & Green, 2002). Specifically, when external, situational (i.e., task-relevant) cues are most salient, the lack of physical appearance cues (such as gender or ethnicity) in distributed environments and the anonymity associated with deindividuation may increase identification with the group and conformity to group norms by focusing attention on the task and not on members' physical attributes.

In sum, the artificial nature of distributed environments (i.e., the team opacity arising from the lack of colocation) makes the application of these motivation theories vital for the development of positive team attitudes (e.g., trust) and efficient team combination processes (e.g., communication and coordination). Interventions guided by these theories can be incorporated to support members during critical phases of the virtual team's interactions (e.g., pre-, in-, and post-process) and to help overcome the detrimental effects of team opacity. In the next section, we discuss how team opacity may also impact the team's shared mental model, another critical component of group productivity.

Shared Mental Models in Virtual Teams

Of particular relevance to virtual teams is research on the concept of shared mental models and its role in enhancing team decision-making performance (Salas, Cannon-Bowers, & Johnston, 1997). According to Cannon-Bowers, Salas, and Converse (1993), shared mental models (SMMs) can be defined as follows:

> *...knowledge structures held by members of a team that enable them to form accurate explanations and expectations for the task, and, in turn, to coordinate their actions and adapt their behavior to demands of the task and other team members. (p. 228)*

A considerable body of research has explored the role of SMMs in team performance and decision making (e.g., Cannon-Bowers et al., 1993; Marks, Zaccaro, & Mathieu, 2000; Mathieu, Heffner, Goodwin, Salas, E., & Cannon-Bowers, 2000; Stout, Cannon-Bowers, & Salas, 1996). These investigations show that SMMs favorably impact performance by improving a team's ability to coordinate efforts, adapt to changing demands, and anticipate the needs of the task and other members.

One underlying mechanism for this beneficial effect may be that teams draw on their SMM of the task and other team-member functions to shift from explicit to implicit coordination, thereby decreasing communication and coordination overhead (Entin & Serfaty, 1999; MacMillan, Entin, & Serfaty, in press; Rouse, Cannon-Bowers, & Salas, 1992; Urban, Weaver, Bowers, & Rhodenizer, 1996). Teams with SMMs would, therefore, be expected to be more adept at adaptively coordinating their behaviors under high levels of stress, time pressure, and workload (Rouse et al., 1992). In contrast, teams with inaccurate or incomplete SMMs would lack this flexibility, and performance would be degraded under such conditions (Entin & Serfaty, 1999). In addition, SMMs may also play a vital role in the development of trust and positive interpersonal perceptions among team members by providing a basis for the team's expectations of each member and by serving as a scaffold for the team members' interactions (Avolio et al., 2001; Fiore et al., 2001).

Because of the potential over-reliance on explicit coordination strategies in distributed environments, the lack of a SMM among virtual team members can lead to uncoordinated efforts, low group productivity, and poorly developed team attitudes, hindering attainment of organizational goals (Espinosa, Lerch, & Kraut, in press; Fiore et al., 2003). As such, Fiore et al. (2003) argued that further strengthening the virtual team's SMM is clearly warranted to overcome these technological subsystem and environmental constraints. An accurate and well-established team SMM of the task and task environment could help overcome the negative impact of the team opacity inherent in distributed environments and, thus, positively affect team combination processes and attitudes and improve virtual team performance.

IMPLICATIONS FOR TRAINING AND PERFORMANCE

As demonstrated throughout this chapter, in distributed environments, the technological subsystem sets significant limits upon the personnel subsystem's actions and creates new demands for optimal group productivity that must be addressed through training interventions and system design. It should also be noted that a virtual team is a dynamic organizational unit, evolving and maturing over time and space as activities strengthen the quality of team member interactions and attitudes. These activities, so critical to team development, occur throughout all phases of team interaction — pre-, in-, and post-process. Based on the organizational psychology theories discussed in this chapter, we next offer guidelines for organizational practice at each of these stages.

Pre-Process Interventions

The negative effects of team opacity can be attenuated through pre-process training interventions that increase social motivation by fostering commitment to the team and to achieving task objectives. This can be accomplished by intensifying personal involvement, clarifying group goals, setting high standards, and promoting collective efficacy and cohesiveness (Forsyth, 1999). In particular, specifying clear, challenging, yet attainable goals for the team during pre-process interactions (e.g., pre-task briefing) may lead to increased effort put on task, better use of strategies, and commitment to the team, thereby enhancing team performance (Forsyth, 1999; Locke, 1968; Locke & Latham, 2002). Moreover, specifying task objectives beforehand could establish a SMM, or shared understanding, of the task demands and the team-level interactions required to meet these demands (Cannon-Bowers et al., 1993). This, in turn, would be expected to increase commitment to attaining the desired outcomes.

Commitment can also be promoted through pre-process interactions that cultivate positive team attitudes such as cohesion and trust. Indeed, recent studies find that manipulations of interaction prior to teamwork (e.g., an initial F-T-F meeting), can facilitate cooperation in virtual teams who had such meetings when compared to those who did not (e.g., Rocco, 1998; Zheng, Bos, Olson, & Olson, 2001). While such pre-task interactions may also benefit traditional teams, such antecedent behaviors are critical for virtual teams in order to "jump start" the development of the team's social identity and trust, which may otherwise be delayed by the team opacity inherent in distributed environments.

Even technology-mediated pre-task interactions (e.g., videoconferencing) were shown to facilitate the development of positive team attitudes among virtual team members (e.g., Bos et al., 2002; Zheng et al., 2001).

Team-building approaches focused on goal setting, roles, interpersonal relations, and problem solving can be aimed at improving the effectiveness of team processes and operations by prompting members to evaluate their behaviors and relationships (Tannenbaum et al., 1992). Goal-setting approaches assist team members in setting individual and group goals and in determining the strategies to meet those objectives. Role approaches focus on identifying each individual's roles and responsibilities in order to minimize any difficulties arising from role conflict or role ambiguity. Interpersonal relations approaches focus on improving the relations among team members. And finally, problem-solving approaches are aimed at guiding team members in developing the skills they need to identify the relevant elements in a problem, such as givens, goals, and obstacles/constraints, and in employing effective strategies to solve the problem.

Each of these approaches can be selectively applied in distributed environments to attenuate the negative effect that technological subsystem constraints and external environmental factors such as team opacity may have on team members' interactions. Goal-setting and problem-solving approaches would be well suited to enhance the processes by which virtual team members use their resources to meet task demands. Role and interpersonal relations approaches would be beneficial for fostering positive team attitudes and commitment to the group. Note that each of these four team-building approaches could also be incorporated as valuable in-process interventions, a topic we turn to next.

In-Process Interventions

Virtual teams would benefit from the use of technological tools during in-process interactions that increase awareness of member actions and provide feedback on performance to enhance combination processes (e.g., coordination and communication) as well as foster the development of positive collective efficacy (e.g., Steinfeld, Jang, & Pfaff, 1999). For instance, Cadiz, Fussell, Kraut, Lerch, and Scherlis (1998) developed a system, called the *Awareness Monitor*, designed to inform distributed work groups of important changes in within-team and external information, without diverting their attention away from the central tasks. However, designers of collaborative groupware systems need to consider the requirements of the individual as well as the group. Specifically, at the group level, these systems need to provide information about member actions to help maintain awareness. Yet, at the individual level, the emphasis should be on providing individuals with powerful and flexible tools with which to interact with the shared workspace and its artifacts (see Gutwin & Greenberg, 1998; in press; Tang, 1991). In addition, although technology may be used to overcome the problem of team opacity, even communication technology affording richer cues (e.g., videoconferencing) can alter the natural exchange of ideas in distributed environments. As such, the judicious use of these technological subsystem components should be guided by an accurate understanding of how the level of media richness may shape the personnel subsystem's social identity and impact the positive or negative influence of deindividuation.

As discussed earlier, researchers specializing in team training and performance stress the importance of establishing SMMs to allow teams to flexibly adapt to high-workload conditions by switching to implicit coordination strategies as needed (e.g., Entin & Serfaty, 1999). Of the several training interventions suggested by Cannon-Bowers et al. (1993) to foster SMM development, cross-training would be particularly beneficial in facilitating in-process interactions among virtual team members. Cross-training may help members better understand the roles and responsibilities of other virtual team members, thereby enabling them to more accurately predict and anticipate each other's behavior and make greater use of implicit team processes. In-process interventions should also focus on developing the team skills (e.g., combination processes such as communication and coordination) that may substantially impact group productivity and performance (Cannon-Bowers, Tannenbaum, Salas, & Volpe, 1995; Espinosa et al., in press). For example, Team Adaptation and Coordination Training (TACT), developed by Entin and Serfaty (1999), emphasizes "the importance of a shared mental model of the situation and task environment, as well as mutual mental models of interacting team members' tasks and abilities" (p. 323). The TACT was shown to be effective in enhancing teamwork behaviors and coordination strategies by increasing the quality and quantity of cues utilized by teams, which in turn, led to improved decision-making performance (Entin & Serfaty, 1999). These improvements were evident under low- and high-stress conditions, indicating that the training's design was adaptive to varying levels of stress and workload. Such in-process training interventions would be expected to be more beneficial for virtual teams than for traditional colocated teams, because technological subsystem constraints may often force virtual teams to rely more on explicit strategies.

Post-Process Interventions

While facilitating pre- and in-process interactions may seem to be the most constructive approach for increasing virtual team productivity, organizations should not underestimate the importance of supporting post-process interactions. In keeping with our conceptualization of virtual teams as open sociotechnical systems, post-process interactions would provide the necessary input for the feedback loops that, in turn, influence the personnel subsystem's subsequent actions. Careful, well-structured dissemination of feedback information following task execution may significantly influence future task efforts (Fiore et al., 2001). Debriefing sessions and after-action reviews involving guided team self-correction could foster positive team efficacy by involving team members in self-regulation of their performances (Cannon-Bowers et al., 1993; Smith-Jenstch et al., 1998). Such post-process interactions could also strengthen the team's SMM by fostering shared knowledge regarding expectations and specific preferences of team members and effective teamwork processes (Smith-Jenstch et al., 1998) as well as by increasing source knowledge of member expertise, another essential component of superior team performance (e.g., Libby, Trotman, & Zimmer, 1987). In particular, research on information sharing and source monitoring in computer-mediated groups suggests that the identification of role knowledge in virtual teams may be diminished, impeding the development of a SMM of team members' competencies (e.g., Durso, Hackworth, Barile, Dougherty, & Ohrt, 1998). As such, well-structured post-process interactions are critical for overcoming the negative effects on virtual team attitudes and processes that may be brought about by decreased awareness of members' actions associated with team opacity.

CONCLUSION

As the prevalence and importance of virtual teams grow, the research community must continue to address issues surrounding their design, implementation, and management. In particular, as researchers, we must identify the sociotechnical factors that help and hinder effective virtual team productivity. Only in this way can the potential of virtual teams be maximized, while mitigating the occurrence of process losses. Adopting a sociotechnical systems approach to investigate how team opacity interacts with these unique task demands and situational constraints to alter group processes and products will enable organizations to effectively utilize the technological subsystem's capabilities to support virtual team productivity. Similarly, a better understanding of the distinct forms of group dynamics that may emerge in virtual teams will advance the design of appropriate training interventions. Unquestionably, the future success of virtual teams in organizations will depend primarily upon the joint optimization of the personnel and technological subsystems comprising this unique sociotechnical system.

ACKNOWLEDGMENTS

The views herein are those of the authors and do not necessarily reflect those of the organizations with which the authors are affiliated. This research was funded by Grant Number F49620-01-1-0214, from the Air Force Office of Scientific Research to Eduardo Salas, Stephen M. Fiore, and Clint A. Bowers. Portions of this chapter were reported at the 46th Annual Meeting of the Human Factors and Ergonomics Society. A special thanks to Barbara Fritzche-Clay of the University of Central Florida for asking the question that inspired this chapter. Address correspondence to Haydee M. Cuevas, UCF Team Performance Lab, 12424 Research Parkway, Room 408, Orlando, FL 32826 or via e-mail at ha651622@ ucf.edu or to Stephen M. Fiore at UCF Team Performance Lab, 12424 Research Parkway, Room 408, Orlando, FL 32826, e-mail sfiore@ucf.edu.

REFERENCES

Anderson, A. H., Smallwood, L., MacDonald, R., Mullin, J., Fleming, A. M., & O'Malley, C. (2000). Video data and video links in mediated communication: What do users value? International Journal of Human-Computer Studies, 52, 165–187.

Avolio, B. J., Kahai, S., Dumdum, R., & Sivasubramanium, N. (2001). Virtual teams: Implications for e-leadership and team development. In M. London (Ed.), How people evaluate others in organizations (pp. 337–358). Mahwah, NJ: LEA.

Bandura, A. (1986). Social foundations of thought and action: A social cognitive theory. Englewood Cliffs, NJ: Prentice-Hall.

Becker, D., & Dwyer, M. (1998). The impact of student verbal/visual learning style preference on implementing groupware in the classroom. Journal of Asynchronous Learning Networks, 2, 61–69.

Bos, N., Olson, J. S., Gergle, D., Olson, G. M., & Wright, Z. (2002). Effects of four computer-mediated communications channels on trust development. Proceedings of CHI 2002. New York, NY: ACM Press.

Cadiz, J. J., Fussell, S. R., Kraut, R. E., Lerch, F. J., & Scherlis, W. L. (1998). The Awareness Monitor: A coordination tool for asynchronous, distributed work teams. Unpublished manuscript. Demonstrated at the 1998 ACM Conference on Computer Supported Cooperative Work (CSCW 1998) (Seattle, WA, November, 1998).

Cannon-Bowers, J. A., Salas, E., & Converse, S. (1993). Shared mental models in expert team decision making. In N. J. Castellan, Jr. (Ed.), Individual and group decision making (pp. 221–246). Hillsdale, NJ: LEA.

Cannon-Bowers, J. A., Tannenbaum, S. I., Salas, E., & Volpe, C. E. (1995). Defining competencies and establishing team training requirements. In R. A. Guzzo & E. Salas (Eds.), Team effectiveness and decision making in organizations (pp. 333–380). San Francisco, CA: Jossey-Bass.

Carey, J. M., & Kacmar, C. J. (1997). The impact of communication mode and task complexity on small group performance and member satisfaction. Computers in Human Behavior, 13, 23–49.

de Greef, P., & Ijsselsteijn, W. (2000, March). Social presence in the PhotoShare tele-application. In: W. I. Jsselsteijn, J. Freeman, & H. de Ridder (Eds.), Proceedings of the 3rd International Workshop on Presence, Presence 2000, Delft, The Netherlands, (p. 1631).

Draper, J. V., Kaber, D. B., & Usher, J. M. (1998). Telepresence. Human Factors, 40, 354–375.

Durso, F. T., Hackworth, C. A., Barile, A. L., Dougherty, M. R. P., & Ohrt, D. D. (1998). Source monitoring in face-to-face and computer-mediated environments. Cognitive Technology, 3, 32–38.

Emery, F. E., & Trist, E. L. (1960). Socio-technical systems. In C. W. Churchman & M. Verhulst (Eds.), Management sciences: Models and techniques (Vol. 2, pp. 83–97). New York, NY: Pergamon.

Entin, E. E., & Serfaty, D. (1999). Adaptive team coordination. Human Factors, 41, 312–325.

Espinosa, J. A., Lerch, F. J., & Kraut, R. E. (in press). Explicit vs. implicit coordination mechanisms and task dependencies: One size does not fit all. To appear in E. Salas & S. M. Fiore (Eds.), Team cognition: Process and performance at the inter- and intra-individual level. Washington, DC: American Psychological Association.

Fiore, S. M., Salas, E., & Cannon-Bowers, J. A. (2001). Group dynamics and shared mental model development. In M. London (Ed.), How people evaluate others in organizations (pp. 309–336). Mahwah, NJ: LEA.

Fiore, S. M., Salas, E., Cuevas, H. M., & Bowers, C. A. (2003). Distributed coordination space: Toward a theory of distributed team performance. Theoretical Issues in Ergonomics Science, 4, 340-363.

Forsyth, D. R. (1999). Group dynamics (3rd ed.). Belmont, CA: Wadsworth.

Fussell, S. R., Kraut, R. E., Lerch, F. J., Scherlis, W. L., McNally, M. M., & Cadiz, J. J. (1998). Coordination, overload, and team performance: Effects of team communication strategies. Proceedings of CSCW 1998 (Seattle, WA, November, 1998), 275–284. New York, NY: ACM Press.

Gibson, C. B. (2001). Me and us: Differential relationships among goal-setting training, efficacy and effectiveness at the individual and team level. Journal of Organizational Behavior, 22, 789–808.

Greenberg, S. (Ed.). (1991). Computer-supported cooperative work and groupware. San Diego, CA: Academic Press.

Gutwin, C., & Greenberg, S. (1998). Design for individuals, design for groups: Tradeoffs between power and workspace awareness. Proceedings of the ACM Conference on Computer Supported Cooperative Work (pp. 207–216). New York, NY: ACM Press.

Gutwin, C., & Greenberg, S. (in press). The importance of awareness for team cognition in distributed collaboration. To appear in E. Salas & S. M. Fiore (Eds.), Team cognition: Process and performance at the inter- and *intra-individual level.* Washington, DC: American Psychological Association.

Hendrick, H. W. (1997). Organizational design and macroergonomics. In G. Salvendy (Ed.), *Handbook of human factors and ergonomics* (pp. 594–636). New York, NY: John Wiley & Sons.

Kanfer, R. (1992). Motivation theory and industrial and organizational psychology. In M. D. Dunnette & L. M. Hough (Eds.), *Handbook of industrial and organizational psychology* (2nd ed., Vol. 1, pp. 75–170). Palo Alto, CA: Consulting Psychologists Press.

Katz, D., & Kahn, R. L. (1966). *The social psychology of organizations.* New York, NY: John Wiley & Sons.

Klein, G., & Miller, T. E. (1999). Distributed planning teams. *International Journal of Cognitive Ergonomics, 3,* 203–222.

Kleinman, D.L. & Serfaty, D. (1989). Team performance assessment in distributed decision making. In R. Gibson, J. P. Kincaid, & B. Goldiez (Eds.), *Proceedings of the Interactive Networked Simulation for Training Conference* (pp. 22-27). Orlando, FL: Naval Training Systems Center.

Kock, N. (1998). Can communication medium limitations foster better group outcomes? An action research study. *Information & Management, 34,* 295–305.

Libby, R., Trotman, K. T., & Zimmer, I. (1987). Member variation, recognition of expertise, and group performance. *Journal of Applied Psychology, 72,* 81–87.

Locke, E. A. (1968). Toward a theory of task motivation and incentives. *Organizational Behavior and Human Performance, 3,* 157–189.

Locke, E. A., & Latham, G.P. (2002). Building a practically useful theory of goal setting and task motivation: A 35-year odyssey. *American Psychologist, 57,* 705–717.

MacMillan, J., Entin, E. E., & Serfaty, D. (in press). Communication overhead: The hidden cost of team cognition. To appear in E. Salas & S. M. Fiore (Eds.), *Team cognition: Process and performance at the inter- and intra-individual level.* Washington, DC: American Psychological Association.

Marks, M. A., Zaccaro, S. J., & Mathieu, J. E. (2000). Performance implications of leader briefings and team-interaction training for team adaptation to novel environments. *Journal of Applied Psychology, 85, 6,* 971–986.

Mathieu, J. E., Heffner, T. S., Goodwin, G. F., Salas, E., & Cannon-Bowers, J. A. (2000). The influence of shared mental models on team process and performance. *Journal of Applied Psychology, 85, 2,* 273–283.

McIntyre, R. E., & Salas, E. (1995). Measuring and managing for team performance: Lessons from complex environments. In R. A. Guzzo & E. Salas (Eds.), *Team effectiveness and decision making in organizations* (pp. 9–45). San Francisco, CA: Jossey-Bass.

McKenna, K. Y. A., & Green, A. S. (2002). Virtual group dynamics. *Group Dynamics: Theory, Research, and Practice, 6*, 116–127.

Morgan, B. B., Jr., Glickman, A. S., Woodward, E. A., Blaiwes, A. S., & Salas, E. (1986). *Measurement of team behaviors in a Navy environment* (Tech Rep. No. NTSC TR-86-014). Orlando, FL: Naval Training Systems Center.

Morgan, B. B., Jr., Salas, E., & Glickman, A. S. (1993). An analysis of team evolution and maturation. *Journal of General Psychology, 120*, 277–291.

Rocco, E. (1998). Trust breaks down in electronic contexts but can be repaired by some initial face-to-face contact. *Proceedings of CSCW 1998 (Seattle, WA, November, 1998)* (pp. 501–529). New York, NY: ACM Press.

Rouse, W. B., Cannon-Bowers, J. A., & Salas, E. (1992). The role of mental models in team performance in complex systems. *IEEE Transactions on Systems, Man, and Cybernetics, 22*, 1296–1308.

Salas, E., Cannon-Bowers, J. A., & Johnston, J. H. (1997). How can you turn a team of experts into an expert team?: Emerging training strategies. In C. E. Zsambok & G. Klein (Eds.), *Naturalistic decision making* (pp. 359–370). Mahwah, NJ: LEA.

Segal, L. (1994). *Effects of checklist interface on non-verbal crew communications*. NASA Ames Research Center, Contractor Report 177639.

Smith-Jentsch, K. A., Zeisig, R. L., Acton, B., & McPherson, J. A. (1998). A strategy for guided team self-correction. In J. A. Cannon-Bowers & E. Salas (Eds.), *Making decisions under stress: Implications for individual and team training* (pp. 271–297). Washington, DC: American Psychological Association.

Steiner, I. D. (1972). *Group process and productivity*. New York, NY: Academic Press.

Steinfeld, C., Jang, C., & Pfaff, B. (1999, November). Supporting virtual team collaboration: The TeamSCOPE System. *Proceedings of GROUP '99: International ACM SIGGROUP Conference on Supporting Group Work*, Phoenix, AZ.

Stout, R. J., Cannon-Bowers, J. A., & Salas, E. (1996). The role of shared mental models in developing team situational awareness: Implications for training. *Training Research Journal, 2*, 85–116.

Straus, S. G., & McGrath, J. E. (1994). Does medium matter? The interaction of task type and technology on group performance and member reactions. *Journal of Applied Psychology, 79*, 87–97.

Tang, J. C. (1991). Findings from observational studies of collaborative work. *International Journal of Man-Machine Studies, 34*, 143–160.

Tannenbaum, S. I., Beard, R. L., & Salas, E. (1992). Team building and its influence on team effectiveness: An examination of conceptual and empirical developments. In K. Kelley (Ed.), *Issues, theory, and research in industrial/organizational psychology* (pp. 117–153). Amsterdam: Elsevier.

Teasley, S., Covi, L., Krishnan, M. S., & Olson, J. S. (2000). How does radical collocation help a team succeed? *Proceedings of CSCW 2000 (Philadelphia, PA, December, 2000)* (pp. 339–346). New York, NY: ACM Press.

Townsend, A. M., DeMarie, S. M., & Hendrickson, A. R. (1998). Virtual teams: Technology and the workplace of the future. *Academy of Management Executive, 12*, 17–29.

Urban, J. M., Weaver, J. L., Bowers, C. A., & Rhodenizer, L. (1996). Effects of workload and structure on team processes and performance: Implications for complex team decision making. *Human Factors, 38*, 300–310.

Van Ryssen, S., & Godar, S. H. (2000). Going international without going international: Multinational virtual teams. *Journal of International Management, 6*, 49–60.

Wittenbaum, G. M., Vaughan, S. I., & Stasser, G. (1998). Coordination in task-performing groups. In R. S. Tindale & L. Heath (Eds.), *Theory and research on small groups. Social psychological applications to social issues*, Vol. 4 (pp. 177–204). New York, NY: Plenum Press.

Zheng, J., Bos, N., Olson, J. S., & Olson, G. M. (2001). Trust with*out* touch: Jump-start trust with social chat. *Proceedings of CHI 2001*. New York: ACM Press.

Chapter II

Effective Virtual Teamwork:
A Socio-Cognitive and Motivational Model

Lynne J. Millward, University of Surrey, UK

Olivia Kyriakidou, University of Surrey, UK

ABSTRACT

While much of the work on virtual teams is grounded in the assumptions that teams are concrete entities, this chapter conceptualizes teams as psychological entities, existing in the minds of teams' members and stakeholders. Drawing from interviews with 40 experts in virtual team building and two focus groups, we offer four principles for the existence of a virtual team: the awareness of its members that they are a "team," identification with the team, commitment to the team goals, and accountability for team success. We then build upon that base to discuss how teams can be made more "intelligent."

INTRODUCTION

The globalization of business and the trend toward leaner, flatter organizations, combined with ubiquitous access to informational technology, has accelerated the need for firms to coordinate activities that span geographical, as well as organizational, boundaries. In addition, the shift from production- to service-related businesses spawned a new generation of knowledge worker not bound to physical work locations. These factors suggest that firms are faced with increased challenges to coordinate tasks across time zones, physical boundaries, and organizational contexts. Consequently, in order to meet the challenges of this new context, the virtual team has begun to emerge as a new form of structure, because it is assumed to bridge inter- and intraorganizational boundaries, to procure expert knowledge from internal and external sources, and to transfer "best practice" information nearly instantaneously (Huber, 1990). However, in spite of pressures for flatter structures, flexible employment strategies (Millward & Brewerton, 1999), empowerment, and semiautomated work guide consider-ations of virtual teamwork as a superior form of organizing, producing a "synergy bonus" (Conway & Forrestor, 1997), there is no clear-cut evidence for the superiority of virtual teamwork.

Moreover, despite the growing enthusiasm for virtual teams, little empirical research exists that explores the dynamics inherent in a virtual work environment (Watson-Fritz, Narasimhan, & Rhee, 1998). Models that could be used to understand better team development and effectiveness have been limited to those based on the traditional colocated group perspective. Although some comprehensive case studies exist documenting the development of virtual teams (O'Hara-Deveraux & Johansen, 1994; Lipnack & Stamps, 1997), theory devel-opment and empirical research are needed to help managers better understand and respond to the challenges that virtual teams face.

The atheoretical nature of virtual teamwork research may be attributable to the atheoretical nature of the field, including the conceptualization of virtual teams based on assumptions that underpin the conventional team literature. Virtual team models are based on the assumption that the team is a singular concrete entity characterized by stability, regular interaction, symbiosis, and team member proximity. However, in the case of virtual teams, these assump-tions are inappropriate. We will try, therefore, to conceptualize the virtual way of working, arguing that the existence of a virtual team is more appropriately located in the mind of its members and stakeholders (i.e., psychological team), as opposed to a physical entity with presence and form (i.e., sociological team). At this end, we emphasize the importance of team cognition as a process in our understanding of effective virtual teamwork.

VIRTUAL TEAMS — CHALLENGES AND TRENDS

Whereas virtual teams undoubtedly face similar challenges to those of traditional teams, it is argued that these dispersed work groups may also face unique issues. More specifically, colocated collectivities are teams with mem-bers who are within close proximity of each other and for whom the dominant mode of communication is face-to-face. Members of colocated teams typically

Table 1: Challenges of virtual teams.

Type of Challenge	Description
Communications	Traditional social mechanisms are lost or distorted; communication dynamics, such as facial expressions are distorted; there is inhibition in building trust; there is communication process dysfunction
Culture	Potential for multiple cultures requires greater communication skills; communication can be distorted through cultural misunderstandings/biases

work in the same physical location or come together regularly and frequently to meet in the same location. On the other hand, virtual collectivities refer to those collectivities of individuals geographically or organizationally dispersed and who are assembled using a combination of telecommunications and information technologies to accomplish an organizational task (Townsend, Demarie, & Hendrickson, 1998). These computer-mediated communication systems (CMCS) (such as desktop conferencing systems, e-mail, group support systems, the Internet, and intranets), used to link team members across time, space, and organizational boundaries, represent fundamentally new types of media with their own advantages, disadvantages, social dynamics, problems, and opportunities (Table 1).

Because communication media may differ in their ability to convey "social presence," information-rich nonverbal cues, such as facial expressions, voice inflections, and gestures, may be lost or distorted through CMCS that lack the social presence inherent to face-to-face environments (Warkentin, Sayeed, & Hightower, 1997). The severity of this information loss will be determined by the richness of the technology being used. Moreover, important social/contextual information, such as a member's social status or level of expertise, may be lost or distorted in virtual team environments characterized by high levels of anonymity (Dubrovsky, Kiesler, & Sethna, 1991). Also, the ability to develop relational links among team members may be hindered, which may negatively affect such outcomes as creativity, morale, decision-making quality, and process loss (Walther & Burgoon, 1992). Finally, the lack of a social context may alter or hinder the process through which team members develop trust (Jarvenpaa, Knoll, & Leidner, 1998).

Although new and innovative modes of communication may be possible through CMCS-enabled work groups, research suggests that virtual teams may still encounter significant problems in processing communication traffic among team members (e.g., Hightower & Sayeed, 1996). In this asynchronous environment, characterized by nonlinear topics, team members may experience information overload as they attempt to cope with a seemingly disjointed set of communications (Hiltz & Turoff, 1985). In such an environment, the nonsequential flow of information may eliminate or significantly reduce points of reference, such that individuals may have difficulty in identifying how messages fit within the overall context of group communication (Hiltz & Johnson, 1990). Additional communication challenges for team members may be created due to cultural misunderstandings and biases (Solomon, 1995).

Finally, given the centrality of technology in virtual team discussions and the role it plays in making teams flexible in time and space, it would be easy for technology and spatial form to obscure the differences among virtual teams. The longevity, interchangeability of skills, and tasks and function range may vary between teams. We can presume that their internal dynamics — the roles adopted, leadership styles, needs for creativity, etc. — will also differ in each case. In this sense, we need to disabuse ourselves of the notion that all virtual teams can be treated as more or less the same, and that a kind of "generic model" of virtual teams can be created. The challenge we face is thus to create a body of knowledge that can inform of research and practices across all types of virtual teams.

These arguments suggest that certain dimensions may be particularly important for virtual team effectiveness. First, given the "altered" social context, a social and cognitive climate must be built and maintained. This is necessary for ensuring adequate levels of virtual team unity and cohesiveness. This is extremely important, because virtual team cohesion was empirically linked to virtual team effectiveness (Millward & Purvis, 1998). Second, the role of managing and coordinating the communications process may take on heightened significance given the challenges noted above; however, this challenge is out of the scope of the present analysis. The potential importance of these dimensions suggests that virtual team effectiveness may be a function of the processes to develop effective, elaborated, and shared virtual team cognitions. The following section draws from a number of expert interviews and focus groups to address the problem of virtual team effectiveness, and challenges are made to the prevailing atheoretical wisdom regarding virtual teams and virtual team effectiveness.

METHOD

Data derived from telephone interviews with a sample of 40 self-classified "experts" in virtual team effectiveness and virtual team building (all of whom were Chartered Psychologists) and from two focus group discussions involving six "experts," each charged with addressing specific virtual team-building problems. The rationale for conducting telephone interviews with virtual team-building experts was based on the understanding that most virtual team-building activity is pursued without formal documentation, such that much of the expertise on this topic remains untapped by the academic community. The analysis reported here, aimed to redress this balance, is in the spirit of the "scientist-practitioner."

Expert telephone interviews. Chartered status or professional affiliation of either the Institute of Personnel Directors or the British Psychological Society was a prerequisite for entry into the expert database. A total of 121 experts were identified and sent letters. Fifteen of them called back to indicate their interest in being "interviewed." A further 25 experts were successfully contacted by telephone over a 2 month period following receipt of the letter. Forty experts were interviewed. Telephone interviews following a semistructured interview format lasted for an average of 15 min. each. Interviews were largely conducted in a conversational vein anchored around a set number of topics. Topics included concepts of "'virtual team" and "team effectiveness," virtual team development process, virtual team technology, theoretical inclinations/preferences, and transfer of learning/maintenance considerations. Notes were taken during the interviews.

Two focus groups comprising six people each were also run. The focus groups were introduced to participants with three objectives: to discuss the concept of virtual team, to identify the kinds of problems and challenges specific to virtual teams that can inhibit effective virtual teamwork, and to form some proposals about how these kinds of problems might be overcome. The focus group was run over a lunchtime period for one hour. Permission to videorecord the session was obtained from participants. The discussion was largely self-managed by the group. Although a facilitator was present, the group created its own modus operandi and monitored its own progress, something that was encouraged by the facilitator, who remained in the background (Millward, 1995).

Interviews were content analyzed by topic/issue [e.g., VT (virtual team) development process, VT technology, transfer of learning], with the material organized into main themes and subthemes where appropriate.

Results: Three Challenges for Virtual Team Effectiveness

From our expert interviews, we uncovered some insights about understanding the "virtual team" concept and meeting the challenges of managing and developing virtual team effectiveness.

Insight 1: Conceptualization of virtual teams. Teams, in general, vary in how members interrelate around the team task (symbiotic/associative) — by the tightness of their boundaries (open/closed) and by the stability of their memberships (fluid/stable) (Hardingham & Royal, 1994). The existence of a virtual team, in particular, is more appropriately located in the minds of its members and stakeholders (i.e., psychological team), as opposed to a physical entity with presence and form in the here and now (i.e., sociological team). In practice, however, sociological and psychological terms are likely to be inextricably linked (i.e., team composition and sociometric cohesiveness is part of a team's psychological reality (Bird, 1975). However, a sociological team may not operate psychologically as a team. Likewise, an effective psychological team need not necessarily have any particular sociological form (e.g., a virtual team). This is not to deny the importance of sociological factors in virtual teamwork (e.g., team composition and process), merely to emphasize the importance of team cognition as well as process in our understanding of effective virtual teamwork (e.g., Moreland & Devine, 1991).

Insight 2: The need to investigate the causes of virtual team effectiveness. There is a need to distinguish the "causes" of virtual team success from the indicators of success (e.g., open communication, few mistakes, low levels of conflict, higher levels of job satisfaction, cooperation, taking responsibility) and the results of success (e.g., the ability of the team to capitalize on opportunity, the meeting of deadlines, decreased costs, effective use of time, and innovative and effective problem solving). Most of our respondents attribute the causes of team success to factors that are within team control in the self-regulatory sense (Varney, 1989), which moves away from process considerations per se to the issue of team self-regulatory ability.

In this sense, a self-regulatory virtual team is a team able to reflect on and manage its own processes, taking a stance on itself in the reflective "helicopter" sense and establishing its own internal criteria of effectiveness. Moreover, an effective virtual team is able to operate with a common language, including a common set of understandings about the nature of their task, team goals, and the nature of the teamwork required; is able to learn from its own experience (captures learning) or is a learning team (i.e., practicing continuous improvement); has fluidity (i.e., able to adapt its processes to requirements), where members successfully reconciled personal interests with team interests; and has members who understand and accept personal roles and contributions. The responsibility of the consultant is said to be one of facilitating the virtual team to become self-regulatory, within a problem-solving framework, drawing on whatever methods or techniques are appropriate for the situation at hand.

Insight 3: The need to pay more attention to virtual team cognition and motivation. Virtual teamwork and team building involve learning. As for any learning event, the issue is not only to secure change (of a permanent kind) but also to ensure that the learning is of the kind that can be transferred and sustained beyond the learning event (e.g., Ford & Kraiger, 1992, p. 31). A test of this is the extent to which a team is able to operate effectively in situations and under conditions (e.g., different people, different problems) that are different from those experienced during the team development event. This presupposes that team members acquire diagnostic power and can adapt intelligently to circumstances beyond those posed in the learning event. The transfer of learning literature tells us that a strong predictor of intelligent transfer (where the team can dynamically adapt to the demands of the situation, often without explicit instruction or communication) is the cognitive representation or mental model developed by participants (Cannon-Bowers, Salas, & Converse, 1990; Ford & Kraiger, 1992).

The virtual team is "intelligent" because of the particular expertise of its members (i.e., technical skill) and the ability of each member to work as an effective "team member" (i.e., team skill). In short, the effective virtual team is one that can operate as a team even without having had the opportunity to "learn to do so," because each member is skilled in teamwork. The effective virtual team is like an amoeba evolving in both form and substance to suit its requirement: it is flexible, having the ability to adapt to circumstances, drawing in resources (e.g., expertise) as and when required.

Another predictor of transfer is termed "metacognition" (i.e., learning strategies and self-regulatory processes that facilitate the generalization of knowledge to novel contexts and circumstances) (e.g., Larson & Christensen, 1993). This is the prescription of particular behavioral processes (as in the typical team-building intervention), which implies that context is a constant and can mean that the team is ill-equipped to respond appropriately to contextual variation and challenge. The criterion of virtual team development success would, in this instance, be whether the team is sufficiently equipped (cognitively and motivationally) to adjust efficiently and effectively to whatever is thrown at it.

A metacognitive orientation reflects the degree to which the team members are cognitively orientated toward effective team working. The clearer team members are as to how each member contributes to the team and how the team contributes to the organization, the more effective the team will be. In practical terms, this suggests that the most effective virtual team development interventions will be those that involve the development and setting of shared goals (Locke, 1968). Furthermore, if this process leads to the optimization of communication between members and an increased valuing of team working, it will again be more likely to improve team performance within the workplace.

To summarize, an effective virtual team is one that can regulate and manage itself. In order to do this, a shift in focus away from process to virtual team cognition and metacognition is required in the way we understand and work with virtual teams.

REDEFINITION OF A VIRTUAL TEAM

The previous discussion leads to a need for the reconceptualization of the virtual team. A virtual team is a collection of individuals who think, feel, and act as an interdependent unit and who are recognized by others to constitute a virtual team. The psychological reality of a virtual team is defined independently of the way the virtual team works, because the exact nature and form of its expression will vary depending on structural (e.g., work design, role sets), compositional (e.g., of whom is the team comprised?), contextual (e.g., team location and distribution of members), and other organizational factors (e.g., reward structures). A virtual team exists to the extent that members:

1. Are aware of themselves as comprising a virtual team
2. Identify with the team (i.e., self-concept and self-esteem are bound up with the team (Dutton, Dukerich, & Harquail, 1994)
3. Commit to and invest heavily in team success (insofar as team success or failure equals individual success or failure; Mael & Tetrick, 1992)
4. Perceive themselves to be accountable (for what they do and contribute to the team and to each other) for team success (Millward & Hopkins, 1997, 1998), counteracting social loafing tendencies in collective contexts where individual contributions are not identifiable (Williams, Karau, & Bourgeous, 1992) and also groupthink (Janis, 1972)

This definition locates our understanding of the virtual team within the cognitive realm, advocating a conceptual distinction between the "causes" of virtual teams' behavior and their generative consequences (i.e., team processes) and outcomes (i.e., output/results). The factors of which a virtual team is comprised are, however, a necessary but not sufficient basis for effective virtual teamwork. Further, elaboration is necessary regarding the development of effective virtual teamwork.

What is an Effective Virtual Team?

It is conventional to conceptualize virtual teamwork at the level of observable behaviors and processes. It can be argued, however, that this approach is limited in focus, insofar as it cannot tell us what makes a virtual team effective in any absolute sense, because what constitutes an effective behavior is likely to be context and time specific: a competent team is one that has transferable skills (Miller, Ross, & Freeman, 1999) and can thus respond flexibly to task demands and contextual changes. Models of virtual team effectiveness, however, should move away from a behavioral focus to try to understand teamwork at a cognitive level. Following Varney (1989), it could be argued that crucial underlying causes of virtual team behavior are role awareness and consideration of other's perspectives and skills, which are independent of context. If these causes are managed properly, the team can correct its behavior, exhibiting the appropriate teamwork behavior for a given situation. In this sense, good virtual teams monitor their performance and self-correct, anticipate each other's actions or needs, and coordinate their actions — that is, a good virtual team can be said to have a SMM (Cannon-Bowers et al., 1990).

Cannon-Bowers et al. (1990) defined a mental model as that which allows individuals to form explanations and expectations of events so that they can decide upon the appropriate action to adopt. With regard to virtual teamwork, practice and experience facilitate the development of cognitive representations of the team task (including teammates' knowledge, skills, abilities, preferences, and tendencies) and of team interaction (including roles and responsibilities, interaction and communication patterns, role interdependencies, and information sources). When individual member's representations (of task, team, and team interaction) overlap, a SMM can be said to exist, enabling members to predict and anticipate their needs and contributions to the team. That is, the more shared knowledge a virtual team has, the better their virtual teamwork potential. This approach does not, however, explain how virtual teams self-regulate or motivate themselves.

A model of virtual team effectiveness is proposed here, therefore, incorporating not only the idea of SMM but also addressing the metacognitive and

Figure 1: The traditional process model of virtual team effectiveness and its implications for virtual team-building focus.

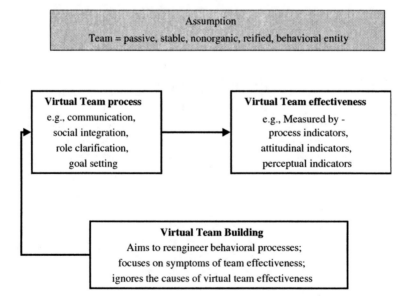

Figure 2: The cognitive motivational model of virtual team effectiveness.

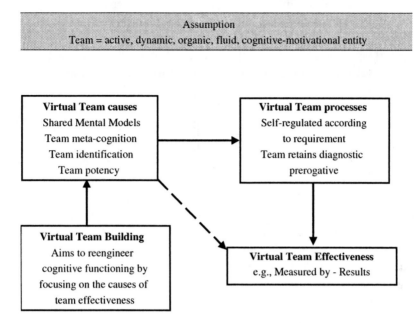

motivational aspects of virtual team functioning. The model suggests that in order for a team to self-regulate, it must have a sound knowledge of itself (its roles, objectives, strengths, and weaknesses) and be able to reflect upon and review its knowledge and practices and subsequently refine or correct these. This is essential for the virtual team to be adaptable and flexible to changing circumstances. This process requires not just a SMM of the team and its task but also cognitions at a metalevel, that is, in the self-regulatory sense (Yzerbyt et al., 1998), as well as a sense of team motivation.

Moreover, we identify two important aspects of team motivation: identity and potency. The identity of the individual is affected by whether the individual is proud to be part of the team, such that self-concept and esteem will be related to the team's success (implying, therefore, that team success takes precedence over individual success) (see Millward & Purvis, 1998). Potency, by contrast, is the collective belief that the team can succeed and be effective in global terms (Guzzo, 1986).

Cognitive approaches to understanding teamwork are gaining status, as it becomes clear that team interventions based upon identifying and changing behaviors have limited impact (Tannenbaum, Lories, & Dardenne, 1992: see Figure 1). This is because behavior is situation, task, team, and individual specific. By examining the cognitive factors influencing team behavior at a deeper level, one can identify the variables that are constant across different situations and upon which pervasive, long-term interventions can be based (see Figure 2).

It could be argued, therefore, that the intelligent virtual team engineers its own processes to suit the requirements. The intelligent virtual team must be as follows:

1. Goal directed — i.e., oriented to the achievement of common goals and objectives. Shared goals and purposes may be instilled by developing team mission statements and core values to help members set objectives, clarify roles, build personal relationships, develop team norms, and establish team identity.
2. Able to reflect on and strategically manage its own processes (interpersonal and task processes) — i.e., virtual team metacognition. A major component of the team's metacognition is the ability to develop ability-based or task-based trust. Building trust in virtual teams requires rapid responses to electronic communications from team members, reliable performance, and consistent follow-through, which should be incorporated into the team's task processes as team norms. Trust in virtual teams grows through team member reliability, consistency, and responsiveness when dealing with teammates.
3. Able to diagnose the "process requirements" of a situation and to respond accordingly.
4. Able to harness and to optimize all of its resources (individually and as a team) as necessary, including "experience" (i.e., with an attitude of "appreciative inquiry").
5. Cognizant of its strengths and weaknesses and can maximize its strengths and take steps to overcome or minimize its weaknesses.
6. Recognizes and rewards the specific contributions and roles of all of its members.
7. Able to learn from its experience (i.e., "capturing learning"), maximizing learning opportunity. "Learning" is stored in the "system" (i.e., within the team as a whole), as opposed to within individual team members (Argote, 1993).
8. Able to reconcile the individual with the team goals and provide opportunity for personal development (Locke & Latham, 1990). Performance data provide a solid foundation for recognizing and rewarding team and individual performances, developing new training programs to assist virtual teams, and identifying individual team members who can benefit from offline mentoring and coaching (Kirkman et al., 2002).

9. Cognizant of the need for diversity within the team and openness of the team to outside influence as a prerequisite to team flexibility and innovative capacity (Conway & Forrestor, 1997).

10. Confident in its self-regulatory ability and success, and is energized accordingly (i.e., team potency or collective belief in a group that it can be effective (Guzzo, Yost, Campbell, & Shea, 1993). Several experts (45%) suggest that training in team skills is part of the process of helping the team become self-regulated (i.e., skills in process analysis, process requirement analysis, process management).

In summary, it is argued that the concept of virtual team pertains to an awareness by members of their existence as a team, a sense of identification with and commitment to the team, and a sense of personal responsibility to and accountability for team success. The concept of virtual team is distinct from the concept of virtual team effectiveness. The effective virtual team is modeled as the self-regulating team, one with a highly articulated knowledge of itself as a team (knowledge of its own processes, and its own strengths and weaknesses, its goals, and so on), a metacognitive ability to reflect upon and adapt its processes according to requirement, and a sense of its own potency (i.e., shared belief in its own ability to be effective).

CONCLUSION

The key operational principle is that virtual team development interventions are addressed to the causes of team effectiveness rather than team processes. In Figure 2, the focus is on virtual team development on the promotion of a team focus and orientation as a prerequisite to team effectiveness and on the promotion of team competence at cognitive (team mental models), metacognitive (higher-order self-regulatory strategies), and motivational levels (team identification and team potency).

In the case of virtual teams, where membership is distributed cross-functionally and is also geographically widely dispersed, team focus and orientation may be absent (because of low proximity and contact) and will be actively engineered and managed by the team leader. A critical issue is for team members not to lose sight of their interdependence and thus the basis of their "teamness." The development of techniques like groupware are of value insofar as they keep the interdependencies (whether goal or task interdependencies) alive on a day-to-day basis for team members, enabling the creation of a virtual working space across the Internet.

REFERENCES

Argote, L. (1993). Group and organization learning curves. Individual, system and environmental components. *British Journal of Social Psychology, 32*, 31–51.

Bird, A. (1975). Development of a model for predicting team performance. *Research Quarterly, 48*(1), 24–32.

Cannon-Bowers, J., Salas, E., & Converse, S. (1990). Cognitive psychology and team training: Training shared mental models of complex systems. *Human Factors Society, 32*, 1–4.

Conway, S., & Forrestor, R. (1997). Innovation and teamworking: Combining perspectives through a focus on team boundaries. Paper presented at the International Workshop on Teamworking. University of Nottingham, 17–18 September.

Dubrovsky, V., Kiesler, S., & Sethna, B. (1991). The equalization phenomenon: Status effects in computer-mediated and face-to-face decision making groups. *Human Computer Interaction, 6*(1), 119–146.

Dutton, J., Dukerich, J., & Harquail, C. (1994). Organizational images and member identification. *Administrative Science Quarterly, 39*, 239–263.

Ford, J. K., & Kraiger, K. (1992). The application of cognitive constructs and principles to the instructional systems model of training: Implications for needs assessment, design and transfer. In C. Cooper & I. Robertson (Eds.), *International review of industrial and organizational psychology*. Mahweh, NJ: Lawrence Erlbaum.

Guzzo, R. A. (1986). Group decision making and group effectiveness. In P.S. Goodman (Eds.), *Designing effective work groups* (pp. 34–71). San Francisco: Jossey-Bass.

Guzzo, R. A., Yost, P., Campbell, R., & Shea, G. P. (1993). Potency in groups: Articulating a construct. *British Journal of Social Psychology, 32*, 87–106.

Hardingham, A., & Royal, J. (1994). *Pulling together: Teamwork and practice*. London: IPD Book.

Hightower, R. T., & Sayeed, L. (1996). Effects of communication mode and pre-discussion information distribution characteristics on information exchange in groups. *Information Systems Research, 7*(4), 451–465.

Hiltz, S. R., & Johnson, K. (1990). User satisfaction with computer-mediated communication systems. *Management Science, 36*(6), 739–764.

Hiltz, S. R., & Turoff, M. (1985). Structuring computer-mediated communication systems to avoid information overload. *Communications of the ACM, 28*(7), 680–689.

Huber, G. P. (1990). A theory of the effects of advanced information technologies on organizational design, intelligence, and decision making. *Academy of Management Review, 15*, 47–71.

Janis, I. L. (1972). *GroupThink: Psychological studies of policy decisions and fiascoes*. Boston, MA: Houghton.

Jarvenpaa, S. L., Knoll, K., & Leidner, D. E. (1998). Is anybody out there? Antecedents of trust in global virtual teams. *Journal of Management Information Systems, 14*(4), 29–64.

Kirkman, B. L., Rosen, B., Gibson, C. B., Tesluk, P. E., & McPherson, S. M. (2002). Five challenges to virtual team success: Lessons from Sabre, Inc. *Academy of Management Executive, 16*(3), 67–79.

Lipnack, J., & Stamps, J. (1997). Virtual teams. In J. Lipnack and J. Stamps (Eds.), *Reaching across space, time, and organizations with technology*. New York: John Wiley & Sons.

Locke, E. A. (1968). Toward a theory of task motivation and incentives. *Organizational Behaviour and Human Performance, 2*, 157–189.

Locke, E. A., & Latham, G. P. (1990). *A theory of goal setting and task performance*. Englewood Cliffs, NJ: Prentice Hall.

Mael, F. A., & Tetrick, L. A. (1992). Identifying organizational identification. *Education and Psychological Measurement, 52*, 813–824.

Miller, C., Ross, N., & Freeman, M. (1999). *Shared learning and clinical teamwork: New directions in education for multi-professional practice*. London: English National Board.

Millward, L. J. (1995). Contextualising social identity in considerations of what it means to be a nurse. *European Journal of Social Psychology, 25*(3), 303–324.

Millward, L. J., & Brewerton, P. (1999). Contractors and their psychological contracts. *British Journal of Management, 10*, 253–274.

Millward, L. J., & Hopkins, L. J. (1997). A psychological contract and identification model of risk ownership. *International Journal of Risk and Project Management*. July, 111–120.

Millward, L. J., & Hopkins, L. J. (1998). Psychological contracts, organizational and job commitment. *Journal of Applied Social Psychology, 28*, 16–31.

Millward, J. L., & Purvis, R. (1998). *Team building techniques — A critical evaluation*. Defence Evaluation Research Agency. Centre for Human Sciences, Farnborough, UK.

Moreland, R. L., & Levine, J. M. (1991). Problem identification by groups. In S. Worchel, W. Wood, and J. Simpson (Eds.), *Group processes and productivity* (pp. 17–47). Newbury Park: Sage.

O'Hara-Devereaux, M., & Johansen, R. (1994). *Global work: Bridging distance, culture, and time*. San Francisco: Jossey-Bass.

Solomon, C. M. (1995). Global teams: The ultimate collaboration. *Personnel Journal, 74*(9), 49–58.

Tannenbaum, S., Beard, R., & Salas, E. (1992). Teambuilding and its influence on team effectiveness: An examination of conceptual and empirical development. In K. Kelley (Ed.), *Issues, theory and research in industrial/ occupational psychology: Advances in psychology* (pp. 117–153). San Francisco: Jossey-Bass.

Townsend, A. M., DeMarie, S. M., & Hendrickson, A. R. (1998). Virtual teams: Technology and the workplace of the future. *Academy of Management Executive, 12,* 17–29.

Varney, G. (1989). *Building productive teams: An action guide and a resource book.* London: Jossey Brown.

Walther, J. B., & Burgoon, J. K. (1992). Relational communication in computer mediated interaction. *Human Communication Research, 19*(1), 850–889.

Warkentin, M., Sayeed, L., & Hightower, R. (1997). Virtual teams vs. face to face teams: An exploratory study of web-based conference systems. *Decision Sciences, 28*(4), 975–976.

Watson-Fritz, M. B., Narasimhan, S., & Rhee, H. (1998). Communication and coordination in the virtual office. *Journal of Management Information Systems, 14,* 7–28.

Williams, K., Karau, S., & Bourgeous, M. (1992). Working on collective tasks: Social loafing and social compensation.

Yzerbyt, V. Y., Lories, G., & Dardenne, B. (1998). *Metacognition: Cognitive and social dimensions.* Thousand Oaks, CA: Sage.

Chapter III

Understanding Composition and Conflict in Virtual Teams

Richard Potter, University of Illinois at Chicago, USA

Pierre Balthazard, Arizona State University West, USA

ABSTRACT

Drawing from several years of empirical research, in this chapter, we look at the impact of the personalities of individual team members on the performance and process outcomes of virtual teams. Our studies showed that both too few and too many extroverts in a virtual team may result in low performance. While conventional wisdom says that teams should be set up on the basis of expertise, we argue that the resulting interaction styles of the members must be considered when establishing a virtual team. We offer suggestions for managers on assessing the potential for constructive interaction styles.

INTRODUCTION

The virtual team is an increasingly common strategic work unit of many organizations. Though research is still developing, at this stage, it is not clear whether virtual teams deliver the level of performance that their face-to-face (F2F) counterparts typically do. Do factors that drive conventional team performance also exist in the virtual environment? Rooted in the personalities of individual team members, a team's *interaction style* was shown to have a great effect on a conventional teams' ability to achieve solution quality and solution acceptance when faced with problem-solving and decision tasks (Hirokawa, 1985; Hirokawa & Gouran, 1989; Watson & Michaelsen, 1988; Cooke & Szumal, 1993). Group interaction styles affect communication and thus team performance by facilitating or hindering the exchange of information among group members. The interaction style of conventional teams can be reliably assessed, and from that assessment, performance problems can be identified. In addition, when forming new teams, managers can identify constellations of personality types that are likely to yield a constructive group interaction style and perform well together.

Methodologies and instruments originally developed at the University of Michigan's Institute for Social Research are commercially available to organization development professionals, consultants, and researchers, who wish to assess a number of vital dynamics of groups and teams. These include group interaction style, influence and leadership, and organizational culture. The authors recreated a variety of these instruments for use with virtual teams, with rigorous validation on hundreds of real-life teams (e.g., Balthazard, 1999). Results show that the dynamics of F2F group interaction styles are also evident in virtual teams. In addition, the effects of the interaction styles are similar to those in conventional F2F teams. However, there are a number of interesting and powerful effects that are a result of the communication mode.

Our research is now at the level of the personalities of the individual team members. Many studies documented the existence of five basic personality types. Our more recent studies focused on one of these, extroversion. Extroversion is considered the most robust and stable of the five types and also received previous attention from information systems and communications researchers. Our novel approach documents the effects not only of the relative amount of extroverted team members but also of the effects stemming from the ratio of extroverts to nonextroverts in the team's composition. These two measures of the personality trait have profound and different effects that drive the formation of the team's ultimate characterization of its interaction style, with the styles' resulting effects on performance and process outcomes.

This chapter draws from several years of empirical research by the authors and their colleagues, much of it presented at academic and consultant conferences and published in a number of information systems, team management, and international management academic journals. Our aim is to introduce readers to this fascinating research and to illustrate how virtual team composition by personality and interaction style drives performance and process outcomes. Common managerial wisdom, along with expense and convenience consideration, dictates that virtual teams be composed strictly on the basis of complimentary expertise. Our research showed that expertise is not likely to drive team performance to its potential when the team is afflicted by a negative interaction style. Negative interaction styles are more common when the team is virtual rather than F2F, and negative interaction styles can easily result in teams with a composition of personalities that is not harmonious.

This research continues to gain wide acceptance by academics and practitioners, because it gives scientific grounding to something that most of us already know: personality clashes in teams or groups drag performance and satisfaction down. In addition — and perhaps most valuable — we show how personality and interaction styles can be assessed in virtual teams, how that assessment can alert members and managers to potential process and performance problems, and how to correct those problems (present or potential). We begin with a discussion of research on interaction styles, performance, and personality in conventional groups and teams and then take a close look at these factors at play in the virtual world.

BACKGROUND
Team Interaction and Performance

Teams involved in intellectual work frequently must create, assess, and exchange information to accomplish their tasks, and like other forms of human work groups, they often have to face conflicting "task" and "social" pressures. The way in which a team deals with these pressures is reflected in the team's *interaction style*. Watson and Michaelson (1988) defined group interaction as the way group members pool their abilities in a collaborative context in order to reach the best decision. Watson and Michaelsen (1988) identified positive and negative behaviors as components of group interaction style. Three groups of behaviors (expectations of performance and integration, leadership, and cohesiveness) contributed to team performance on an intellective task, while one group of negative behaviors (e.g., noninvolvement, withholding of information) detracted. These communication behaviors are rooted in the stable personality characteristics of group members, and the aggregation of these individual behaviors characterizes a group or team's interaction style.

Building on the Watson and Michaelsen typology and others (Maier, 1967; Hoffman, 1979), Cooke and Szumal (1994) found that group interaction takes one of three general styles: constructive, passive, and aggressive. The *constructive style* is characterized by a balanced concern for personal and group outcomes, cooperation, creativity, free exchange of information, and respect for others' perspectives. The constructive style enables group members to fulfill needs for personal achievement as well as needs for affiliation. The *passive style* places greater emphasis on fulfillment of affiliation goals only, maintaining harmony in the group, and limiting information sharing, questioning, and impartiality. The *aggressive style* places greater emphasis on personal achievement needs, with personal ambitions placed above concern for group outcome. Aggressive groups are characterized by competition, criticism, interruptions, and overt impatience.

Constructive, passive, and aggressive teams each achieve different levels and patterns of effectiveness. Specifically, predominantly constructive groups produce solutions that are superior in quality to those produced by passive groups and superior in acceptance to those produced by either passive or aggressive groups. Groups with predominantly passive styles produce solutions that are inferior in quality to those of constructive (and possibly aggressive) groups and inferior in acceptance to those of constructive groups. Similarly, groups with predominantly aggressive styles produce solutions that are not as consistently of high quality as those generated by constructive groups but not as consistently of low quality as those produced by passive groups. The solutions produced by aggressive groups generate less overall acceptance than those developed by constructive groups and about the same level of acceptance as those generated by passive groups (Cooke & Szumal, 1994).

Ultimately, group interaction styles affect performance, because they can impede or enhance team members' ability to bring their unique knowledge and skills to bear on the task and the extent to which they develop and consider alternative strategies for approaching the task (Hackman & Morris, 1975). This is particularly critical for groups with heterogeneous levels and areas of expertise, as communication by most expert group members is positively correlated with group performance.

Assessing Interaction Styles and Performance

The Group Styles Inventory (GSI) was developed to measure group interaction styles that are theoretically linked to the quality and acceptance of group solutions (Cooke & Lafferty, 1988). The GSI is a self-report survey made up of 72 statements regarding the demeanor of members, the atmosphere of the problem-solving session, and the impact of the group on the behavior of individual members. The items (short phrases) assess 12 styles that aggregate into three distinct, yet interrelated, group style clusters — constructive, passive/defensive, and aggressive/defensive. Each style is measured by six items that describe specific collective behaviors that might characterize a group *to a very great extent* (Response 4) or, at the other extreme, *not at all* (Response 0). The scores on four related styles are then aggregated to derive the three style cluster scores.

The 12 styles measured by the GSI are (1) humanistic-encouraging, (2) affiliative, (3) approval, (4) conventional, (5) dependent, (6) avoidance, (7) oppositional, (8) power, (9) competitive, (10) perfectionistic, (11) achievement, and (12) self-actualization. The selection of these styles and their placement on the circumplex reflect the distinctions between "security" versus "satisfaction" needs and "people" versus "task" orientations. Maslow's (1954) work on lower- and higher-order needs led to the distinction between styles oriented toward the fulfillment of security needs (the conventional, dependent, avoidance, opposi- tional, and power styles in GSI) and styles oriented toward higher-order or satisfaction needs (the humanistic-encouraging, affiliative, perfectionistic, achievement, and self-actualizing styles in GSI). When divided another way, the circumplex reflects the distinction between people and task orientations implicit in most theories of leadership. A concern for people is reflected in the humanistic-encouraging, affiliative, approval, conventional, and dependent styles; a concern for tasks is reflected in the oppositional, power, competitive, perfectionistic, and achievement styles (Cooke & Lafferty, 1982).

Yet another interpretation of GSI splits the circumplex into the three general clusters defined above, each of which contains four styles. The four styles that constitute the *Constructive* cluster facilitate high-quality problem solving and decision making (humanistic-encouraging, affiliative, achievement, self-actual- izing). The other eight styles are grouped into either the *Passive/Defensive* or *Aggressive/Defensive* clusters, and they detract from effective performance.

The GSI is typically used after a team decision-making or problem-solving task, such as a survival or business situation simulation. The preliminary task engages participants to solve a decision problem on their own and then asks them to solve the problem as a group. From the exercise, individual performance as well as performance as a team can be evaluated against a standard, typically the ideal solution promulgated by one or more domain experts. Objective perfor- mance measures include average individual performance, team performance gain or loss, the average individual scores, and the team's gain over the solution of its best member. Following this task, the GSI is used to capture individual team member's perceptions of team process. It assesses process outcomes, such as group solution acceptance, and identifies the team's dominant interaction style. It then becomes the format for giving the group members insight into factors explaining the group's performance, including their individual interaction styles with regard to decision making, problem solving, and relating to one another. By using the instrument to develop shared perceptions of the group's (and its individual members') functioning during the problem-solving process, the group can determine what it needs to do to make the group process more effective. Used in combination with a decision-making or problem-solving task, the tools give teams a means for measuring and monitoring team performance, for developing a creative and open team culture, for improving analytical skills and consensus problem-solving and decision-making skills and, ultimately, improving team synergy and performance.

Digging Deeper: Personality and Interaction Style

Five personality factors were identified that constitute the fundamental dimensions of personality (Fiske, 1949; Hogan, 1991; McCrae & John, 1992). These dimensions or factors are extroversion, agreeableness, conscientiousness, openness, and neuroticism. They provide a broad, yet inclusive and empirically tested way, of looking at personality in the work environment (Hogan, 1991; Barry & Stewart, 1997). Extroversion refers to the degree to which individuals are gregarious, friendly, compliant, cooperative, nurturing, caring, and sympathetic, versus introversion, which is characterized by the degree to which individuals are shy, unassertive, and withdrawn. Conscientious describes those who are achievement oriented, well organized, neat, dependable, and hard working, versus those who are disorganized, impulsive, careless, unreliable, and lazy. Openness refers to the degree to which individuals are intelligent, imaginative, curious, original, and creative, versus the degree to which they are more conservative in their opinions, dull, literal-minded, and set in their ways. Neuroticism can be characterized by individuals who are tense, self-doubting, depressed, irrational thinkers, moody, low in self-esteem, and ineffective in coping, versus those who are emotionally stable and exhibit self-confidence, high self-esteem, and calmness. Agreeableness describes individuals who are cooperative, warm, tactful, and considerate, versus those who are independent, cold, rude, harsh, and unsympathetic.

Of these five factors, extroversion received the greatest attention from researchers and has shown to be the most stable of the constructs. Barrick and Mount (1991) found that extroversion and conscientiousness were the two, out of the five, traits that consistently related to success in the workplace (Barrick & Mount, 1991). They concluded that extroversion correlates positively with individual performance in jobs involving social interaction. Barry and Stewart (1997) found that at the individual level, extroversion was the "key" personality correlated with individual impact on group performance. There was a positive relationship between extroversion and impact on group performance at the individual level. Extroverts are usually active participants in group interactions and often have high intragroup popularity (Barry & Stewart, 1997).

But, extroversion is a two-edged sword. While extroverts have strong tendencies to be articulate and expressive, and may be able to persuade and influence others (Goldberg, 1990; Watson & Clark, 1997), an important behavioral characteristic of extroversion is dominance (Trapnell & Wiggins, 1990). House and Howell (1992) described dominance as a tendency to "take initiative in social settings, to introduce people to each other, and to be socially engaging by being humorous, introducing topics of discussion, and stimulating social interaction" (p. 85). The proportion of group members who are high in extroversion may be related to the groups' interaction style, which in turn, relates to group performance. Barry and Stewart (1997) found that the proportion of high-extroversion group members was related curvilinearly to task focus and group performance. Too few extroverts may result in low performance, whereas too many extroverts may lead to a decrease in group performance due to the group's lessened ability to remain focused on task completion (McCrae & Costa, 1992). Two possible reasons are as follows: extroverts may be more concerned with pleasurable social interactions than task completion (Barry & Stewart, 1997), and too many extroverts may result in intrateam conflict. Recalling that one of the characteristics of extroverts is dominance, conflict can occur when there are too many dominant individuals (Mazur, 1973).

Interaction, Performance, and Personality in the Virtual World

In recent studies, it was demonstrated that when operating in teams via computer-mediated communication channels, individual team members' behavioral and psychological communication characteristics are essentially the same as their conventional F2F counterparts. As with F2F teams, virtual team members can express themselves and discern each other's communications sufficiently well to characterize the style of that communication, in turn, resulting in a team interaction style. In addition, group interaction styles have the same effects on performance outcomes, such as decision quality, as well as process outcomes, such as solution acceptance, in both modalities (Potter, Balthazard, & Cooke, 2000; Potter & Balthazard, 2002a). These studies also provided detail on the development, validation, and technology of the virtual team version of the GSI and two preliminary decision-making/problem-solving tasks (Balthazard, 1999a, b). The first of these studies used 139 members of 31 virtual teams, and the second used 186 members of 42 virtual teams.

However, a more recent study comparing 69 virtual and 78 F2F teams directly showed that there are some significant differences that arise when teams work virtually (Balthazard, Potter, & Cooke, 2002). First, virtual teams typically do not perform as well as F2F teams and have much less propensity for achieving a better solution than either the average individual or the team's best member. Perhaps more important, virtual teams displayed significantly less team synergy, solution acceptance, cohesion, and group commitment. Members of virtual teams perceived their interactions to be less effective than members of F2F teams. A lack of solution acceptance, poor cohesion, and weak group commitment are compelling predictors of longer-term performance difficulties of virtual teams.

In addition, the development of a group interaction style appears to be dependent, at least in part, on the communication mode [i.e., computer-mediated communication (CMC) versus F2F]. Virtual teams, in comparison to F2F teams, have fewer tendencies to develop constructive or aggressive styles and more tendencies to develop passive interaction styles. Moreover, while communication mode is related to group interaction styles and performance, the moderator–mediator regression analysis used in that study suggested that, in fact, mode may contribute to outcomes only through its effect on interaction style. In other words, the effect of mode on outcomes tends to dissolve when interaction type is taken into account: Constructive teams tend to do well regardless of the communication mode, and passive teams tend to do poorly regardless of the communication mode. Aggressive teams tend to do poorly, and more so in virtual settings.

Finally, the findings of that study echoed those of earlier studies, again showing that group interaction styles predict performance in both modes. Teams with a predominantly constructive interaction style produce more team synergy and promote increased solution acceptance, healthy cohesion, and group commitment. Members of such teams perceive their interactions as effective. Teams with a passive interaction style produce more team errors and less team synergy. The passive style discourages solution acceptance and group commitment and promotes poor cohesion. Members of such teams do not perceive their interactions as effective. Although teams with a predominantly aggressive interaction style can produce good or bad team performance in the short term, in the longer term, aggressive teams also discourage solution acceptance and group commitment and promote poor cohesion. Members of such teams also do not perceive their interactions as effective.

The final study we discuss here examined the role of extroversion in virtual teams (Balthazard, Potter, & Warren, 2002; Balthazard et al., 2002). In that study with 248 members of 63 groups, we saw that extroversion led to constructive or aggressive styles, and that differences in the proportion of extroverted individuals on a team led to passive styles. Perhaps most important, we found that it is mostly group styles (and not individual personality or the expertise of one individual) that have predictive power on outcomes in virtual teams. This study used a preliminary task that asked participants to make a business decision regarding ethics (Balthazard, 2000).

Consistent with McCrae and Costa (1992), who found that too much extroversion can lead to decreases in performance, increased extroversion in these virtual teams also decreased a team's objective performance on the decision task. Variances in extroversion within virtual teams (which connotes the presence of extroverts and nonextroverts) appeared to trigger largely negative interaction characteristics. For example, large variances in extroversion were associated with passive interaction styles and nonconstructive behaviors. These intrateam variances in extroversion also decreased process outcomes, such as commitment.

The Bigger Picture for Virtual Teams

Three overarching implications can be drawn from the theory and research we presented above, each important for those involved with virtual teamwork. First, individual personality and its effects on others in one's group do not go away just because the group or team is doing its collaborative work online rather than F2F. Though some researchers showed that dominance behaviors often displayed by extroverts in conventional team settings (e.g., talking a disproportionate amount or otherwise limiting the input of others) can be ameliorated to some degree online by virtue of the technology's capacity for parallel input processing, extroverts can still dominate by other means, such as by using stronger language or voicing more vehement objections to others' input. And, the effects in virtual teams mirror those found in conventional teams: a little extroversion can be a plus, but a little goes a long way. A high proportion of extroverts on a team invites conflict and pushes nonextroverts into passivity.

Second, interaction styles have the greatest effect on virtual team performance and process outcomes, far stronger than the mode, and also stronger than the level of extroversion (and most likely the other individual personality characteristics taken separately). Computer-based communication mode, that is, working via e-mail or threaded discussion Web pages, was held by many to be the leading suspect in virtual team performance problems. Our results soundly refute this for two reasons. First, prior research in this area did not consider the role of interaction styles and member personalities. Second, CMC modes are now sufficiently "rich" to allow unambiguous and largely unaffected communication to support many group processes. Our methodology obviously did not account for all types of team behaviors supportable by modern CMC technology, but it does assess information sharing, group synergy, decision quality, and process outcomes, all surely core elements of the behavior of any team engaged in knowledge work.

Our third point is a caveat to this second point. Interaction styles profoundly influence team performance and process outcomes. Communication mode, by comparison, has little direct effect. But it does have an important, if indirect, effect. By reducing the salience or social presence of the team and its members, the CMC mode facilitates passivity. Members can ignore communication, and the team may function passively for some time before a norm about communication amount and frequency develops. The norm may act to reduce passivity (if it is not too late), or it may simply reflect it.

Reducing passivity and encouraging communication and participation are behaviors strongly associated with the constructive interaction style, the style associated with high-performing teams. Unfortunately, teams working via the CMC mode are significantly less likely to display this style. Why? These behaviors have physical components such as eye contact, vocal inflection, posture, and gesturing that are used to induce participation, diminish negative domination, and otherwise regulate and encourage healthy group participation and processes. These cannot be used to fight passivity or aggression in a mode that does not permit them to be seen.

Putting the Tools to Work

While the conventional team versions of the tools and methodologies discussed here have been used for over two decades by organizational development professionals around the world, the virtual versions are just now becoming available for practitioners and researchers. In their traditional guise, they are chiefly used to diagnose performance problems in teams and groups, often as part of a larger organization development initiative. In addition, when used proactively, they permit managers to assess how a potential team's members are likely to interact and, thus, perform. The virtual instruments can be used in the same manner. As noted, conventional wisdom on virtual teams seems to be that the teams are to be assembled solely on the basis of complimentary expertise needed for a project. Although the formation of a virtual team of dispersed experts may have apparent cost and convenience advantages over a conventional F2F team, there is no guarantee that either type of team is going to exhibit a constructive interaction style and perform to its potential. In actuality, a virtual team is more likely to suffer the handicap of a nonconstructive interaction style. Cost and convenience advantages suddenly disappear when the nonconstructive virtual team's performance lags.

Fortunately, forewarned is forearmed. Virtual team managers, like their conventional counterparts, can now assess a team's interaction and performance potential before cutting it loose. If project expertise requirements dictate a lineup that exhibits a nonconstructive interaction style, team-building exercises or other organization development interventions can be used to reduce behaviors that contribute to those styles and to groom a constructive interaction style. If an established virtual team is not performing up to desired standards, the tools can be used at any later stage to diagnose the interaction style and the role it is playing. In addition, personality inventories, such as the Myers–Briggs test, can be used, along with our methodologies, to dig deeper into the root sources of the interaction style.

FUTURE DIRECTIONS

We described our work at individual and team levels and will continue with more studies (a more complete description of our methodology and results can be found in Potter and Balthazard, 2002b), and we are continuing our research and development on virtual versions of tools for the assessment of influence and leadership and organizational ethics in teams. But increasingly, organizations deploy larger units in virtual forms, and some entire organizations operate completely virtual. At some point, often beginning at the departmental level, organizational units form their own cultures. Many years of organizational culture research findings point to the positive and negative ramifications of culture at these various levels. In addition, mergers, acquisitions, partnerships, and global or multinational organizations all connote a meshing of previously independent organizational cultures. Our current research agenda focuses on these larger forms and the assessment and effects of culture. As we did with the team-size instruments, we are developing and validating instruments to assess culture and its effects on the virtual organizational unit.

CONCLUSION

In this chapter, we introduced the reader to our work aimed at understanding virtual team performance. We showed that a major key to team performance — particularly with knowledge-based teams — is the team's interaction style. This style stems from stable personality characteristics, such as extroversion, and prompts a number of behaviors that team members exhibit. A passive or aggressive style diminishes information sharing, participation, and critical thinking in any team, and virtual teams are more likely than their conventional counterparts to suffer performance problems from these nonconstructive styles. The good news is that virtual team managers and members can now assess their potential for achieving a constructive interaction style and the performance pluses that come with it. And, ailing virtual teams can now be properly diagnosed, most likely to find good old-fashioned human conflict, rather than technology, to be the ghost in the machine.

REFERENCES

Balthazard, P. A. (1999a). In R. A. Cooke, & J. C. Lafferty, *Virtual version of the Group Styles Inventory*. Arlington Heights, IL: Human Synergistics/Center for Applied Research.

Balthazard, P. A. (1999b). In J. C. Lafferty, & A. W. Pond, *Virtual version of the Desert Survival Situation*. Arlington Heights, IL: Human Synergistics/Center for Applied Research.

Balthazard, P. A. (2000). In R. A. Cooke, *Virtual version Ethical Decision Challenge*. Arlington Heights, IL: Human Synergistics/Center for Applied Research.

Balthazard, P. A., Potter, R. E., & Cooke, R. A. (2002). Process and performance in face-to-face and virtual teams: the mediating role of group interaction styles. Working Paper #106. Chicago, IL: Department of Information and Decision Sciences, University of Illinois at Chicago.

Balthazard, P. A., Potter, R. E., & Warren, J. (2002). The effects of expertise and extroversion on virtual team interaction and performance. In *Proceedings of the 53rd Annual Hawaii International Conference on System Sciences*, Honolulu, Hawaii.

Balthazard, P. A., Potter, R. E., & Warren, J. (2002a). Expertise, extroversion, and group interaction as task and contextual performance indicators in virtual teams. *Data Base, 56,* 1-21.

Barrick, M. R., & Mount, M. K. (1991). The big five personality dimensions and job performance: a meta-analysis. *Personnel Psychology, 44,* 1–26.

Barrick, M. R. et al. (1998). Relating member ability and personality to work-team processes and team effectiveness. *Journal of Applied Psychology, 83*(3), 377–391.

Barry, B., & Stewart, G. L. (1997). Composition, process and performance in self-managed groups: the role of personality. *Journal of Applied Psychology, 82*(1), 62–78.

Cooke, R. A., & Lafferty, J. C. (1988). *Group styles inventory.* Plymouth, MI: Human Synergistics.

Cooke, R. A., & Szumal, J. L. (1993). Measuring normative beliefs and shared behavioral expectations in organizations: the reliability and validity of the organizational culture inventory. *Psychological Reports, 72,* 1299–1330.

Cooke, R. A., & Szumal, J. L. (1994). The impact of group interaction styles on problem-solving effectiveness. *Journal of Applied Behavioral Science, 30*(4), 415–437.

Fiske, D. W. (1949). Consistency of the factorial structures of personality ratings from different sources. *Journal of Abnormal and Social Psychology, 44,* 329–344.

George, J. M. (1990). Personality, affect, and behavior in groups. *Journal of Applied Psychology, 75,* 107–116.

Goldberg, L. R. (1990). An alternative "description of personality": the big-five factor structure. *Journal of Personality and Social Psychology, 59,* 1216–1229.

Hackman, J. R., & Morris, C. G. (1975). Group tasks, group interaction process, and group performance effectiveness: a review and proposed integration. *Advances in Experimental Social Psychology, 8,* 45–99.

Hirokawa, R. (1985). Discussion procedures and decision-making performance: a test of a functional perspective. *Human Communication Research, 12*(2), 203–224.

Hirokawa, R., & Gouran, D. S. (1989). Facilitation of group communication: a critique of prior research and an agenda for future research. *Management Communication Quarterly, 3*(1), 71–92.

Hoffman, L. R. (1979). Applying experimental research on group problem solving to organizations. *Journal of Applied Behavioral Science, 15,* 375–391.

Hogan, R. T. (1991). *Personality and personality measurement. Handbook of industrial and organizational psychology* (pp. 873–919). Palo Alto, CA: Consulting Psychologists Press.

House, R. J., & Howell, J. M. (1992). Personality and charismatic leadership. *Leadership Quarterly, 3,* 81–108.

Maier, N. R. F. (1963). *Problem-solving discussions and conferences: leadership methods and skills.* New York: McGraw-Hill.

Maslow, A. H. (1954). *Motivation and personality.* New York: Harper.

Mazur, A. (1973). Cross-species comparison of status in established small groups. *American Sociological Review, 38,* 513–529.

McCrae, R. R., & Costa, P. T. J. (1989). The structure of interpersonal traits: Wiggin's circumplex and the five-factor model. *Journal of Personality and Social Psychology, 56,* 586–595.

McCrae, R. R., & John, O. P. (1992). An introduction to the Five-Factor Model and its applications. *Journal of Personality, 60,* 175–215.

Potter, R. E., & Balthazard, P. A. (2002a). Virtual team interaction styles: assessment and effects. *International Journal of Human–Computer Studies.*

Potter, R. E., & Balthazard, P. A. (2002b). Understanding human interaction and performance in the virtual team. *The Journal of Information Technology Theory & Application.*

Potter, R. E., Balthazard, P. A., & Cooke, R. A. (2000b). Virtual team interaction: assessment, consequences, and management. *Team Performance Management, 6*(7-8), 131–137.

Trapnell, P. D., & Wiggins, J. S. (1990). Extension of the interpersonal adjective scalers to include the big five dimensions of personality. *Journal of Personality and Social Psychology, 59,* 781–790.

Watson, D., & Clark, L. A. (1997). *Extroversion and its positive emotional core.* In R. Hogan, J. A. Johnson, & S. R. Briggs, *Handbook of personality psychology* (pp. 767–793). San Diego, CA: Academic Press.

Watson, W. E., & Michaelsen, L. K. (1988). Group interaction behaviors that affect group performance on an intellective task. *Group & Organization Studies, 13*(4), 495–516.

Section II:

Leading Virtual Teams

Chapter IV

Leading from Afar:
Strategies for Effectively
Leading Virtual Teams

Stacey L. Connaughton, Rutgers University, USA

John A. Daly, The University of Texas at Austin, USA

ABSTRACT

Leadership is central to effective virtual teams. Yet leading people from afar constitutes a challenge to practitioners and an underinvestigated research area to scholars. Based on a series of in-depth interviews with project leaders, senior managers, and executives of global organizations, this chapter advances 13 propositions about effective virtual team leadership. These propositions aid leaders of dispersed teams in overcoming leadership challenges they face.

INTRODUCTION

Virtual teams afford organizations many opportunities. They can maximize productivity and lower costs (Davenport & Pearlson, 1998). And, they can enable organizations to serve international customers and capitalize on globally dispersed talent (Zaccaro & Bader, 2003). Despite these benefits, virtual teams also exacerbate challenges that traditional teams face and create new ones. One challenge relates to leadership. In a recent study of 500 virtual managers, 90% of them perceived managing from afar to be more challenging than managing people on-site. Furthermore, 40% of these virtual managers perceived team members to produce less when physically separated from each other than when colocated (Hymowitz, 1999).

Leadership of virtual teams is more complex than that of colocated teams for several reasons: a leader's "social presence" may be more difficult to achieve in distanced settings (Kiesler & Sproull, 1992; Warkentin, Sayeed, & Hightower, 1997); trust among leaders and team members may be swift and fleeting (Jarvenpaa, Knoll, & Leidner, 1998); members' identification with the team, organization, and leader may be challenged over distance (Connaughton & Daly, in press); and communication among leaders and team members may be complicated by diverse ethnic, communication, and organizational backgrounds (Cascio, 1999; Cascio & Shurygailo, 2003).

The purpose of this chapter is to advance 13 propositions about how successful leaders of dispersed teams meet these challenges. These propositions are based on a series of semistructured interviews with leaders who manage teams globally. These individuals operate from an organization's headquarters and have worldwide or regional responsibilities for leading people in distanced locations. They also have limited physical access to their team members. Most of the individuals interviewed for this project led a number of distanced teams, in various industries, over the last decade.

Following Cascio and Shurygailo (2003), we define "dispersed teams" as teams that are separated by some degree of time and distance, and we conceptualize "distanced leadership" as leadership in those contexts. In our work, we found it critical to conceive of distanced leadership as being a function of both physical distance and perceived access to the leader. Leaders who successfully shape the perception that they are accessible can overcome many of the challenges of distanced leadership. We also recognize that there are varying degrees of virtuality (Zigurs, 2003) and various types of virtual teams (Cascio & Shurygailo, 2003). In this chapter, we examine global virtual teams in which a designated team leader is located in the United States and team members are scattered across the globe. Thus, although we believe there are similarities among leadership in various types of virtual teams, we acknowledge that our chapter looks specifically at leadership in remote teams. To do so, we first present background on our topic and examine some of the leadership challenges in dispersed contexts; next, we explain the methods used to conduct the study; then, we offer 13 propositions based on our research; and, we conclude by discussing future trends in this area.

BACKGROUND: CHALLENGES TO LEADING FROM AFAR

Distanced leadership is a topic of interest to practitioners, yet it is underexplored in scholarly investigations. Management and communication scholars have long studied leadership, typically in colocated settings (e.g., Bass & Avolio, 1994; Burns, 1978; Fairhurst, 2001; Fiedler, 1967; Mintzberg, 1994, 1973; Yukl, 1989, 1981). But discussions of distanced leadership have primarily appeared in popular management books [e.g., *The Distance Manager* (Fisher & Fisher, 2001); *Mastering Virtual Teams* (Duarte & Snyder, 1999); *Virtual Teams* (Lipnack & Stamps, 1997)], training and development journals (e.g., Geber, 1995; Nelson, 1998), and business periodicals such as *Fortune* and *Business Week*. While scholars examined issues of trust in virtual teams (Jarvenpaa, Knoll, & Leidner, 1998) and the use of communication technologies in virtual teams (Scott et al., 1999), the leadership dimension of virtual teamwork is often absent from those investigations. Hiltz and colleagues argued that team leadership in distributed settings is critical to team effectiveness (Fjermestad & Hiltz, 1998–1999; Hiltz & Turoff, 1985; Hiltz, Dufner, Holmes, & Poole, 1991). Kayworth and Leidner (2002) contributed to our discussions of these matters by noting the managerial behaviors of leaders in global virtual teams. And other organizational scholars coined the term "e-leadership" to refer to leaders who conduct many leadership processes primarily through electronic channels (see Avolio & Kahai, 2003; Cascio & Shurygailo, 2003; Zaccaro & Bader, 2003). But scholars still know little about what leaders believe to be effective leadership tactics in these virtual organizational forms. The current project begins to fill that void.

The challenges inherent in distanced leadership become apparent when we acknowledge the advantages of physically proximate offices. Traditional office settings provide more opportunities for organizational members to communicate frequently and spontaneously with each other; the potential to interact immediately for troubleshooting; a forum in which to directly access information; and the chance to develop and maintain relationships (Davenport & Pearlson, 1998). The immediacy of others can foster a sense of connectedness among people and between members and their organization.

But, when individuals are scattered across the globe, fewer opportunities to incorporate informal communication exist. Instead of feeling connected to their organization and leader, distanced employees often feel isolated from their leaders and from events that take place at the central organization (Fisher & Fisher, 2001; Lipnack & Stamps, 1997; Van Aken, Hop, & Post, 1998; Wiesenfeld, Raghuram, & Garud, 1998). As a result, distanced leaders often must cope with their geographically dispersed employees' feelings of isolation from other organizational members, from their leadership, and from "their organization" (Lipnack & Stamps, 1997).

Although face-to-face (F2F) teams can experience these same challenges, these issues are more pronounced in dispersed teams (Solomon, 1995; Zaccaro & Bader, 2003) for two reasons. First, geographic dispersion greatly enhances the complexity of establishing effective interactions for meeting leadership challenges. In a previous project (Connaughton & Daly, in press), we uncovered that, conceptually, the major challenges of distanced leadership revolve around issues of isolation and trust that, in turn, challenge members' senses of identification with the organization and with the leader. On a global level, we also found that these issues are further complicated by cross-cultural communication differences. The second reason these challenges are more pronounced in dispersed teams is that virtual teams today are more likely to be formed for a limited time and then disbanded when tasks are completed. This is a leadership challenge, because the dynamics that help teams become effective require time to develop (Cramton, 2002).

In an empirical study of virtual teams in an international educational setting, Kayworth and Leidner (1998) found that the leaders rated as "effective" by their members demonstrated a "mentoring" quality characterized by understanding, empathy, and concern for team members. In other words, effective distanced leaders are adept at building and maintaining relationships with those they lead from afar. Kayworth and Leidner (1998) concluded that a primary difference between leading virtual teams and colocated ones is limited opportunities for virtual team leaders to project these qualities to their members. In this chapter, we offer some suggestions to virtual team leaders who seek to exhibit these qualities over time and space.

THE STUDY

The data for this project came from semistructured, extended interviews conducted with organizational leaders who frequently lead from afar. Marshall and Rossman (1995) classified this type of interviewing as elite interviewing, which is an appropriate choice for the current research project, because it allows the participant's perspective on distance leadership to emerge.

Twenty-one leaders with global responsibilities in organizations were interviewed for this study. All participants were executives or divisional directors who were currently leading globally remote employees. The organizations included a large hardware manufacturer, an integrated computer company, an energy company, two semiconductor manufacturers, and a military unit. Nineteen respondents were male and two respondents were female. All had significant experience managing projects and people from afar. All had experience supervising many people, both in F2F settings and in distanced settings. All would be considered senior managers with significant responsibilities.[1]

A series of open-ended interview questions probing the dynamics of leading from afar was crafted into an interview protocol. Most of the interviews took place either in a private meeting room or in the interviewee's office. A few were conducted via videoconferencing, e-mail, or telephone.[2] After securing permission, each interview was audiotaped and later transcribed.

A thematic content analysis (McCracken, 1988) was used to identify strategies for leading from afar. Emergent themes consisted of recurrent topics of discussion, action, or both on the part of the actors being studied (Glaser & Strauss, 1967). To ensure accurate coding, the constant comparison method (Strauss & Corbin, 1990) was used. The interviews took place over a number of weeks. This allowed us to regularly check the outcomes of any one interview with other interviewees. Respondents were also visited after the thematic analysis was completed in order to verify the interpretations presented in this chapter.

PROPOSITIONS ABOUT DISTANCED LEADERSHIP

From this investigation, 13 propositions for effective distanced leadership emerged. They relate to the nature of leader's communication (Propositions 1, 2, 3); expectations and ground rules for distanced leadership (Propositions 4, 5, 6); awareness of potential leadership challenges (Propositions 7, 8, 9); other tools for distanced leadership (Propositions 10, 11, 12); and, what we propose are the stages of distanced leadership (Proposition 13).

Proposition 1: F2F Communication is Critical

Although virtual teams are, by definition, geographically separated, research suggests that F2F communication is still important to achieving organizational outcomes (Cohen & Prusak, 2001; Weisband, Schneider, & Connolly, 1995; Zack, 1993), specifically for performing particular organizational tasks such as initiating group projects, negotiating issues, and solving problems (Sproull & Kiesler, 1991). F2F communication enables people to build shared meaning (Zack, 1993), and it affords people more opportunities to disclose individuating information to each other (Weisband, Schneider & Connolly, 1995). In addition, F2F communication allows people to observe others' responses to situations (Giddens, 1984) and to grasp personal nuances revealed through others' facial expressions, gestures, vocal intonations, as well as status markers, such as clothing and office size (Daft & Lengel, 1986).

Given the importance of F2F communication, the challenge for distanced leaders becomes how to incorporate F2F communication into their routines, even though the use of communication technologies makes it appear to be unnecessary. Our research indicates that one critical moment for long-distance leaders to utilize F2F communication is when they are building the relationship with those they will be leading from afar. Relationships have many dimensions, all of which are difficult to establish and sustain even in local situations. Distance work relationships are further complicated by less frequent contact and greater reliance on mediated communication. The leaders we spoke with found that trust, perhaps the key to building relationships with people over distance, is built with a person they met, not with a voice on a phone or with an author of an e-mail.

One interviewee related a story of a new manager who, soon after having acquired global responsibility, assumed that the work relationships that his predecessor built with distanced employees would still be intact for him. Thus, when he visited the remote sites for the first time, he greeted the employees there by saying, "Hello, I'm from XYZ corporation. We've had a great relationship in the past. I'd like to continue it." Almost every individual responded by saying, "We have no relationship. We had a relationship with [his predecessor]." The new global manager learned quickly that trust was something built between two people in F2F contact and must be nurtured over time. Another interviewee explained some reasons why:

> I need to see what contexts they work in. I think that in order to be accepted, I need to show my willingness to come on their turf. And, I need to get to know them on a personal level. A lot is happening in technology where you can do videoconferencing. I do a lot of teleconferencing with [city]. But there's nothing that replaces face-to-face. When I took over the leadership role, I went to the different locations in Europe. I think when you see each other face-to-face you don't start to wonder what the agenda is. You see each other face-to-face and you can talk through it. I think I was able to demonstrate that I was going to listen to what was going on.

Proposition 2: Personalization and Small Talk Matter

In an age where time is money and efficiency is key, organizational leaders may be tempted to communicate only about task-related topics when they interact with their distanced employees. Whereas locally, a leader can have a casual conversation with an employee in the cafeteria or in the hallway at any time during the day, distanced leaders have fewer opportunities to interact, and thus, must make the most of the time they have. Yet, interviewees cautioned distanced leaders against thinking that "making the most of their time" means avoiding informal, personalized interactions with distanced employees. In fact, they refer to these informal interactions as integral to building and maintaining relationships.

Successful distanced managers find ways to create personal relationships with employees even though they are far away. One technique that we discovered among some of the best leaders was the use of brief narratives and personal disclosures. For instance, Vincent is an executive with a large technology firm. He manages teams located in a number of locations around the world. Every Friday, Vincent sends an e-mail message to all team members updating them about the business — what is happening and where the business is going. At the end of each weekly message, Vincent appends a brief story about something that happened to him during the week. It might be about a delayed flight, his daughter's argument about what color of braces she will be getting, or a fender-bender in which he was involved. Why does Vincent spend time creating and delivering these narratives? He says that the stories connect him with his team members in ways that no other method of communicating would. His measure of success, he says, is that when he is visiting an office 2000 miles from his own, one of his employees will pop up and ask him about that flight, the color of braces his daughter selected, or the accident. His goal, he told us, was to ensure that when he traveled to visit his employees, they could engage in the simple, but very important, personal "chit-chat" that is a hallmark of an office where people work F2F. These little life stories bond team members, creating intimacies that lubricate the work relationship. Distance often precludes this.

Our findings suggest that relationships can, and should, be built through technological means (see Walther, 1995, 1992; Walther & Burgoon, 1992). Organizations are held together, culturally, by a number of "stories" that personify the organizations and provide the members with rules for behavior. Stories such as these are critical, because they reveal to the audience how the leader makes sense of his or her world (Browning, 1992). The person engaged in that story will not only feel more connected to corporate headquarters, but will also know, to some extent, what makes the executive or manager at headquarters tick.

Small talk also helps to build and maintain these relationships. Research on small talk's functions tells us that talk is the essence of relational maintenance, and that everyday conversations bind people together (Knapp & Vangelisti, 2000). The importance of small talk in building relationships should not be forgotten in distanced settings. As one interviewee noted:

> *The frequent interactions with people you have here [at the geographically proximate location] are often attributed to trust. And over distance you have a complete void there. So, you are missing one of your fundamental tools. Somehow you've got to overcome that. And that's where the one-on-one calls come in because you really have to have meaningful interaction with these people somehow. So, during the calls I spend time trying to*

*get to know the person well, not just the work stuff. For example,
I know that our engineering manager over in Europe likes to go
sailing on his vacations and I know the way he manages his day,
and I know when I can catch him and when I can't, and I know
what worries him. When I'm over there, we'll go out to dinner,
usually one-on-one and have some very good conversations over
dinner that are work kinds of things, but they are more of the
deeper thinking that's going on inside him over what's going on
at work. When I go to Asia, I sit down with the engineering
director there for dinner usually every time I'm there. It's a
mixture of personal and work but you've got to make time for the
personal talk when you can do it.*

In organizations, it is often tempting to distinguish between small talk — chattering, gossiping, conversing about "unimportant" everyday things — and the more serious "business talk." Our research revealed the primacy of small talk for maintaining distanced relationships.

We typically think of using small talk in F2F interactions, but our research suggests that it is also necessary to incorporate small talk into computer-mediated communications. For instance, one interviewee reported successfully using what he calls "free-flow chatter" at the beginning of his monthly videoconference meeting with individuals at distant locations. He asks questions such as "How have you been since the last time we talked?" or "Did you go skiing like you had been talking about last time?" Here, small talk functions to build and maintain the relationships between the leader in one location and those individuals around the world who are important to his company's future. This talk is crucial for teamwork. It is how leaders and employees get to know one another, and how they maintain their relationships.

Proposition 3: Overcommunicate

*It is easy to undercommunicate outside of your immediate sphere
of contact everyday. And that means that people feel lost and
disconnected. When they hear about something that everyone
back here [headquarters] knew for weeks was coming and
nobody told them they feel they have wasted time, effort, and
personal investment. That's a real problem.*

As this interviewee noted, it is "easy" for distanced leaders to neglect remote sites. Indeed, interviewees expressed that combating feelings of remoteness is one of their biggest challenges, for perceived isolation can adversely affect performance, satisfaction, and turnover.

In our work, it quickly became obvious that the most effective leaders overcommunicated with their distanced team members. They did this in a number of ways. Commonly, they tended to use at least two different media for any message of importance: telephone calls were followed by e-mails summarizing the conversation; phone calls came quickly after e-mails to ensure clear understanding.

Leaders also made an effort not to inform local people before informing distant people of issues affecting the organization. This is especially important in times of change, as one interviewee noted:

In a recent downsizing I made it a point not to communicate anything to the local group before it was communicated to the distant group. I did the communication via a teleconference [speaker phone]. This seemed to be key to making the groups seem equivalent.

Additionally, leaders establish a mechanism that encourages information to be exchanged across functions, projects, and organizations. One leader uses the Internet to post a company "newsletter," updating individuals in remote sites not only about developments in their functional division but also in other divisions.

Once an exchange mechanism is established, it is important to consider the nature of the information exchanged. Some leaders maintain Web sites where project managers post their "lessons learned" and share best practices with other organizational leaders. Leaders use this forum to advertise what "works" in the regions and to propagate those ideas to headquarters and other remote sites. In conjunction with a Web site, companies successfully developed internal electronic bulletin boards where leaders can ask and answer questions as well as receive suggestions from each other. Leaders must communicate not only the facts surrounding an organizational development but also the implications of the developments for those in geographically separated locations (see Davenport & Pearlson, 1998, for details).

Leaders must encourage participation by remote sites' members in the information exchange process. Soliciting remote employees' opinions gets them involved. Research shows that once individuals become involved in a project, their commitment to it intensifies. For this reason, leaders of remote-site employees must make a concerted effort to regularly give feedback to long-distance employees and to frequently solicit feedback from them. Soliciting feedback from remote-site individuals who have extended experience working in a specific region may bring to the fore cultural and environmental barriers that may be impeding a project's development. Long-distance leaders are not privy to that information, because they are not at the remote site to observe events taking place.

Proposition 4: Discipline is Key to Distanced Leadership

One of the more interesting observations of some respondents is the critical place of discipline in distanced business relationships. What we mean by discipline may be explained by some examples:

- Since meetings need to be scheduled and people have to attend (physically or through electronic means), people need to come prepared; the meeting has to start on time and end on time.
- People need to follow through on their commitments with less supervision. Given the distance, it is impossible for distanced leaders to closely monitor employees.
- Deadlines are real in business, and they are magnified in distanced settings where, because of time zones, everything takes more time. A business in Chicago has sales representatives in Almady (12 time zones away). The sales representative files an order with the Chicago office that then communicates it to the shipping center in Warsaw. By the time all of this gets communicated, the Almady customer is waiting two to three days for a response. A delay at any point in this communication chain creates problems.
- Colleagues need, in a disciplined way, to continually communicate updates and decisions to others. Nothing is more isolating to employees than to find that a decision was made at headquarters to cancel some activity and that message was not promptly communicated to them. They wasted good time doing something that was unnecessary.

These are examples of disciplined management, especially relevant in a distanced leadership environment. A consistent refrain of people who led distanced teams is that leaders need to have much more discipline about everything from returning calls and e-mails to managing meetings and tasks. Otherwise, things quickly fall apart. Clearly, the leader needs to be disciplined. Promises must be kept, and deadlines must be adhered to. But, just as importantly, team members must be disciplined, for dispersed teams face a constant pull toward entropy.

Proposition 5: Expectations and Ground Rules about Communication Need to be Established at the Start

Effective communication is difficult in any setting. It is much more difficult in distanced settings. Part of the challenge revolves around the communicative behaviors and misbehaviors of team members. Informants who led successful distanced teams related that they learned, from prior experience, to quickly establish some ground rules for how the team would communicate. For example, one leader established the following as ground rules for meetings based upon her experiences leading distanced teams:

- We will identify meetings as "must" attend and "may" attend meetings. We will all attend "must" meetings.
- When we miss a meeting, we each agree to go along with the decisions made at the meeting.
- Each meeting will have an agenda distributed before the meeting.
- People will log-on, connect, or show up at the scheduled start of the meeting.
- Meetings will end on time.
- There will be no side conversations (by whatever media) during meetings.
- F2F team meetings will, when possible, be rotated across regions.

The reason why rules should be established when a team is created is interesting. Respondents said that if a leader waits to establish rules until some problem has arisen, then any rule the leader makes will reflect someone's misbehavior. If six weeks into leading a team the leader establishes a new rule that says people must answer their e-mails within 24 hours, everyone on the team knows that the reason the leader is creating the rule is because of one person on the team who already gained a reputation of not promptly responding to e-mails.

When employees are geographically separated from their manager or executive, they do not have the day-to-day frequent contact to figure out what makes their leader "tick." To overcome this lack of F2F contact, one leader highlighted the importance of articulating his expectations — both for performance and interaction — with distanced individuals up front. A leader's expectations for interaction with others, both local and distanced, are rarely articulated explicitly. Leaders should consider creating, for example, an "e-mail protocol" that they follow and encourage others to follow. The protocol may state that leaders should try to respond to e-mails within one business day. When a thorough response is impossible in one day, leaders may then wish to send a brief reply acknowledging receipt of the message. Another e-mail protocol may be to limit the length to less than one page. If e-mails will exceed a page, the sender should be encouraged to send an attachment.

Proposition 6: Meeting Management is Critical to Distanced Teams

There are two aspects to successful meeting management over distance: articulating norms for preparing for and engaging in meetings; and ensuring that meetings are regularly and publicly scheduled. Research shows that individuals tend to respond more favorably when they know what to expect from an interaction. This is especially important for meetings, whether videoconference or teleconference. Meetings will be more productive and more efficient if attendees are given access to the meeting agenda and pertinent data prior to the meeting. One interviewee shared his successful tactics for facilitating teleconference meetings with participants in the Middle East:

What we would do to make communication more effective is we . . .would come up with half a dozen issues each before hand. Each of us would do some pre-work beforehand to make the telephone call more productive rather than just leaving it up for grabs.

By e-mailing or faxing agenda items to be discussed, spreadsheets to be reviewed, as well as copies of presentation slides that will be used during the meeting, leaders can increase the efficiency and productivity of long-distance meetings.

The second piece of virtual meeting management is ensuring that meetings are regularly and publicly scheduled. When leaders and subordinates are colocated, leaders do not consciously think about establishing and adhering to a formal pattern of communication. There are inadvertent conversations by the coffee machine, small talk in the elevator, and plenty of scheduled F2F meetings in which to exchange information. If an immediate situation arises, the leader can walk to the local individuals' workstation to initiate discussion. It is also questionable whether regularly scheduled meetings (e.g., the Monday morning meeting held each week) are useful for teams that work F2F constantly. Much of what is accomplished at those regular get-togethers can be accomplished more efficiently in less formal ways.

When some or all members of a team work at a distance, however, regularly scheduled meetings are critical. As more than one of our informants pointed out, if you do not have regular meetings, people get forgotten. And, even when they are not forgotten, they may assume that others "know" things they do not. This seems especially true with what might be called semidispersed teams, in which some members are colocated and others are at a distance. The colocated people, because of their proximity, are often perceived to be "in the know." Thus, distanced leaders must establish regular communication patterns with distanced employees. These interactions must be ones that leaders and followers can anticipate. Interviewees report successfully using one-on-one weekly or bi-weekly phone calls with distanced employees.

One concern with establishing these weekly, structured conversations is that there will be nothing to talk about, and both parties will lose valuable business time. But, the interviewed leaders said that even if they did not have a pressing issue on the agenda, they still engaged in conversation with employees. They may have talked about the weather for a while, but inevitably, halfway through the conversation, one of them would raise a business-related issue. If nothing else, these one-on-ones provide frequent opportunities to build relationships.

Proposition 7: Cultural Nuances Matter

In the fast-paced business world, misunderstandings can spell disaster. Even when unintentional, misinterpretations can result in project delays, missed opportunities, and strained business relationships. To do global business successfully, distanced leaders must appreciate culture differences in interaction norms and they must also adapt their behaviors accordingly.

While there has been a good deal of research surrounding broad cultural differences (e.g., Hofstede's notions of collectivism versus individualism; high versus low context; 1980, 1991), the results of our studies suggest that smaller, more nuanced cultural differences may be as important. Just as Van Ryssen and Godar (2000) found that language and socializing differences affect students' teamwork across cultures, we found that similar types of misunderstandings jeopardize effective teamwork in global teams. Different cultures have different holidays; members work at different times; and they have different beliefs about what is, and what is not, ethical. We found that it is critical for leaders to stay attuned to these cultural matters.[3]

The interviewees pointed to two strategies for meeting cultural challenges: attending to communication style and choosing appropriate timing for communication. One interviewee, for instance, reported how the Irish's direct communication style caused Irish employees to misinterpret a directive. In this case, the distanced leader at the U.S. headquarters stated to the Irish: "Here's an idea that you might think of implementing in your area." Irish individuals at that site understood headquarters' statement as advocating an optional activity, not a mandatory one. But, what the American leader really meant in that statement was "Here's something I'd like to get your 'buy in' on because you really ought to do it." The American leader chose to subtly state the objective, because the Irish complained previously about how headquarters was constantly sending them directives without getting their input. In the leader's attempt to avoid coming across as insensitive, the leader chose an indirect approach to getting a "mandatory" objective across. The indirect approach backfired, however, because it did not accommodate the Irish's direct communication style. The miscommunication resulted in costly project delays.

In addition to different communication styles, it is important to be sensitive to foreign nationals' sense of time. One manager at a large software firm who worked in Israel claimed that his U.S.-based company *said* they were global but always assumed his weekends were on Saturday and Sunday, as in the United States. When scheduling meetings and phone and videoconferences, the U.S. team preferred Friday meetings, and although they were sensitive to time (always scheduling them early in the morning, U.S. time) they did not "get" that he had to come into work from home on his weekend (Friday and Saturday). Another respondent described the differences in how people celebrate and his fear of insulting team members.

Varying sense of time also comes into play when considering communication norms across cultures. Some of our U.S. leaders, for instance, reported frustration with some Asian groups' slow response times to e-mails. This complaint demonstrates how Americans' "need for speed" reacts adversely to Japanese interaction norms. In responding to e-mail, the Japanese people are not only using a second language. They also may be following cultural interaction norms of thoughtfully drafting a response as well as developing group consensus before responding (Grove & Hallowell, 1998).

All of these examples demonstrate that adaptation is critical to global success. As one interviewee perceptively warned, "Don't try and make the recipe that you use locally apply internationally. It's not a cookie cutter. You have to stand by the basic foundation, but be able to alter for unique cultural and regional needs."

Proposition 8: Media Choices and Equal Access Matter

Communication is the essence of distanced teamwork. Although F2F communication is important, distanced leaders often must, by definition, use technological media (e.g., e-mail, videoconferencing, computer-assisted meetings) to communicate with distanced employees. Which media are used, as well as access to equal media, are critical to effective distanced teamwork.

One part of the challenge is to use the appropriate media for each message. When leaders opt for inappropriate media choices, they challenge teamwork. Given the increasing assortment of media, which are appropriate under what conditions for leading from afar?

Work on media richness (Daft & Lengel, 1984, 1986) and social presence (Fulk & DeSanctis, 1995; Rice, 1993) reveals that some media are better than others for certain kinds of messages. Media richness theory posits that media vary in the number of cues available to interactants. F2F communication is considered the "richest" medium, because it allows for immediate feedback and engages multiple information-processing cues. Slightly less rich is the telephone, because communicators are unable to pick up on visual cues. The media richness hypothesis (Daft & Lengel, 1984, 1986; Lengel & Daft, 1988) purports that managers ought to use rich media to communicate highly equivocal information and lean media for less equivocal information, as leaner media, such as written messages or e-mail, do not allow for immediate feedback (Kiesler, Siegel, & McGuire, 1984). Electronic means of communication are efficient and effective for many sorts of tasks — updating peers about the status of projects, setting and responding to short-term objectives, and discussing everyday challenges at work. Other forms of communication such as F2F are more effective for other tasks, such as sharing a vision and making important policy decisions.

In a geographically dispersed setting, however, physical separation often entices leaders to choose lean rather than rich media, even when a richer medium would be more appropriate. For instance, rather than traveling across some time zones to handle a crisis, the leader opts to send an e-mail. Appraisals, conflicts, and even recognitions are best done F2F for three reasons. First, F2F communication represents the richest media with the most cues. The probability of misunderstanding is lowest with F2F exchanges, according to our respondents. Second, F2F communication permits rich interactions. If a person does not understand something, he or she can ask right away. Third, there is a symbolic dimension to the communication media one chooses to use. A senior boss who flies across the Atlantic to congratulate a team for a successful quarter is doing something symbolically far more important than the same leader who sends an e-mail offering congratulations.

In addition, there are a number of new communication skills distanced team members need to learn. Some seem simple (e.g., when doing a telephone meeting, head nods do not communicate, because people at a distance cannot see the nods); other skills are more complex (e.g., juggling, as one large company does, instant messenger chats while negotiating with other companies using teleconferencing).

The second leadership challenge related to media use involves access to equal media. All team members, regardless of their physical locations, should have access to equal media in order to work effectively as a virtual team. For example, if two team members (one located in New York and one in Paris) have access to one videoconferencing system and a team member located in London has an inferior videoconferencing system, problems may arise.

Distanced team members often suffer from distinctly different levels of access to communication technologies: Some locations will have highly sophisticated media (e.g., videoconferencing, high-speed broadband access), while other locations will have limited equipment (e.g., telephone and 56K baud modem connections). The consequences of this disparity are enormous. The "sophisticated" team members communicate in very different ways than the "poor" members. The poor team members are, de facto, excluded, and, as one person said, "ghettoized" by their limited access to communication technologies. A consistent finding in our research is the importance of team members having equally sophisticated technology for communication. When there is inequity in technological support, it creates a sense of extreme isolation and an implied status hierarchy. In the words of one respondent, "when your technology is weak compared to others on the team, you simply do not count."

Relatedly, virtual leaders should only use media that everyone intimately understands. One executive in the oil industry related a time when a worldwide videoconference was scheduled to begin at 5:30 a.m., Houston-time. People from Europe, the United States, and Japan were all scheduled to be part of the meeting. Although people were at their respective locations on time, the meeting did not actually start for another 45 minutes, as people at different locations struggled to make the equipment function. A few participants never could get their technology to work, and at least one location's members came and left three times. One setting did not have sound; another did not have picture. After this very expensive debacle, the company dropped videoconferencing, opting instead for e-mail discussion groups.

Small things can make the difference with media. One executive said that she is always amazed during teleconference calls when some people forget that people on the other end of the line cannot see their nodding or shaking of heads. So often, she said, she will raise an issue or question in a teleconference meeting and hear nothing from others. They're agreeing with her, she later finds out, but she would not have known that from their lack of vocalized responses.

Proposition 9: Overcome the Challenge of Multiple Leaders

In distanced settings, matrix organizational management is common. One might have a functional head, a team leader, and perhaps a country or regional director. Unless these leaders are consistent in the goals, messages, and standards, the distanced employee can face a difficult group of challenges. Who is the "real" boss? Who do I listen to? How do I play the politics? In one case, we interviewed an employee located in a Scandinavian country working for a U.S. company. His challenge was that his country head wanted him to work on certain projects that were not the choices of his functional boss located in Minneapolis.

In many cases, the distanced employee will have a variety of managers making assignments. These assignments may be contradictory, placing the distanced employee in a difficult position. In one organization, for example, a six sigma "master black belt" who was assigned to work in South America reported directly to his country manager but was expected to be responsive to almost 20 other people located in the United States, who were leading a quality initiative in different parts of the company.

The key to the multiple management challenge is communication among managers. Respondents in our interviews were clear that a major task of a team leader is to ensure that the multiple leaders coordinate and offer consistent direction. Someone must be responsible for prioritizing tasks for the employee and for clarifying the reporting structure.

Juggling the "hassle factor" of multiple managers is only one challenge when it comes to leading dispersed team members. Managers must also be smart about selecting the right people, maintaining trust, and coping with the challenges of emergent leaders. In F2F settings, leaders can directly manage people they have working for them. They are able to, if necessary, closely supervise and monitor the work of those employees offering constant reinforcing and redirecting feedback. In distanced settings, leaders are far less able to constantly oversee the work of their subordinates. The implications of this are many. First, leaders need to select employees who are able and comfortable working independently from supervision. Some employees need the predictability and discipline of being physically proximate to managers. For those individuals, if the boss is not around, work does not happen. Other individuals perform flawlessly without day-to-day supervision. They are, as one manager said, "self-starters." They seek projects and accomplish them with little or no supervision. Optimally, these are the individuals who should be working from afar.

Second, trust is critical, and it is a two-way street. While most of the work on distance talks about the role of the subordinate's trust in their boss and the organization, the opposite is just as important: the boss and organization must deeply trust their distanced employees. O'Hara-Devereaux and Johansen (1994) go so far as to contend that only trust can prevent geographic distance from becoming psychological distance. In practical terms, leaders of geographically distanced others need to "trust" that others intend to get the job done and that they have the expertise to accomplish specific objectives and vice versa.

Third, the distanced leader must deal with the emergence of informal leaders at different locations. Work on teams reveals that oftentimes, individuals on a team emerge as leaders without any official pronouncement. These people emerge because of their task or social skills. In many teams, the informal leader has more influence on team members than the formal leader. In distanced settings, informal leaders are to be expected. The issue is how the formal, assigned leader handles this emergence. Smart distanced leaders celebrate informal leaders, understanding that these individuals can aid them in getting tasks accomplished. They are going to arise, so why not use them?

Proposition 10: Knowledge Management Tools are Essential to Successful Distanced Teams

Working in the same physical location allows people to garner information from one another. If a leader needs something that a colocated team member is working on, the leader can simply walk to the member's cubicle and ask. If the member is not there, the leader can grab the binder on the shelf where the information lies. At a distance, this information propinquity is not available.

Successful distanced teams quickly develop and diligently maintain sophisticated knowledge management services. The most common sorts of knowledge management are Web-based repositories of information that are religiously maintained. All of the issues of knowledge management matter for effective distanced teamwork. For instance, team members have to take the extra time to constantly add new information to the repository, because a knowledge management system is only as good as the materials within it. Key terminology needs to be agreed upon; and, the system needs to be constantly pruned of old information. Many of our informants said that poor knowledge management was a weakness of many dispersed teams.

Proposition 11: Symbols Matter

Leadership is, in many ways, the manipulation of symbols. In F2F settings, effective leaders recognize they are on something akin to a soundstage. They decorate their offices to communicate a particular message or image; they eat at certain places and with certain people to announce what they value and what they do not value. Because people in remote sites often have little everyday communication with leaders, the symbols the leader uses matter even more. Do employees always visit the leader, or does the leader make it a point to visit them? What is on the walls of offices at headquarters and on those at a distance? Are distanced members included in pictures that are hanging on the walls at headquarters, and vice versa?

In one organization, the manager of a globally dispersed team keeps flags of each nation represented on the team in his office. Another company, a Korean organization with a large presence in the United States, understood the symbolic value to Korean employees working in the United States of ensuring that cafeterias in U.S. locations served both American and Korean food. Contrast these positive symbolic moves to those in a U.S.-based software company, where a major complaint of distanced employees is that although the organization purports to be international, all "family" or "social" events happened only on the headquarters campus. Or, contrast those positive examples to an energy services company that refuses to offer financial support for employees who request language training for the country they will be working in. The key thing about these examples is not the specific behaviors or policies. It is the positive (or negative) symbolic value that these actions communicate to employees.

Many interviewees felt that one of the most important tactical and symbolic steps leaders can take is to make regular personal visits to the remote sites. Personal visits function not only to increase the long-distance leader's understanding of the remote employees' point-of-view, but they also increase the visibility of the long-distance leader. One interviewee, for example, commented that F2F interaction decreases the "us" versus "them" mentality. Personal visits allow leaders and distant individuals to realize their commonalities and to get to know one other on an interpersonal basis.

Symbolically, leaders from headquarters taking the time to travel to remote sites sends the message that headquarters is committed to individuals at remote sites and that they are an integral part of the organization. Many of these visits will be planned in advance. However, executives and managers must be willing to go to the remote sites whenever they are needed, even without much notice.

According to one interviewee, doing so sends a powerful message of dedication and inspires remote employees to work hard for that individual.

These on-site visits have bottom-line importance as well. When functional teams are geographically dispersed, communication networks become the links holding people together. Remote individuals' ease, willingness, and comfort in interacting with distanced leaders may determine how successful they are in carrying out an objective. Thus, providing opportunities periodically to interact in a F2F setting becomes not only a social matter, but also a productivity one. One executive reported how visiting a remote site was critical to getting individuals there focused on the issues that were integral to the company's performance goals:

> *The reality is that when I went down there [to a remote site] a month and a half ago they were still working all the wrong issues. So, I had to intervene and had to learn and listen and talk to people. I had to go to the location and get blown off by the customs guy there. I had to experience that for half a day. It's the most frustrating thing, it's such a waste of time, but yet, if you don't understand the subtleties of what exactly that means, then you can't help them deal with it. But, after being down there 10 days we can provide them different resources, different ways to work on it.*

One way to reduce the "us" versus "them" mentality even further is to meet for the first time at a "neutral site" (Grove & Hallowell, 1998). For example, if a leader who offices in Austin leads individuals located in China, Great Britain, and Brazil, he or she should choose a different location (e.g., Germany) to hold the initial meeting. Gathering in a neutral site sends a powerful message — no one's site is favored, including corporate headquarters. The neutral location is as unfamiliar to one group member as it is to another.

Proposition 12: You "Sell" to Distanced Locations, You Do not "Tell" Them

One could easily argue that great work is done voluntarily; it is not coerced. All people come to work every day. Some do a great job; some do just enough to keep their jobs. Effective leaders approach their employees as volunteers, and they try to sell them business agendum and changes. Many of our respondents said that although leaders often work hard to sell changes to employees at headquarters, they often merely give distanced employees announcements of what was already decided.

In F2F environments, managers can scrutinize their employees to ensure that those individuals are attaining specific objectives. But in a distanced environment where scrutiny is often impossible, successful leaders have to entice employees to internalize the overall vision and goals. As several interviewees commented, if distanced individuals are not "bought into" an idea or a project, they may not engage in the desired action, they may drag their feet, or they may leave the organization. For this reason, long-distance leaders' ability to influence becomes an indicator of their effectiveness. If long-distance employees truly internalize an idea or philosophy, they will be inspired to perform. Building relationships is also critical:

> *Influencing from a distance is extremely difficult. It requires a basic relationship with the person before you can begin [to influence]. For example, what is the person's history in the company; what are their goals, hopes, and aspirations; what are the person's likes and dislikes? This basic relationship must be developed in person, usually in a "facilitated" session, and then followed up with at least four hours of one-on-one conversation. Only then can true long distancing influencing occur.*

As this interviewee indicated, leaders must consider the context of the people they are trying to influence.

Successful influencers are those who not only build relationships with the person they are attempting to influence, but also with those around the people who hold critical roles in that individual's professional life. One interviewee spoke to the reality of the corporate world for remote individuals:

> *In my experience, even when in a particular role, the likelihood that they [remote individuals] will be taking 100% direction from the U.S. is stated in the extreme. Reality for that person is that his or her long-term success, their personal advancement, their career is not in your hands. It's in the hands of the management team back home [at the remote sites], who will place them in their next job, who will determine long term what their raises and pay are, their rewards. And even if you could have certain amount of control over their salary during the time they report to you, there's not two ways around it, their future is in the hands of the people in the country.*

As this quotation illustrates, successful influencers are those who leverage and align critical players. The long-distance leader's responsibility is to identify those credible third parties and influence them as well.

Another key part of influencing others over time and space is communicating the big picture. One of the major challenges leaders report with some distanced teams is the tendency for employees located at a distance to have a "job shop" mentality. People at a distance execute demands rather than make them. And, they often do not understand why the demand was made in the first place. While employees clearly want to know what they are suppose to be doing and the criteria for success on those tasks, they also want to know the whys of the task: why is this task important, how does it fit with the agenda and strategy of the organization, what is the strategy, and so on. Successful managers keep distanced employees aware of corporate issues as much as everyday issues.

Proposition 13: There are Two Stages to Long-Distance Leadership

In the interviews with seasoned distanced leaders, it became clear that there are two stages to leading a team from afar. The initial stage happens when a team is first created or when a new leader is announced for an existing team. Successful leaders understand that this is the stage where F2F communication is essential, for during this time, people are building trust and coming to know one another. Trust is of paramount importance in creating and maintaining effective relationships over distance (Lipnack & Stamps, 1997; Nilles, 1998). Trusting relationships promote open, substantive, and influential information exchange (Early, 1986) as well as reduce transaction costs (Cummings & Bromiley, 1996; Handy, 1995). Trust is the glue of the global workspace (O'Hara-Devereaux & Johansen, 1994). The second stage, which we call the "maintenance" stage, occurs after a trusting relationship between manager and subordinate is established.

This is not to suggest that leaders should forget about using F2F communication after establishing a relationship, however. In the maintenance stage, F2F communication is still critical for some issues, but the leaders can successfully manage the day-to-day issues of their teams from afar, mostly by using technologies such as telephone, e-mail, and video. The problem is that if a leader does not engage in F2F exchanges during the initial phase, it becomes difficult for that leader to successfully manage during the maintenance phase. When employees have spent time with their manager, misunderstandings are far less likely to occur and negatively impact the relationship.

FUTURE TRENDS

National newspapers, industry journals, and trade magazines reported that thousands of companies in diverse industries now have long-distance leaders (see Apgar, 1998; Bryan & Fraser, 1999; Hymowitz, 1999; McCune, 1998). Although the exact number of long-distance leaders is constantly changing, companies such as Dell Computers, IBM, Hewlett-Packard, AT&T, Proctor & Gamble, and Compaq integrated virtual teams into their regular operations (Davenport & Pearlson, 1998). Leaders within these organizations have the complex task of managing people who are thousands of miles away from their home offices. As distanced leadership becomes increasingly common in organizations, understanding leadership strategies that work, and those that do not, is critical to organizational success.

In this chapter, we summarized 13 propositions about distanced leadership. These propositions, drawn from our interviews with experienced distanced leaders, represent testable hypotheses. While they seem intuitively reasonable, and were supported in our interviews, they still await empirical testing.

In addition to empirically exploring the validity of the propositions included in this chapter, future research will need to develop theoretical models of leadership that incorporate distance as a major component. Theoretically, future researchers should approach the issues involved in distanced leadership in at least two ways. First, what are the key theoretical dimensions of distanced leadership? In previous work, we suggested that distance challenges trust and community (isolation). These two constructs are critical, we would suppose, to understanding distanced leadership, for they affect individual's identification with and sense of connectedness to the organization, which, in turn, affect important organizational outcomes such as productivity. Central to any theoretical model is communication, the implicit focus of this chapter. Second, we need to clarify what is meant by a "distanced work relationship." We argue that these relationships have both physical distance and access components to them. One could imagine other considerations as well. This sort of theoretical explication is important, because they relate to the question: what is distinctive about distanced relationships? Some would argue that many of the variables discussed in research on virtual teamwork could just as easily apply to F2F teams. It is important to attend to those variables that are specific to dispersed relationships. These will be determined by thoughtful empirical work.

Current and future organizational trends related to virtual teams may also be fruitful avenues for research and also important for practitioners to keep in mind. Consider these trends:

1. The rise of geographically dispersed ad hoc teams that are assembled for short-term projects.
2. The increasing use of contractors and consultants who do not have loyalty to the organization — how do you manage them from afar?
3. Trends in international customer service — how do organizations effectively serve and lead customers from afar?

Practitioners and researchers may also wish to consider other emergent issues related to distanced leadership. First, generational differences may be important to note. Those who grew up using the technologies now utilized for dispersed teams may have different leadership experiences than those who are unaccustomed to using the technologies in everyday life. Today's youth who talk on the phone, e-mail, and use (computer) Instant Messenger all at the same time and think nothing of it may experience fewer difficulties managing the complexities of long-distance leadership than older generations. There may, as well, be a learning curve for distanced leadership. Some of the challenges cited in this chapter may become obsolete when younger generations assume leadership roles. Legal issues may also arise in distanced leadership. In a distanced relationship, everything is potentially "on record" if it is written in e-mail or taped via audio or video means. Practitioners and researchers may wish to consider the potential chilling effects of this information permanency on how people lead distanced teams.

One important issue is the presumption made by many that distanced teams have more difficulty than F2F teams. That may or may not be true. Some of the individuals involved in this study raised an interesting thought — some people may actually prefer to work in a distanced setting far from their managers. It will be important to probe when, and with whom, this might be the case, and, more importantly, why this would be true.

CONCLUSION

While geographically dispersed teams afford exciting business possibilities, they also bring new leadership challenges. We know that both the task and affective dimensions of leadership are critical to leading from afar. We also know that although some leadership strategies are just as appropriate in geographically proximate settings as they are in distanced ones, other tactics must be incorporated in order to compensate for the lack of routine and F2F interaction, which is often taken for granted. One interviewee noted the following:

Leading from a distance is an absolute necessity in our industry. It will be that way in more and more industries. It is a hard skill. People who have never done it don't even recognize it as a separate skill. You'll say, "Well, you don't have any worldwide experience," and they'll say, "Well, what's worldwide experience except putting me in a worldwide job?" [interviewee laughs] There are just so many aspects that many people don't understand.

Because the globalization of business and recent corporate restructuring trends increasingly demand distanced leadership, the focus of this project will be of continuing importance to organizations in the 21st century. Suggested in this chapter are practical communication skills for leaders and employees engaged in dispersed teams. Continued research in this area will advance theory and provide further understanding of virtual organizations, knowledge organizations, and other emergent organizational forms.

REFERENCES

Apgar, IV, M. (1998, May–June). The alternative workplace: Changing where and how people work. *Harvard Business Review*, 121–136.

Avolio, B. J., & Kahai, S. S. (2003). Adding the "E" to e-leadership: How it may impact your leadership. *Organizational Dynamics, 31*, 325–338.

Bass, B. M., & Avolio, B. J. (1994). *Improving organizational effectiveness through transformational leadership.* Thousand Oaks, CA: Sage.

Browning, L. D. (1992). Lists and stories as organizational communication. *Communication Theory, 2*, 281–302.

Bryan, L. L., & Fraser, J. N. (1999). Getting to global. *The McKinsey Quarterly, 4*, 28–37.

Burns, J. M. (1978). *Leadership.* New York: Harper & Row.

Cascio, W. F. (1999). Virtual workplaces: Implications for organizational behavior. In C. L. Cooper & D. M. Rousseau (Eds.), *Trends in organizational behavior* (pp. 1–14). Chichester: John Wiley & Sons.

Cascio, W. F., & Shurygailo, S. (2003). E-leadership and virtual teams. *Organizational Dynamics, 31*, 362–376.

Cohen, D., & Prusak, L. (2001). *In good company: How social capital makes organizations work.* Cambridge: Harvard University Press.

Connaughton, S.L., & Daly, J.A. (2003). Long distance leadership: Communicative strategies for leading virtual teams. In D.J. Pauleen (Ed.), *Virtual Teams: Projects, Protocols, and Processes* (pp. 116-144). Hershey, PA: Idea Group Inc.

Cramton, C. D. (2002). Finding common ground in dispersed collaboration. *Organizational Dynamics, 30*, 356–367.

Cummings, L. L., & Bromiley, P. (1996). The organizational trust inventory (OTI): development and validation. In R. M. Kramer, & T. R. Tyler (Eds.), *Trust in organizations: Frontiers of theory and research* (pp. 302–330). Thousand Oaks, CA: Sage.

Daft, R. L., & Lengel, R. H. (1984). Information richness: A new approach to managerial information processing and organization design. In B. Staw, & L. Cummings (Eds.), *Research in organizational behavior* (pp. 199–233). Greenwich, CT: JAI.

Daft, R. L., & Lengel, R. H. (1986). Organizational information requirements, media richness and structural design. *Management Science, 32*, 554–571.

Davenport, T. H., & Pearlson, K. (1998). Two cheers for the virtual office. *Sloan Management Review, 39*, 51–65.

Duarte, D. L., & Snyder, N. T. (1999). *Mastering virtual teams: Strategies, tools, and techniques that succeed.* San Francisco: Jossey-Bass.

Earley, P. C. (1986). Trust, perceived importance of praise and criticism, and work performance: An examination of feedback in the United States and England. *Journal of Management, 12*, 457–473.

Fairhurst, G. T. (2001). Dualisms in leadership research. In F. A. Jablin, & L. L. Putnam (Eds.), *The new handbook of organizational communication* (pp. 379–439). Thousand Oaks, CA: Sage.

Fiedler, F. E. (1967). *A theory of leadership effectiveness.* New York: McGraw-Hill.

Fisher, K., & Fisher, M. D. (2001). *The distance manager: A hands-on guide to managing off-site employees and virtual teams.* New York: McGraw-Hill.

Fjermestad, J., & Hiltz, S. R. (1998–1999). An assessment of group support systems experiment research: Methodology and results. *Journal of Management Information Systems, 15,* 7–149.

Fulk, J., & DeSanctis, G. (1995). Electronic communication and changing organizational forms. *Organization Science, 6,* 337–349.

Geber, B. (1995). Virtual teams. *Training, 32*(4), 36–40.

Giddens, A. (1984). *The constitution of society.* Berkeley: University of California Press.

Glaser, B., & Strauss, A. (1967). *The discovery of grounded theory.* Chicago: Aldine.

Grove, C., & Hallowell, W. (1998). Spinning your wheels? Successful global teams know how to gain traction. *HR Magazine, 43,* 24–28.

Handy, C. (1995, May–June). Trust and the virtual organization. *Harvard Business Review,* 40–50.

Hiltz, S. R., & Turoff, M. Structuring computer-mediated communication systems to avoid information overload. *Communications of the ACM, 28,* 680–689.

Hiltz, S. R., Dufner, D., Holmes, M., & Poole, M. S. (1991). Distributed group support systems: Social dynamics and design dilemmas. *Journal of Organizational Computing, 2,* 135–159.

Hofstede, G. (1980). *Culture's consequences.* Beverly Hills, CA: Sage.

Hofstede, G. (1991). *Cultures and organizations: Software of the mind.* London: McGraw-Hill.

Hymowitz, C. (1999, 6 April). Remote managers find ways to narrow the distance gap. *The Wall Street Journal,* p. B1.

Jarvenpaa, S., Knoll, K., & Leidner, D. E. (1998). Is anybody out there? Antecedents of trust in global virtual teams. *Journal of Management Systems, 14,* 29–64.

Kayworth, T. R., & Leidner, D. E. (2002). Leadership effectiveness in global virtual teams. *Journal of Management Information Systems, 18,* 7–40.

Kiesler, S., & Sproull, L. Group decision making and communication technology. *Organizational Behavior and Human Decision Processes, 52,* 96–123.

Kiesler, S., Siegel, J., & McGuire, T. (1984). Social psychological aspects of computer-mediated communication. *American Psychologist, 39,* 1123–1134.

Knapp, M. L., & Vangelisti, A. L. (2000). *Interpersonal communication and human relationships* (4th ed.). Boston: Allyn & Bacon.

Lengel, R. H., & Daft, R. L. (1988). The selection of communication media as an executive skill. *Academy of Management Executive, 2,* 225–233.

Lipnack, J., & Stamps, J. (1997). *Virtual Teams: Reaching across space, time, and organizations with technology.* New York: John Wiley & Sons.

Marshall, C., & Rossman, G. B. (1995). *Designing qualitative research.* Thousand Oaks, CA: Sage.

McCracken, G. (1988). *The long interview.* Sage University Paper Series on Qualitative Research Methods, 13, Beverly Hills, CA: Sage.

McCune, J. C. (1998). Telecommuting revisited. *Management Review, 87,* 10–16.

Mintzberg, H. (1973). *The nature of managerial work.* New York: Harper & Row.

Mintzberg, H. (1994, Fall). Rounding out the manager's job. *Sloan Management Review,* 11–26.

Nelson, B. (1998). Recognizing employees from a distance. *Manage, 50*(1), 8–9.

Nilles, J. M. (1998). *Managing telework: Strategies for managing the virtual workforce.* New York: John Wiley.

O'Hara-Devereaux, M., & Johansen, R. (1994). *Global work: Bridging distance, culture, & time.* San Francisco, CA: Jossey-Bass Publishers.

Rice, R. E. (1993). Media appropriateness: Using social presence theory to compare traditional and new organizational media. *Human Communication Research, 19,* 451–484.

Scott, C. R., Frank, V., Cornetto, K. M., Sullivan, C., & Forster, B. (1999, November). *Communication technology use and key outcomes in novice groups: A comparison of site and virtual teams.* Paper presented at the meeting of the National Communication Association, Chicago, IL.

Solomon, C. M. (1995). Global teams: The ultimate collaboration. *Personnel Journal, 74,* 49–58.

Spradley, J. S. (1979). *The ethnographic interview.* New York: Holt, Rinehart, & Winston.

Sproull, L., & Kiesler, S. (1991). Connections: New ways of working in the networked organization. Cambridge, MA: MIT Press.

Strauss, A., & Corbin, J. (1990). *Basics of qualitative research: Grounded theory procedures and techniques.* Newbury Park, CA: Sage.

Van Aken, J. E., Hop, L., & Post, G. J. J. (1998). The virtual organization: A special mode of strong interorganizational cooperation. In M. A. Hitt, J. E. Ricart I Costa, & R. D. Nixon (Eds.), *Managing strategically in an interconnected world.* Chichester: John Wiley & Sons.

Van Ryssen, S., & Godar, S. H. (2000). Going international without going international — multinational virtual teams. *Journal of International Management, 6,* 49–60.

Walther, J. B. (1992). Interpersonal effects in computer-mediated interaction: A relational perspective. *Communication Research, 19,* 52–90.

Walther, J. B. (1995). Relational aspects of computer-mediated communication: Experimental observations over time. *Organization Science, 6,* 186–203.

Walther, J. B., & Burgoon, J. K. (1992). Relational communication in computer-mediated interaction. *Human Communication Research, 19,* 50–88.

Warkentin, M. E., Sayeed, L., & Hightower, R. (1997). Virtual teams versus face-to-face teams: An exploratory study of a web-based conference system. *Decision Sciences, 28,* 975–996.

Weisband, S. P., Schneider, S. K., & Connolly, T. (1995). Computer-mediated communication and social information: Status salience and status differences. *Academy of Management Journal, 38,* 1124–1151.

Wiesenfeld, B. M., Raghuram, S., & Garud, R. (1999). Communication patterns as determinants of identification in a virtual organization. *Organization Science, 10,* 777–790.

Yukl, G. (1981). *Leadership in organizations.* Englewood Cliffs, NJ: Prentice-Hall.

Yukl, G. (1989). Managerial leadership: A review of theory and research. *Journal of Management, 15,* 251–289.

Zaccaro, S. J., & Bader, P. (2003). E-leadership and the challenges of leading e-teams. *Organizational Dynamics, 31,* 377–387.

Zack, M. H. (1993). Interactivity and communication mode choice in ongoing management groups. *Information Systems Research, 4,* 207–238.

Zigurs, I. (2003). Leadership in virtual teams: Oxymoron or opportunity? *Organizational Dynamics, 31,* 339–351.

ENDNOTES

[1]   After conducting these formal interviews, we talked with 20 other distanced leaders in various industries who also had global responsibilities. We include their commentary in this chapter as well.

[2]   Each interview began with a general, nondirective, open-ended question about the challenges that leaders faced when leading from a distance. These "grand tour" questions (Spradley, 1979) functioned to encourage the interviewee to talk without specifying the substance of his or her response. The rest of the interviews consisted of a series of "category questions" (McCracken, 1988) that asked the respondents about their strategies for leading from afar. With each topic area, the interviewer asked the respondent to reveal an "exceptional incident" that reflected what the respondent was talking about.

[3]   As we share the insights of our interviewees, it is critical to note that these are *perceptions* of cultural differences. Future researchers should test hypotheses about these cultural nuances to determine how representative they are of reality.

Chapter V

Creating Positive Attitudes in Virtual Team Members

D. Sandy Staples, Queen's University, Canada

Ann Frances Cameron, Queen's University, Canada

ABSTRACT

Patterns of what is required to enhance a virtual team member's satisfaction with their work and with being part of the team, their commitment to the team, and their motivation with the project were identified via case studies of six employee virtual teams. Positive patterns were found between two or more of these outcome attitudes and the following input variables: significance of the task, task autonomy, interpersonal skills, team potency, and team spirit. Managing these input variables well would be important for organizations with virtual teams, because doing so could positively affect the team members' attitudes toward the work, leading to enhanced productivity and effective behavior. Implications for practitioners and researchers are offered.

INTRODUCTION

Groups and teams in organizations have been formally studied for over half a century, resulting in thousands of studies and a huge body of literature (Guzzo & Shea, 1992). Virtual teams, or teams with geographically distributed members, have been growing in popularity over the last decade or so but have not yet been extensively studied. Although working in geographically distributed teams is becoming more widespread in organizations today, how to do it effectively is not yet fully understood. Typical team effectiveness models (e.g., Cohen, 1994 — see Figure 1) are based on colocated teams and usually assess two main groups of effectiveness outcome variables: performance outcomes, such as quality, productivity, and controlling costs; and attitudinal outcomes, such as satisfaction with the job, satisfaction with the team, motivation, and organizational commitment. The focus of this chapter is on the latter, examining the factors and processes that affect attitudinal outcome variables of virtual team members. Concentrating on attitudinal outcomes will add to our understanding of how to make virtual teams effective. To accomplish this, attitudinal outcomes in six case studies of existing virtual teams are examined.

This chapter is organized as follows. The research framework used to guide the case studies is presented in the second section. The following section discusses the methodology used in the case studies and describes the characteristics of the teams studied. Then, in the next section, the results of the analysis are presented. Finally, discussed in the last section are implications for practitioners and researchers, and suggestions for future research are provided.

Figure 1:   Virtual team effectiveness model.

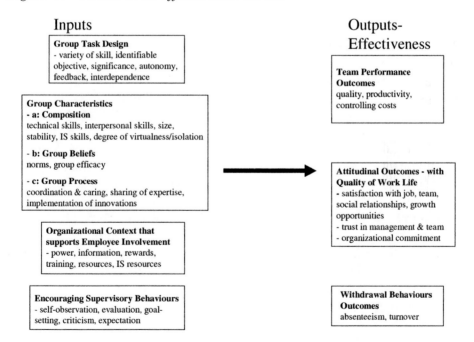

Source: Adapted from Cohen (1994).

RESEARCH FRAMEWORK

A self-managed team effectiveness model developed by Cohen (1994) was used to guide the case studies. Cohen developed her model based on an extensive review of the relevant research literature and an examination of other team effectiveness models. As can be seen in Figure 1, Cohen's model consists of four categories of input variables that potentially impact team effectiveness. These inputs are proposed to impact the three output categories of team effectiveness: team performance, attitudes, and behaviors. Note that the large arrow in Figure 1 considerably simplifies the complex relationships between input and output variables.

Because Cohen's model pertains to various outcomes of traditional self-managed teams, modifications were made to the model to make it fit a virtual work setting. First, it is important for team members in a virtual setting to have information technology skills as well as the ability to use such skills. In addition, team members need to be given appropriate tools and opportunities to use technology skills to accomplish their work. As such, the variable *Information System (IS) Skills* was added to the Group Composition list of variables, and *IS Resources* was added to Organizational Context.

Second, the degree of virtualness could potentially affect attitudes of geographically disperse team members. Degree of virtualness measures how often the team works from different locations and can vary from never meeting face-to-face (F2F) to occasionally working virtually. Team members working in a highly virtual team may experience higher degrees of isolation from other team members as well as other members of the organization. Thus, *Degree of Virtualness* was added as a Group Composition variable.

Third, the scope of this study will be limited to a subset of Cohen's model. While the original model includes three categories of outputs, the focus of this chapter is only on attitudinal outcomes. In particular, the chapter will examine factors and processes that enhance a team member's satisfaction with work, satisfaction with the work of other team members, commitment to the team, and motivation with the project. On the input side, supervisory behaviors were not included in this study due to practical limitations and the fact that Cohen, Ledford, and Spreitzer's (1996) test of Cohen's 1994 model did not find any significant relationship between supervisory behavior variables and effectiveness measures. The three groups of input variables that were included in the study are explained below, followed by discussion of previous research results supporting the links between the input variables and the attitudinal outcomes.

Task Design

Hackman and Oldham's job characteristics theory and sociotechnical theory suggest that group task design is critical for employee motivation, satisfaction, and performance (Cohen, 1994). Both theories suggest that to positively impact performance and attitudes, the task should be designed so that a variety of skills are required; it should be a whole and identifiable piece of work so that members can see the outcome of their efforts; the task should be perceived to have significant impact on the lives of other people; the team should have considerable autonomy and independence in determining how the work will be done; and regular and accurate feedback should be provided so that the team can understand how it is performing.

Sociotechnical theory suggests that group task design influences outcomes through team self-regulation (i.e., by developing the capacity in team members to develop good strategies to deal with technical and environmental changes, and how to cope with uncertainty). Job characteristics theory, which has fairly strong empirical support (Cohen, 1994), suggests that task attributes influence effectiveness through their impact on critical psychological states (supporting the importance of studying attitudes in this study).

Group Composition

The collective knowledge and skills of a team will impact the team's ability to carry out its task. This includes technical skills, information systems (IS) skills, and interpersonal skills. IS skills are needed to use the information technology tools and systems that are available to communicate and share information. The size of the team can also affect the ability of the team to do its task. If team size is too big, higher coordination costs result. If it is too small, it will not have the resources needed to complete its work, and it is less likely that team members will be committed to the team. Stability of team membership is also an important factor. If turnover is high, time and effort will be spent orientating new members, performance norms will not develop, and performance will suffer. However, some turnover can be beneficial, in that it could revitalize a stagnant team and enhance creativity. There has been limited empirical evidence to suggest that greater geographic distribution of a team leads to lower performance (e.g., Cramton & Webber, 1999). This is presumably due to reduced F2F contact, reduced opportunities to build social relationships, and difficulties in communicating and coordinating virtually. This implies that higher virtuality could be negatively related to team performance and satisfaction with the work and the team.

Group Beliefs

Group performance beliefs were found to be a strong predictor of group effectiveness in previous research. In this study, group beliefs were assessed via a concept called group potency. Group potency captures efficacy beliefs at the group level. According to Gibson, Randel, and Earley (2000), group potency (sometimes referred to as group efficacy) is "a collective belief in the capability of the group to meet a task objective" (p. 71). The group potency scale developed by Guzzo, Yost, Campbell, and Shea (1993) was used in this study, because it had established reliability and validity characteristics to assess general team efficacy (Gibson et al., 2000).

Group Process

Three groups of variables pertaining to group process were examined: coordinating and caring (i.e., team spirit), sharing expertise, and implementing innovations. Good coordination among team members leads to working together without duplication and wasted efforts. Caring about each other implies working together with energy and team spirit. Sharing and benefiting from others' knowledge and expertise are important in supporting effective cross-training and decision making and to fulfilling interdependencies. Implementation of innovations describes a team's ability to create and adopt new ways of working to better complete their tasks. This ability is important so that a team can adjust to changing conditions and make improvements in its work processes. These three group process variables are part of most models of group effectiveness and were found to be associated with group effectiveness in previous research.

Organizational Context

The organizational context in which a team works can create the conditions for a team to be successful or for it to fail. The team with the best internal processes may still perform poorly if it lacks the resources or information needed to do its task. A team will not be able to make good decisions without proper information, sufficient training, and adequate resources. Therefore, a series of organizational context variables was examined. These variables potentially interact to create an environment where the employee wants to be involved and can participate to complete tasks effectively. Specific variables examined were the reward system (it should be designed so that it is tied to performance and development of capability and contributions to the team); the availability of training (it should enable employees to develop the skills and knowledge required to complete their tasks); the access to needed information (without this, employees will not be able to effectively complete their tasks); and the resources available, including information technology infrastructure to communicate and share information electronically in the virtual setting (adequate resources are needed to enable employees to complete their tasks).

Motivation

Task design variables were found to be significantly related to motivation (Colquitt, LePine, & Noe, 2000; Coovert & Thompson, 2001; Rhoades &

Eisenberger, 2002). Colquitt, LePine, and Noe's (2000) review of training motivation found that a process variable, caring for others in the group, was related to training motivation. Their review also found organizational context variables, rewards and resources, were significantly related to motivation.

Commitment

The link between commitment and team processes was shown by several researchers. Mathieu and Zajac's (1990) meta-analysis of organizational commitment found that group cohesion and sharing of expertise was related to commitment. Meyer and Allen (1997) also found support for the relationship between commitment and team processes, as did Cohen et al. (1996) in the test of the Cohen (1994) model. Support for relationships between commitment and organizational context variables, such as power, information access, rewards, training, and resources, was found in the work of Cohen et al. (1996), Mathieu and Zajac (1990), Meyer and Allen (1997), and Rhoades and Eisenberger (2002).

Satisfaction with Own Work and Satisfaction with the Team

Support for the relationships between task design factors (e.g., variety of skill, significance, autonomy, and feedback) and satisfaction was found in the work of Cohen et al. (1996) and Spector (1997). Cohen et al.'s (1996) study found significant associations between team composition variables (i.e., technical skills, interpersonal skills, and team stability) and satisfaction, and between team process variables and satisfaction. The research findings of Gardner and Pierce (1998) and Zellars, Hochwarter, Perrewe, Miles, and Kiewitz (2001) demonstrated support for the relationship between team beliefs and satisfaction. Positive relationships were also found between satisfaction and organizational context variables, such as power, information access, rewards, training, and resources (Cohen et al., 1996; Rhoades & Eisenberger, 2002; Spector, 1997).

The Cohen (1994) model was designed for traditional teams, and the results reported above were largely based on studies of nonvirtual work. Examination of the relationships between input variables and attitudinal outputs in a virtual team context is warranted and will be explored in this study using a case study methodology, as described in the next section.

METHODOLOGY

Provided in this section are details about how the data were collected and analyzed and details of the teams that participated in this study.

Data Collection and Analysis

Case studies

Case studies of six virtual teams from three different companies, in different industries (i.e., high-tech, consulting, and manufacturing), were conducted. Face-to-face or telephone interviews were conducted with 39 team members. In addition to the team members, the managers and business sponsors of each team were interviewed in order to learn their perspectives on the effectiveness of the teams. The semistructured interviews typically lasted 1.5 hours each, and a case-study protocol was followed to ensure consistency across the interviews. The specific questions that were asked to collect data about the output variables and input variables are provided in Appendix A. Most interviews were audiotaped (a few participants did not allow this). Transcripts were prepared from the interviews (resulting in over 1000 pages of text) and entered into a qualitative analysis software package (N6 from QSR International). Each transcript was coded, as described below.

Coding the transcripts

A tree of nodes was initially built, where the nodes represented the constructs of interest and the levels within the construct. The initial list of nodes was based on the model guiding the study and the questions used in the interview. Two coders then separately coded one complete interview with the initial list of nodes. The list of nodes was modified slightly by collapsing a few nodes and creating a few new ones to capture findings not initially anticipated. After this initial training and development period, both coders coded a random sample of 10% of the transcripts to assess inter-rater reliability. Inter-rater reliability was determined using the Bourdon (2000) ICRV (Inter-Coder Reliability Verification) technique. Inter-rater reliability was 80%. This was deemed acceptable, so the list of codes (i.e., the nodes) was finalized, and the rest of the transcripts were coded by one person.

Analysis

Once the coding of the transcripts was complete, analysis was done to identify patterns of factors that potentially affected the virtual team members' attitudes regarding their work. Initially, within-case analysis (i.e., at the specific team level) was done (Miles & Huberman, 1994); however, variance was limited within some of the teams. Because we were interested in individual attitudes, across-case analysis was then completed using the individual as the unit of analysis. Matrices were created for each of the outcome variables and for each of the blocks of input variables (see Appendix B for a sample matrix that contains a small number of respondents' records). These matrices were then examined to see if any patterns appeared to emerge for respondents who were high on the specific outcome variable versus respondents who were low on the outcome variable. High for the outcome variables was defined as a score of six or greater (on the 1 to 7 scale — see Appendix A for details). Low was defined as a value less than six.

Characteristics of the Teams in the Sample

In order to provide context to the reader, short descriptions of each team are provided below. The nature of the task, the type of team, and the degree of virtuality present (i.e., how geographically distributed the team was) are described. To ensure confidentiality and anonymity, the identities of the companies, the teams, and the team members are not provided.

Nature of the tasks and duration of the teams

Teams A and B were developing new product lines within their organization. Both teams were in existence a few months and felt the teams would stay together assuming the product lines they were developing were successful. These teams can be thought of as long-term project teams. Teams C and D were developing new product features for an existing product and had just about completed their tasks when the interviews took place. These teams were together approximately nine months, so they can be thought of as medium-term project teams. Teams E and F were ongoing teams that provided products to internal service groups, and most people were on the teams for at least one year. Therefore, these were permanent teams. Teams A through D felt that their tasks were complex and that there was a great deal of interdependence among the team members to get the task completed. Teams E and F felt that their tasks were more routine and that usually they had relatively low dependence on other team members to complete their tasks. Varying degrees of complexity and interdependence were experienced by Teams E and F, depending on the specific task being completed.

Technology used

All teams used teleconferencing and e-mail heavily. Teams A, B, E, and F frequently used Lotus Notes to share information and coordinate activities. Teams C and D used an internal intranet system to share documents and resources. NetMeeting was used occasionally, and videoconferencing was rarely used. Teams E and F heavily used instant messaging.

Degree of virtuality

Teams A, B, and D were spread across multiple cities in North America. Team C was similar, except there was also one member located in India. Teams E and F were more distributed, with members in North America, Europe, and Asia. F2F contact varied considerably across the teams. Members from Teams A and B met F2F a few times per year or more. Members from Team C met F2F once during the duration of the project. Members from Team D never met F2F. Members from Teams E and F met F2F approximately once per year.

Reporting structure

Teams A through D were self-managed. Their members reported to directors or to a panel of business sponsors. The management relationships were typically described as hands-off. Teams E and F had a more direct reporting relationship to a manager and had more structure in place. Members of Teams A through D felt the team was given a great deal of autonomy to carry out its task. Members of Teams E and F felt the autonomy was fairly limited, as their work was fairly structured and routine.

Construct Measurement

Four outcome attitudinal variables were measured: motivation, commitment, satisfaction with own work, and satisfaction with the team (see Appendix A for details on the measurement). Five sets of input variables were assessed: task design, team composition, group beliefs, team process, and organizational context. Five indications of the task design were collected from team members. We asked about the variety of skills needed for the task, the significance of the task, the autonomy given to the team to carry out its work, the amount of feedback provided on the team's performance, and if the responsibility for the task was shared equally among the team members. Six indications of team composition were collected from team members. Three types of skills (technical, IS, and interpersonal skills), team size and stability, and degree of virtuality were examined. Group beliefs were assessed using the team potency scale (see Appendix A). Individual average values varied from 6 to 9.6 (out of a possible range from 1 to 10, with 10 being high potency). Four indications of team process were used: team coordination, team spirit, sharing of expertise, and implementation of innovations. Six aspects of organizational context were examined. These were reward systems, training availability and support, access to needed information, access to needed resources, provision of information technology resources, and power/decision-making authority. Provided in Appendix A are specific details on how all the variables were measured.

RESULTS FOUND

Presentation of the results is organized sequentially by the four outcome variables that were examined in this study: motivation with the work, commitment to the team task, satisfaction with own work, and satisfaction with being part of the team. For each outcome variable, patterns that were identified between the blocks of input variables and the outcome variables are presented.

Motivation with the Work

Two of the task design variables were found to be associated with motivation. Patterns indicated that team members with low motivation tended to have lower beliefs in the significance of the task and believed that their team had low autonomy. No other obvious patterns were found. The only discernible pattern for the team composition variables was between interpersonal skills and motivation. Individuals who felt that interpersonal skills were lower among the other team members did not tend to be as motivated to do the task. Analysis of the group potency results showed that people who had low motivation generally had lower beliefs about their team's abilities (i.e., potency). The only distinguishable pattern in the team process variables dealt with team spirit. A team member who had low motivation also perceived that the team's spirit was low. No clear patterns emerged from the analysis of the matrices for the organizational context variables and motivation.

Commitment to the Team Task

Two patterns were found for task design variables and commitment. Team members with lower beliefs in the significance of the task felt that their team (including themselves) had lower levels of commitment. Team members who felt their team had low autonomy also tended to believe that the team was less committed to the task, as compared to team members who perceived their team as having high autonomy. No clear patterns were found between the team composition variables and commitment. A pattern was found between team potency and commitment. Team members with low team potency beliefs also felt their team had lower commitment levels. One pattern emerged regarding the process variables and commitment. Team members who felt that team spirit was low, also generally felt that commitment to the team task was low. No clear patterns were found between the organizational context variables and commitment.

Satisfaction with Own Work

Autonomy was the only task design variable that showed a pattern with the satisfaction team members had with their own work. Team members who felt their team had low autonomy had lower levels of satisfaction with their work. With respect to team composition variables, individuals with lower satisfaction with their own work tended to assess their team's interpersonal skills lower and often felt that the team lacked some technical skills. Respondents who had lower beliefs about their team's abilities (i.e., team potency) also had lower satisfaction with their own work. One pattern was found with the team process variables. Team members who had lower satisfaction with their own work generally felt there was not a strong team spirit. No patterns were found between organizational context and satisfaction with the task, although when examined at the team level, the team with the most supportive organizational environment had the highest average satisfaction levels.

Satisfaction with the Team

Two patterns were found among the task design variables and satisfaction with the team. Individuals with lower satisfaction with the team were more likely to believe that responsibility for the task was not shared equally and that the team had lower autonomy. Two patterns were also found in the team composition variables. Team members with lower satisfaction with their team tended to assess their team's interpersonal skills lower and often felt that the team lacked some technical skills. A strong pattern was found between satisfaction with the

Table 1:   A summary of the patterns found.

Input Variables	Output Variables			
	Motivation	**Commitment**	**Satisfaction with Own Work**	**Satisfaction with the Team**
Significance of the task	X	X		
Responsibility shared equally				X
Autonomy	X	X	X	X
Interpersonal skills	X		X	X
Technical skills				X
Team potency (efficacy)	X	X	X	X
Team spirit	X	X	X	X
Coordination				X

team and group potency perceptions. Team members who felt their team had high capabilities (i.e., a high group potency rating) had high satisfaction with their team. Two patterns were found between the process variables and satisfaction with the team. People who had lower satisfaction with their team felt that there was not a strong team spirit and often felt that coordination could be improved. No distinct patterns emerged from the analysis of the organizational context variables responses and the satisfaction with team responses.

In the next section, the findings and present implications for organizations that have virtual teams will be discussed, and suggestions for future research will be made. The overall findings are summarized in Table 1, where an "X" in the cell indicates that a pattern was found between the input variable and the output variable. Note that the input variables included in Table 1 are only those that were found to have patterns with one (or more) output variable(s). In all cases, the nature of the patterns was positive (e.g., low perceptions of the input variable were found with low perceptions of the output variables).

DISCUSSION

The findings suggest that, within the teams studied, motivation was positively associated with perceptions of task significance, autonomy, interpersonal skills, beliefs about the team's ability to do the task, and team spirit. Although our research design does not allow us to make any conclusions of causal direction, previous research (see the second section of this chapter) would suggest that improving these input variables would lead to increased motivation to work on the team's task. Along similar lines, the findings would also suggest that commitment could be increased by strengthening the perceived significance of the task, providing more autonomy to the team, enhancing perceptions of the team's abilities, and improving the team's spirit. Satisfaction with one's work could also be enhanced by providing higher autonomy to the team, developing stronger interpersonal skills, enhancing team potency, and improving team spirit. These same processes, along with designing the task so responsibility is shared equally, ensuring that technical skills are adequate for the task, and having good coordination with the team, could be used to increase satisfaction with the team. The discussion below deals with each of the input variables in turn and offers several implications of these variables for virtual teams and their organizations.

Significance of the task appears to be positively linked to motivation and commitment. This implies that managers and leaders of virtual teams should work hard to make individuals aware of how important the task is and to whom. How can organizations do this? The director of the team examined in this study whose members had by far the highest perceived significance of the task suggested that you need to build a shared sense of cause within the team. Building this shared sense of cause will allow team members to feel their work is important. As a result, they may pull together to achieve greater success. This director stated:

> *If you can create a cause around something you usually get passion for it.... [You] can create this passion by gathering the stakeholders together... the business team participants all together in one place and allow them to see the direct impact of their project...*

One mechanism used by this director was to take the entire team to the site of a future customer. On-site, the team worked with that customer to understand his or her needs as well as how he or she and future customers could potentially be impacted by the team's product. The director also used a second mechanism for creating high significance. As illustrated in the quote below, this director made sure that the team members understood the career-enhancing opportunity that being part of the team gave them:

> *[You] can also have passion when the management can demonstrate how the project will result in significant outcomes for the [team members] themselves because they will grow with this business opportunity. They will get to do things that they never thought they were going to do before.*

Equal responsibility for the outcome of the team's efforts was found to be associated with satisfaction with the team. Therefore, shared responsibility for the outcome is an important task design variable for organizations to consider. One of the teams studied was clearly not designed for all members to have equal responsibilities. In this team, there was a "leadership" subgroup and a "worker" subgroup. People in the leadership subgroup felt team spirit was good and communications were fine. People in the worker subgroup felt they were not involved with key decisions and did not feel they equally shared responsibility for the outcome of the project. They also had a significantly more negative view of the team's spirit and communication processes. Therefore, organizations should be careful not to intentionally or unintentionally create subgroups. In virtual teams, where part of the team may be collocated and part of the team remote, this can be particularly challenging. The supervisor of another team was aware of this potential problem. With three team members on-site and the remaining team members remotely located, he was very careful to treat all team members equally. He attempted to communicate, share information, and share responsibilities for the team's task equally among the colocated as well as dispersed members of the team.

High autonomy was found to be positively associated with all the output variables examined. This is consistent with research findings on effective collocated teams. According to Cohen and Bailey (1997), the organization needs to give team members autonomy in their work. Worker autonomy has been shown to have clear benefits; it enhances worker attitudes, behaviors, and performance (whether measured objectively or rated subjectively by team members). Organizations should give team members the power to take action and make decisions about work and business performance.

In the study, interpersonal skills were related to all of the output variables except commitment. This highlights the importance of training and developing strong interpersonal skills in virtual team members. Organizations can provide basic interpersonal skills to teams through training or through team member selection. Because team members are interdependent, one important interpersonal skill is the ability to communicate effectively. This skill can be especially important in virtual teams, where effective communication is difficult. Time zones may be frequently crossed. Participants may have different national cultures that influence their natural communication patterns. Virtual team communications often rely heavily on asynchronous electronic media, which has limited feedback mechanisms. This limited feedback may lead to team members making false attributions about each other's behaviors. As Cramton (2001) found in her research, in the absence of other information, people often attribute things like nonresponse to laziness or lack of interest, when in fact, it could be due to nonreceipt or other legitimate reasons. Thus, virtual team members need to agree on norms and expectations for communications so that false attributions, which could damage group cohesiveness and motivation, are not made. Skills have to be developed in this area as well. Some examples of how communication in virtual groups can be improved were suggested by participants. Team members have to be responsive, quickly returning telephone calls and responding to e-mails, even if it is just to say, "I don't have time right now, but I'll get back to you in two days with the answer." Further, two virtual team managers suggested that the recipient actually confirm that the message was received and ensure that the major points in the message were understood. Developing communication skills such as these could help to avoid misinterpreting interpersonal situations or behaviors.

Two other sets of skills were identified as being positively associated with satisfaction with the team: technical skills and coordination abilities. Previous research supports the need for having adequate technical skills among team members to complete the team's task and the importance of effectively coordinating efforts so time is not wasted and work is not duplicated (e.g., Cohen, 1994). To accomplish this, organizations can ensure that members on a team collectively have the skills required to complete the task. The organization can do this by carefully selecting team members whose skills complement each other or by providing training and development opportunities so that the needed skills can be acquired. Routine, frequent communications were mentioned by many of the team members as contributing to good coordination (see quote below). Good communication between members ensures that the team members know what each are doing and how their pieces of the project fit together, and this helps to avoid duplication.

> *I would think so [the team's efforts were well coordinated] because we had weekly meetings so I would say it was very structured. We had weekly meetings and to follow up the weekly meetings were weekly minutes. You know and then the following week we followed up on any outstanding items. And then aside from that there were individual e-mails that might have gone, you know, between meetings, back and forth, so I would say it was well structured.*

In the teams studied, most routine meetings were carried out via teleconferencing. Another mechanism that was identified as aiding coordination was the use of Lotus Notes databases. Such technology can be used to store project information so team members and management can track the status of tasks, and to generally help teams manage their schedules. Project management tools such as Gantt charting software were also used by some of the teams.

Team potency was found to be positively associated with all the output variables, implying that if an organization can increase team members' beliefs in the abilities of the team, the team members will be more motivated and committed to the team and be more satisfied with being part of the team. To increase team potency, organizations can select team members who have the required skills and abilities. However, this is not enough. Team members have to know about the skills and abilities that others bring to the team and develop a belief that the team will collectively succeed. Celebrating and recognizing achievements as they occur should also help build beliefs in abilities. We know from the extensive work on self-efficacy (e.g., Bandura, 1977, 1982) that previous successes enhance perceived efficacy and that self-efficacy is a powerful predictor of performance (Stajkovic & Luthans, 1998). Generally, it appears that if one does not believe that the team will succeed and operate well, one is less satisfied with one's own contribution to the team, less committed to the team, and less motivated to contribute to the team.

Team spirit was positively associated with all the output variables, suggesting the importance of this concept for organizations. Team spirit is demonstrated through working together with energy and caring about fellow team members (Cohen, 1994). Many of the team members felt that because F2F interaction is limited, creating strong team spirit in virtual teams can be difficult. For example:

It is hard for the people who are far away to feel this [i.e., team spirit], especially if they are isolated and working on their own. In that case, they do not get exposed to the [company] culture and learn about it. This is also a problem for new people. It is hard to share culture and build team spirit, especially when remote from others.

*Yeah, I believe there was [a team spirit]... Like I said, it would
have been better if we could all have gotten together for beers
more often but, cheers, we have virtual beers.*

One team leader explained why team spirit was so strong in his virtual team:
*Yeah, I think so [a team spirit was present in the team] even
though it was a virtual ... yeah it had a virtual spirit. But I mean
I would get on the call and in the first five minutes, you know,
talking about what's happening in everybody's personal lives...
I mean it's ... we were interested in what everybody else was
doing.*

Getting to know team members on a personal basis and demonstrating
genuine interest in what they are doing should help build team spirit. Although this
can be done effectively through F2F social settings, the quote above illustrates
that it can also be accomplished at a distance. Setting aside time in teleconference calls for social time or a virtual coffee break can help people get to know
each other better and enable them to better appreciate each other's situation. In
two of the teams, synchronous instant messaging was heavily used. Team
members reported that many of the messages were of a social nature and that
such messages helped them feel connected to the rest of the team. Future
research efforts to help organizations understand how to establish team spirit in
a virtual setting would be valuable.

The discussion so far has focused on the relationships that were found
between input variables and output variables. However, it would be equally
interesting to determine where relationships were *not* found. When there is
ample evidence in previous team effectiveness research, why were no significant patterns found for many of the other input variables? The most probable
explanation is that the teams in this study did not exhibit enough variance in some
of the input variables. For example, the variety of skills required was high for all
teams, turnover was low in most teams, and little duplication of effort was found.
In addition, few innovations were developed by the teams, team size was
perceived to be adequate for most teams, and information technology resources
provided to the teams and the team members' abilities to use them were both
good. Finally, training support was similar for all teams, few team-based rewards
were provided, and access to information and resources was usually not a
problem. The fact that many of these input variables had little variance and were
often well-done by all teams is one limitation of this study. Therefore, we cannot
conclude that these variables are not important inputs for effective virtual teams.
Future research is needed to further understand these input variables and their
significance for effective virtual teams. For example, future research could

advance our understanding of degree of virtuality. In this study, the degree of virtuality varied, but no clear patterns were observed. This may indicate that degree of virtuality is not a strong predictor of effectiveness or is only important if other components are not strong (e.g., information technology support, coordination, communication, etc.). The validity of these conclusions can only be determined by future research into virtual team effectiveness.

In conclusion, the geographic dispersion of team members in virtual teams makes it a significant challenge for organizations to develop and maintain effective virtual teams. Via case studies of six virtual teams, we identified patterns and indications of what it takes to enhance virtual team members satisfaction with their work and with being part of the teams, their commitment to the teams, and their motivation with the projects. Positive patterns were found between two or more of the attitudes and the significance of the task, task autonomy, interpersonal skills, team potency, and team spirit. Managing these input variables well would be important for organizations with virtual teams, because doing so could positively affect the team members' attitudes toward the work, leading to enhanced productivity and effective behavior. Although we know from previous research that attitudes are important indicators of team effectiveness and are associated with behaviors, future research needs to be done to look at other effectiveness outputs, such as team performance and withdrawal behaviors. It is hoped that this chapter provides insights to organizations that are wrestling with the challenges of designing and maintaining effective virtual teams, and that it identifies additional areas that researchers should focus on in the future.

REFERENCES

Bandura, A. (1977). Self-efficacy: Toward a unifying theory of behavioral change. *Psychological Review, 84*(2), 191–215.

Bandura, A. (1982). Self-efficacy mechanism in human agency. *American Psychologist, 37*(2), 122–147.

Bourdon, S. (2000). *Inter-coder reliability verification using QSR Nud*Ist.* Paper presented at Strategies in Qualitative Research: Issues and Results from Analysis Using QSR NVivo and QSR NUD*IST, September 30. The Institute of Education, University of London, UK.

Cohen, S. G. (1994). Designing effective self-managing work teams. In M. M. Beyerlein, D. A. Johnson, & S. T. Beyerlein (Eds.), *Advances in interdisciplinary studies of work teams: Vol. 1. Theories of self-managed work teams.* Greenwich, CT: JAI Press.

Cohen, S. G., & Bailey, D. E. (1997). What makes teams work: Group effectiveness research from the shop floor to the executive suite. *Journal of Management, 23*(3), 239–290.

Cohen, S. G., Ledford, G. E., Jr., & Spreitzer, G. M. (1996). A predictive model of self-managing work team effectiveness. *Human Relations*, *49*(5), 643–676.

Colquitt, J. A., LePine, J. A., & Noe, R. A. (2000). Toward an integrative theory of training motivation: A meta-analytic path analysis of 20 years of research. *Journal of Applied Psychology*, *85*(5), 678–707.

Coovert, M. D., & Thompson, L. F. (2001). Computer supported cooperative work: Issues and implications for workers, organizations, and human resource management. In J. Barling, & K. Kelloway (Eds.), *Advanced topics in organizational behavior*. Thousand Oaks, CA: Sage Publications.

Cramton, C. D. (2001). The mutual knowledge problem and its consequences for dispersed collaboration. *Organization Science*, *12*(3), 346–371.

Cramton, C.D., & Webber, S. S. (1999). Modeling the impact of geographic dispersion on work teams. Working paper, George Mason University.

Gardner, D. G., & Pierce, J. L. (1998). Self-esteem and self-efficacy within the organizational context: An empirical examination. *Group & Organization Management*, *23*(1), 48–70.

Gibson, B. G., Randel, A. E., and Earley, P. C. (2000). Understanding group efficacy: An empirical test of multiple assessment methods. *Group & Organizational Management*, *25*(1), 67–97.

Guzzo, R. A., & Shea, G. P. (1992). Group performance and intergroup relations in organizations. In M. D. Dunnette, & L. M. Hough (Eds.), *Handbook of industrial and organizational psychology: Vol. 3* (2nd ed., pp. 269–313). Palo Alto, CA: Consulting Psychologists Press.

Guzzo, R. A., Yost, P. R., Campbell, R. J., & Shea, G. P. (1993). Potency in groups: Articulating a construct. *British Journal of Social Psychology*, *32*, 87–106.

Mathieu, J. E., & Zajac, D. M. (1990). A review and meta-analysis of the antecedents, correlates, and consequences of organizational commitment. *Psychological Bulletin*, *108*(2), 171–194.

Meyer, J. P., & Allen, N. J. (1997). Commitment in the workplace: Theory, research and application. In J. Barling, & K. Kelloway (Eds.), *Advanced topics in organizational behavior*. Thousand Oaks, CA: Sage Publications.

Miles, M. B., & Huberman, A. M. (1994). *Qualitative data analysis: An expanded sourcebook*. Thousand Oaks, CA: Sage Publications.

Rhoades, L., & Eisenberger, R. (2002). Perceived organizational support: A review of the literature. *Journal of Applied Psychology*, *87*(4), 698–714.

Spector, P. E. (1997). Job satisfaction: Application, assessment, causes and consequences. In J. Barling & K. Kelloway (Eds.), *Advanced topics in organizational behavior*. Thousand Oaks, CA: Sage Publications.

Stajkovic, A. D., & Luthans, F. (1998) Self-efficacy and work-related performance: A meta-analysis. *Psychological Bulletin, 124*(2), 240–261.

Zellars, K. L., Hochwarter, W. A., Perrewe, P. L., Miles, A. K., & Kiewitz, C. (2001). Beyond self-efficacy: Interactive effects of role conflict and perceived collective efficacy. *Journal of Managerial Issues, 13*(4), 483–499.

APPENDIX A: CONSTRUCT MEASUREMENT

Task Design Assessment

Five indications of the task design were collected from team members. We asked about the variety of skills needed for the task, the significance of the task, the autonomy given to the team members to carry out their work, the amount of feedback provided on the team's performance, and if the responsibility for the task was shared equally among the team members. Specific questions were as follows:

- What are the skill sets required to complete the task? How are these skills distributed among the team members?
- On a scale of 1 to 7 points, with 1 = very little, and 7 = very much, how would you answer the following question: How does the work, or project, affect the lives or well-being of others?
- How much autonomy does the group have in determining the parameters of the task, the methods for achieving the task, or even the task itself?
- What kind of feedback is provided to the group on performance? Is feedback provided regularly, and is this feedback useful?
- Is responsibility for the final outcome shared equally among all members?

Team Composition Assessment

Three types of skills (technical, IS, and interpersonal skills), team size and stability, and degree of virtuality were examined for the proposition related to group composition summary. Specific questions were as follows:

- Are there adequate technical skills among the group members to complete the task? Do you feel that your individual technical skills are sufficient for the required task?
- On a scale of 1 to 7 points, with 1 = very low, and 7 = very high, how would you rate the general level of interpersonal skills in your group? Probe for additional comments — ask why.
- What level of relevant IT training and abilities do the team members have? Is it adequate for the existing IT tools? What level of IT training and experience do you, as an individual, have? Do you feel it is adequate?
- How many team members are there? Are there enough team members to do a good job? Are there too many?
- How long has the group been working together? Is there a high turnover in group membership? How was the team first started? How did team members get to know each other?
- How many members of the team are geographically dispersed? How dispersed is the team — number of time zones spread out among members? How often do they meet face to face?

Group/Team Potency

In this study, group beliefs were assessed via a concept called group potency. The group potency scale developed by Guzzo, Yost, Campbell, and Shea (1993) was used in this study. Respondents were asked to indicate how accurately, on a 1 to 10 scale, a series of eight statements described their team. The eight statements are listed below. A potency value was created for each respondent by averaging their eight responses.

1.   My team has confidence in itself.
2.   My team believes it can become unusually good at producing high-quality work.
3.   My team expects to be known as a high-performing team.
4.   My team feels it can solve any problem it encounters.
5.   My team believes it can be very productive.
6.   My team can get a lot done when it works hard.
7.   No task is too tough for my team.
8.   My team expects to have a lot of influence around here.

Team Process Assessment

Several questions were asked to get at three sets of process variables: coordination and caring (i.e., team spirit), sharing of expertise, and implementation of innovations. The specific questions asked were as follows:

- How would you characterize your team's level of coordination? What is the level of duplication that occurs (or does any duplication occur)?
- Is there a sense of team spirit in your group? Why or why not?
- How comfortable are your team members with sharing important information within the team? How comfortable are your team members with taking advice from or deferring to someone in the team with greater knowledge or skill?
- Has the team adopted or created any new innovations or inventions to improve your way of doing required tasks?

Organizational Context Assessment

Several questions were asked to get at five sets of process variables: reward system, training availability, access to needed information, access to needed resources, and power/decision-making authority. The specific questions asked were as follows:

- What is the reward system? How are rewards distributed?
- How adequately is training available and supported?

- Who has the information you need to do your job? How easy is it to get the information you need?
- Does your geographic location hinder or increase your access to required resources? How difficult is it to acquire resources as the need arises; does your location make a difference? What resources (if any) do you feel are missing in your off-site work, compared to on-site work?
- IT tools provided: What kinds of IT tools and infrastructure are present?
- Power/authority: What is the power structure in your team? What level of authority does your team have in making important decisions?

Team Outcome Variables

Motivation with the task
- On a scale of 1 to 7 points, with 1 = very low, and 7 = very high, how would you answer the following question: How would you characterize your level of motivation with your current project? Probe for reasons and comments.

Commitment to the team's project/work
- How would you rate the level of commitment of members of the team to achieving the overall goals of the team (scale: 1 to 7; 1 = very low commitment, and 7 = very high commitment)? Why?

Satisfaction with own work
- On a scale of 1 to 7 points, with 1 = very low, and 7 = very high, how would you answer the following question: How would you describe your level of satisfaction with *your* work? Why?

Satisfaction with being part of the team
- On a scale of 1 to 7 points, with 1 = very low, and 7 = very high, how would you answer the following question: How would you describe your level of satisfaction with your team? Why?

APPENDIX B: SAMPLE DATA MATRIX WITH A SUBSET OF THE RECORDS

Variety of skills	Significance to society	Autonomy	Feedback	Responsibility for the task shared equally?	Motivation
High	6 — "Our new product line will be recyclable, whereas what we are trying to replace is not."	High	Nothing formal; fairly high profile so there is interest from the executive level	"I think we may all be equally responsible, but there is one person ultimately accountable."	High
High	7	Medium	At the end of the year, the team's funding will be renewed or pulled by senior management, so that will provide feedback. "We tend to get more informal feedback passed down through our group leader."	"I guess some don't have as big a stake, because they might be less time involved in the program if they are spread out amongst other programs."	High
High	7	High	The feedback is provided as often as basically we request it	Yes, shared responsibility	High
High	7	Medium	Feedback to the project team is from the business manager or the local manager		High
High	4	High	Do not know, but expect some	Two key members have most responsibility	Low
High	6	Low	"Feedback is not consistent and not given directly. Some informal feedback is provided, and this is valuable, but not everybody gets this as not everybody is interacting with senior management."	Some have a more vested interest but all are responsible for the final outcome	Low
High variety	2	High	"The only thing we've received so far is just from the portfolio management team, and so far it's been good... We get, you know, feedback as we go, and we get feedback from our own functional managers as well."	Yes	Low
High	1	High	"There wasn't a lot of feedback, and there wasn't a lot of ... you know ... this is a great direction and you are doing a good job with this ... there wasn't anything like that."	"All the members were collectively responsible for doing their parts."	Low
High	4	High	Little feedback from outside the team	Equal responsibility for outcome	Low

Chapter VI

Trust in Virtual Teams

Wray E. Bradley, The University of Tulsa, USA

George S. Vozikis, The University of Tulsa, USA

ABSTRACT

Discussed in this chapter are the role and importance of trust in virtual teams. It is suggested that the nature and degree of this trust are related to the culture and management philosophies of a firm, the interpersonal skills of management and team leaders, and the psychological characteristics and prior experiences and expectations of the team members. Trust and trust building are examined at three different levels: the firm level, the manager or team leader level, and the individual member level. A better understanding of the dynamics of trust in virtual teams will assist management in developing more efficient and effective virtual collaborative teams.

INTRODUCTION

Virtual teams can be identified by several characteristics. The teams make extensive use of information and communication technology (ICT) systems. They typically use a computer-mediated communication (CMC) system. They often use technology enablers, such as Lotus Notes/MS Exchange and Groove, and may use video- and audioconferencing and group decision support systems (GDSS). In some cases, the team has its own dedicated virtual workspace. The team members rarely, if ever, meet face-to-face, and the individual team members may represent different cultures, languages, and organizations. Frequently the teams are temporary, being formed and dissolved over a short period of time. Occasionally, virtual teams will be semipermanent. However, even in semipermanent teams, members frequently move on and off the team. Virtual teams are usually charged with interdependent tasks that have common goals.

In order to achieve these goals, team members may have different competencies and different technical specialties (Townsend, DeMarie, & Hendrickson, 1998; Picolli & Ives, 2000; Bos, Olson, Gergle, Olson, & Wright, 2002; Bell & Kozlowski, 2002).

In this kind of environment, it is difficult for managers to supervise employees and to assess individual employee behavior. For employees, typical factors contributing to team cohesion, such as close physical location and common backgrounds and experiences, are often absent. In this self-directed, sometimes isolated environment, trust becomes a pivotal element of success. Without trust, or with low levels of trust, virtual workers may engage in dysfunctional behavior designed to avoid interaction with other team members, such as low commitment to a project, lack of information sharing, and unilateral alterations of task structure and sequence. These behaviors limit the overall efficiency and effectiveness of a virtual team. Furthermore, customers dealing with virtual teams may perceive a lack of trust among team members as a lack of reliability or lack of concern for the customer's needs.

Management can ill afford dysfunctional geographically diverse teams that operate in cyberspace with a minimum of supervision. It is generally agreed that trust and trust building are essential if an organization is committed to virtual teams. Management has a vested interest in creating an environment that is conducive to the development of high trust levels among virtual team members. Several researchers suggest that trust is perhaps the most important determinant of success for virtual teams (O'Hara-Devereaux & Johansen, 1994; Lipnack & Stamps, 1997).

This chapter begins with a brief background review of the topic of trust. This review includes definitions of trust, briefly discusses some research findings from F2F studies that have implications for virtual team trust, and presents research findings from several empirical studies on trust in virtual teams. The background review is followed by additional discussion of building and maintaining virtual team trust. This additional discussion describes some of the roles that management philosophy, manager/team leader behavior, and individual characteristics and behavior play in virtual team trust and trust building. We conclude with a short summary and suggestions for future research.

BACKGROUND

Trust has been defined in variety of ways. Trust has been framed in terms of an employee's belief that the organization's management and fellow workers will interact honestly and fairly and in a reliable and predictable manner (Lipnack & Stamps, 1997). Trust has also been defined as a willingness on the part of organizational members to allow themselves to be vulnerable and undertake actions based on the belief that other parties will perform their parts effectively without supervision or control (Mayer, Davis, & Schoorman, 1995). Cummings and Bromiley (1996) take an even broader view of trust:

> *Trust will be defined as an individuals' belief or a common belief among a group of individuals that another individual or group (a) makes good-faith efforts to behave in accordance with any commitments both explicit and implicit, (b) is honest in whatever negotiations preceded such commitments, and (c) does not take excessive advantage of another even when the opportunity is available. (p. 303)*

The foregoing definitions show the highly relational nature of trust. Trust usually develops over a period of time through regular interpersonal contact. This suggests that F2F interaction is often an important factor for trust building.

Face-to-Face Advantage

Bos et al. (2002) conducted an experiment using 66 three-member teams operating in different media. Teams were divided into F2F groups, videoconference groups, phone-conference groups, and computer chat room (CMC) groups. Each group participated in social dilemma games that were previously used in trust research (Komorita, 1994). Bos et al. (2002) found that in the computer-mediated groups, there was a larger incidence of defections in terms of breakdown of trust, and retaliatory action. This study suggests that F2F is the best way to develop and maintain trust in a team. After F2F interaction, rich communication media seems to be the next best means to develop and maintain trust.

Face-to face also appears to be important for trust building when firms are forming virtual teams that work through interorganizational alliances. Scott and Gable (1997) examined the formation of the alliance between The University of Texas, Queensland University of Technology, and SAP AG. Their study emphasized that developing and maintaining trust in a large interorganizational alliance requires F2F meetings and exchange of personnel, even if virtual teams will ultimately accomplish the majority of the actual work. They note that in order to be successful, an interorganizational alliance must share common goals and purposes and must develop agreed-upon means to assess the fulfillment of these goals. This means that each organization within such an alliance must create an atmosphere of trust within its own organization before employees can operate and interact in a trusting manner toward members of other firms. There must be trust-building mechanisms in place, such as frequent communication and open sharing of information, on both an intrafirm basis and an interfirm basis. All of these issues are nearly impossible to address on an entirely virtual basis.

Handy (1995) characterized the importance of F2F meetings in virtual settings as "trust needs touch" (p. 46). It may well be that virtual teams that operate on a long-term basis will need to periodically meet F2F in order to develop and sustain high levels of trust. If F2F meetings are difficult to arrange (as is the case for some virtual teams), the richer the communication media and the more trust oriented the corporate culture, the better the atmosphere for developing and maintaining virtual team trust.

Selected Empirical Research on Trust in Virtual Teams

In a F2F environment, trust develops incrementally over time through a socialization process. During this process, trust is not merely an abstract concept. Rather, it binds together all relationships and provides the foundation from which a group or organization operates, leadership flourishes, and changes occur. However, sometimes the F2F socialization process is not available to the virtual team member, who is often located at a geographically distant workstation. Because the normal socialization process associated with developing trust is not available, virtual team members have almost no choice but to rely on trust expectations based on their past experiences. Jarvenpaa, Knoll, and Leidner (1998) found that virtual teams acted as if trust existed from the beginning of the virtual team formation. This type of trust was characterized as "swift trust" (Meyerson, Weick, & Kramer, 1996). Swift trust is based on team members' prior experiences and expectations. If a team member previously worked in a team setting (any team setting, not necessarily virtual) where high trust was the norm, then the member assumes that a high level of trust exists in the new virtual team setting, from the beginning. However, in a second study using 12 teams for in-depth case analyses, Jarvenpaa and Leidner (1999) found that swift trust is fragile and can be readily modified, either positively or negatively, by the early communication behavior among team members.

The link between communication behavior and virtual team trust is further supported by the research of Warkentin and Beranek (1999). They found that teams containing virtual team members who were given interpersonal communication training prior to joining the team exhibited higher levels of trust than did those teams whose members were not given communication training. Similarly, Bradley, Haines, and Vozikis (2002), in a computer laboratory experiment of 15 five-member virtual teams, found that individual team members' trust levels were impacted by simple directions or complete lack of direction regarding initial team organization. These findings indicate that it is important for management to assist in the planning of initial communication strategy and to provide some initial organizational direction for virtual teams.

Individual team member attributes also play an important role in virtual team trust. Jarvenpaa et al. (1998) examined the personal trust attitudes of virtual team members from 75 virtual teams consisting of four to six members each. Many team members lived in countries different from other members. The researchers used the trustee/trustor paradigm of Mayer, Davis, and Schoorman

(1995). This paradigm suggests that trust is a function of how an individual team member perceives fellow team members in three areas: perceived ability (domain competence), benevolence (care and concern for others), and integrity (dependability, reliability). The study found that individual perceptions of the trustworthiness of fellow team members was at first highly related to the perceived ability (competence) of other members, but this decreased as time went by. The perception of integrity early on was important but not as important later. The perception of benevolence had little impact on perceived trust in the virtual team setting. In addition, perceptions of high team trust were found to be a function of an individual's general personality trait, known as "propensity to trust." This propensity to trust is viewed as a composite personal trait formed by experiences, personality type, culture, education, and socioeconomic factors. Propensity to trust was found to be important in virtual team trust, invariably, throughout the life of the teams. That is, team members with high propensity to trust perceived that the team and other team members operated at high levels of trust, whereas, team members with low propensity to trust perceived that the team and team members exhibited lower levels of trust.

Propensity to trust was also investigated by Galvin, Ahuja, and Agarwal (2002), who performed a content analysis of the e-mail of 90 individuals from six organizations and 23 different virtual teams. The e-mails discussed 15 different projects. The study found that the three most important variables associated with trust were recent and past virtual team experience, structural assurance, and disposition to trust (propensity to trust). Individuals with virtual team experience were found to be more likely to take a positive view of trust in the virtual context. Further, subjects with recent virtual team experience were found to exhibit higher levels of trust than subjects with less recent virtual team experience. The

Table 1: Precursors of virtual team trust based on empirical research.

- F2F meetings and rich communication media are important for trust in virtual teams
- Communication training for all virtual team members may improve team trust
- Initial organizational direction for virtual teams is essential for the early development of trust
- All team members must be competent and reliable for trust to continue to develop
- Selection of team members who have a high "propensity to trust" may improve the overall team trust environment
- Individual team members perceive that a system of structural assurances is important for preventing heretofore unknown virtual members from taking advantage of them
- Team members with recent prior virtual team experience are likely to positively influence high trust levels

second construct, structural assurance, is based on the idea that an individual perceives that the organization has mechanisms in place that will protect them from actions of other employees. Examples would be things like written policy guidelines that contain penalties for noncompliance and grievance procedures. As to propensity to trust, Galvin et al. (2002) went so far as to suggest that propensity to trust might be a factor in initial hiring decisions, and it should be a factor to be considered when assigning employees to virtual teams.

Some of the key points found in the empirical literature are summarized in Table 1.

BUILDING AND MAINTAINING
TRUST IN VIRTUAL TEAMS

In this section, the discussion of virtual team trust is extended beyond the summary findings listed in Table 1. First, building and maintaining virtual team trust at the firm level is discussed. This is followed by discussions of building and maintaining virtual team trust from the team leader and individual team member perspectives.

Trust at the Firm Level

Firm-level management plays the *sine qua non* key role in establishing an atmosphere where virtual team trust can develop and thrive, regardless of overall organizational structure. Different organizational forms face different problems in respect to trust in virtual teams. The following is a limited discussion of the impact that firm culture and management philosophy can have on virtual teams. The framework for the discussion is based on the four organizational types and management philosophies outlined by Creed and Miles (1996), namely, functional, divisional, matrix, and network organizational structures. In addition to the four organizational types, a brief discussion of interorganizational aspects of virtual team trust is included as a subsection of this firm-level discussion. Creed and Miles (1996) related trust to the four organizational forms as follows: "Comparatively, in functional forms, trust failures reduce efficiency; in divisional forms, they reduce effectiveness and raise costs; in matrix forms, they cause the form to fail; and in networks, they cause the firms to fail" (p. 26).

Functional Organizations

Functional organizations are usually vertically integrated and generally operate in a hierarchical centralized "management by exception" scheme. A failure of trust at the firm level will undoubtedly reduce efficiency, but virtual teams working in this organizational structure face a potential problem that will also reduce the effectiveness of the team. Virtual teams operating in vertically integrated organizations are likely to be involved with tasks that require the expertise of functional specialists (production, marketing, etc.). Oftentimes, in this type of organization, many key decisions are made above the functional specialist level. If this is the case, functional specialist virtual team members may not be empowered to make important decisions without consulting higher management. This may cause other team members to perceive the functional specialist as not being competent or reliable, creating a low team trust atmosphere. It is doubtful that actual domain competence and high integrity on the part of a functional specialist team member can overcome a deficit in decision-making authority. If a functional organization is going to use virtual teams, then a managerial system that promotes trust and decision making on the part of functional specialists must be in place.

Divisional Organizations

Divisional organizational forms offer a particular challenge for a virtual team. Traditionally, organizations operating in a divisional form are highly competitive from an internal firm standpoint. Divisions may compete on the basis of divisional profits or divisional market share, and often, division managers are compensated at the expense of peer division managers. This environment often breeds distrust and win–lose situations. A virtual team member operating in this type of environment would be dealing with team members in other divisions or other organizations. A divisional type of organization that plans to use virtual teams must, by necessity, engage in a program of division-wide teambuilding, but it must also address the issue of how a virtual team member deals with fellow team members who are not privy to and may not care about the internal competitive structure of the division or the firm.

Matrix Organizations

Unlike the divisional form, a well-functioning matrix organizational form should be fertile ground for virtual teams that operate at high trust levels. In the ideal matrix system, decision-making responsibility largely resides with project teams or team leaders, where the swift trust expectations of virtual team members are high. Often, the competencies and reliability of distant team members was already established by prior contact or by reputation. Nevertheless, upper management can erode the high trust environment normally attendant to this form of business by moving toward a more centralized approach to decision making.

Network Organizations

Network forms of organizations are where one would expect to find wide use of virtual teams, because, for these organizational types, trust is the cornerstone. Powell (1990) indicated that these organizations operate on the basis of strict allegiance to the network, even at the expense of self-interest. Virtual teams with high levels of trust based on firm loyalty and individual experience are expected to be the norm for this type of organization. As Creed and Miles (1996) pointed out, a trust failure for network firms can result in firm failure. Therefore, management in network organizations has a vested interest in developing and maintaining an organizational culture with high levels of trust throughout the entire organization.

Interorganizational Considerations

Interorganizational virtual teams are often given complex tasks that require a high degree of coordination and exchange of ideas and information, and depend on specific individuals to perform highly specialized tasks. Teams operating in this environment need high levels of trust in order to ensure success. The different organizations within an alliance may be internally structured and organized in any of the aforementioned forms; however, there are certain issues that must be addressed on a common basis if the teams are to operate effectively and efficiently. Kasper-Fuehrer and Ashkanasy (2001) suggested that swift trust, in an interorganizational context, must be nurtured in several ways. They argued, first, that there must be ongoing "communication of trustworthiness."

Table 2: Firm-level considerations for building and maintaining trust of virtual teams.

Organizational form	
Functional	• Have a system in place that promotes trust and allows for key decision-making authority at the functional specialist team member level
Divisional	• Provide a division-wide team-building training program • Discourage competitive relationships among virtual team members, even though this is almost counterculture in this type of organizational form
Matrix	• Maintain decentralized approach to decision making • Ensure that mechanisms are in place to foster an overall high trust environment
Network	• Maintain overall high trust in corporate culture
Interorganizational	• Have reliable, media-rich, standardized communication systems in place • Adopt a system of agreed-upon product standards and specifications • Formalize terms of cooperation • Adopt a code of business ethics

This is accomplished by ensuring that the information and communications technology (ICT) system(s) that will be used by virtual teams are highly reliable and interorganizationally standardized. The ICT system should also be designed to transmit facial expressions and allow for the transmission of emotional cues. Second, building blocks of trust must be in place. These building blocks include agreed-upon product standards and specifications, agreed-upon terms of cooperation, some "sense of shared identity," and a formal code of business ethics in place for each of the firms involved. Successful interorganizational virtual teams demand high levels of trust.

The main points of the foregoing organization level elements of trust building are summarized in Table 2.

Trust at the Facilitator/Team Leader Level

In order for trust to emerge in a virtual team, it is important to have a designated leader for all virtual teams, from the start. Virtual teams comprised of self-starters can certainly self-organize. However, as mentioned earlier, there is a strong likelihood that fragile swift trust will quickly dissipate in a self-organized virtual team. This is why the initial appointment of leaders and facilitators who are knowledgeable in virtual team management is important. Organizationally, there needs to be a manager–facilitator who is responsible for getting a virtual team started and for monitoring the progress as well as securing the effective performance of the team. The designation of this person requires careful consideration, especially in an interorganizational setting that is organized in a matrix or network form. In an interorganizational setting, it may be helpful to diagram the overlapping reporting relationships of team members in order to determine the most logical candidate. Ideally, this same facilitator will also be the operational team leader.

The behavior of virtual team leaders or middle management team facilitators is a key factor in developing and maintaining trust within a virtual team. Because team members join the team with the expectation that trust already exists, it is incumbent upon the team leader to maintain and reinforce these initial swift trust expectations. An important aspect of enhancing the initial level of team trust is the team leader's communication discipline. Research shows that the most effective team leaders adhere to specific communication guidelines and standards when dealing with team members. These include promptly replying to team member inquiries, providing a large quantity of accurate and unbiased feedback regarding team activities, and communicating in a manner that is not arrogant or distant (Duarte & Snyder, 2001; Bell & Kozlowski, 2002; Kayworth & Leidner, 2002). Additionally, frequency of contact seems to be important. The communication discipline can be reinforced by standardized routines (i.e., set contact schedules) and should include rules of protocol and etiquette among members. If team members have not heard from the leader in some time, they usually begin to speculate as to whether or not they were overlooked or ignored. This diminishes the trust level. Platt (1999) suggested an initial "contracting discussion" among virtual team members for the purpose of discussing team member expectations. This contracting discussion will determine frequency of contact with each other and cover specific and detailed expectations for all team members.

Also consistent with previous research is the idea that team leaders should precisely outline the team's mission with explicit objectives and clearly defined division and assignment of tasks. Kayworth and Leidner (2002) even suggest that there is a definite social integration aspect of virtual teams. In this social context, it becomes important for the team leader to be sensitive to the opinions of team members, consulting them before time deadlines are set, and carefully acknowledging and considering their suggestions. It may even be helpful to establish social chat sessions and post personal information on a team Web site. However, team leaders need to be careful that social interaction does not give the appearance of exploitation or overt competitiveness, as this will diminish trust in a virtual team.

Finally, global team leaders must be prepared to deal with the cultural dimensions of team trust. Duarte and Snyder (2001) discussed some cultural dimensions of virtual team trust in terms of a concept called "trust-radius." They point out that team leaders need to take into account that some cultures place more importance on relationship building than others. Quaddus and Tung (2002) found that cultural differences significantly impact decision making. They state that facilitators and team leaders need to "increase their sensitivity to differences in cultural dimensions across groups of different cultures." They recommended the use of Hofstede's (1984) cultural dimensions to assist in this task. Hofstede divided international culture into four dimensions: power distance, uncertainty avoidance, individualism, and masculinity. Understanding these concepts is a must for the global virtual team leader. The task of building and maintaining trust in culturally diverse global virtual teams is not to be taken lightly. Training of team

Table 3: Individual team leader traits and behaviors that enhance trust in virtual teams.

- Leader should be highly qualified and virtual team "aware"
- Leader should establish a formal communication discipline early on
- Leader should precisely outline the team mission with explicit objectives and clearly defined division of tasks
- Leader should consider the social aspects of team development
- Leader should consider the cultural dimensions of the team

leaders in the cultural aspects of virtual teams is a worthwhile investment for any organization.

Some of the team leader traits and behaviors that help build and maintain trust in virtual teams are summarized in Table 3.

Trust at the Team Member Level

Individual virtual team members need to be carefully selected by management. They must first and foremost be skilled with the technology that will be used by the team, capable of self-direction, and comfortable with working independently in a multiple role capacity. They must also possess and exhibit high ability in respect to their functional specialty, as well as a demonstrated record of integrity. Additionally, because an individual's propensity to trust is important throughout the life cycle of a virtual team, and because propensity to trust is often influenced by a virtual team member's identity with the organization, management should be careful to select virtual team members who demonstrated that they are real team players who gain satisfaction from the success and effectiveness of their work unit. Because the initial swift trust environment of a virtual team is fragile, trust may start at high levels, but it will quickly diminish if any of the team members have a low propensity to trust or are perceived as lacking in ability or integrity.

There are specific behaviors on the part of individual team members that will enhance or detract from virtual team trust. Poor communication on the part of an individual team member is often interpreted by other team members as lack of motivation. An individual team member should always be aware of the activities within the team by regularly reviewing team message traffic, even if no action is required on the part of the specific team member. A periodic "how is it going with your part of the project" communication to other team members indicates interest in the project. Compliance with deadlines is a must, even if the individual team member thinks that the deadline is not important. Often, team members are waiting to hear that a deadline has been met before they can start a special task assigned to them.

Kayworth and Leidner (2002) found that virtual team members in low-trust teams sometimes thought that fellow team members were not open-minded and lacked common goals. Virtual team members need to be receptive to new ideas and new ways of doing things. Additionally, like virtual team leaders, individual virtual team members who work in multicultural interorganizational virtual teams need to be sensitive to cultural differences that may affect how a project is managed and completed. Individual virtual team members also need to be sensitive to the social dimensions of intercultural virtual teams. Ultimately, the success of a virtual team, and the level of trust manifested in a virtual team, rests with the individual virtual team member. A lack of understanding of the dynamics

Table 4: Individual team member traits that enhance trust in virtual teams.

- Team members must be skilled with the technology used by the team
- Team members must be self-starters
- Team members must have a high degree of functional area competency
- Team members must exhibit high integrity
- Team members should have a high "propensity to trust"
- Team members should adhere to a good communication discipline
- Team members should be open to the ideas of others
- Team members should be sensitive to cultural differences within the team
- Team members should be sensitive to the social aspects of the team

of virtual team trust or a poor attitude on the part of the individual virtual team member will hamper the effectiveness and efficiency of any virtual team.

Individual team member traits and behaviors that enhance trust in virtual teams are summarized in Table 4.

CONCLUSION AND SUGGESTIONS FOR FUTURE RESEARCH

Trust is established on relationships and built through a socialization process based on historical interaction. This places virtual teams that operate in a geographically and culturally diverse cyberspace environment, often on a short-term basis, at a disadvantage. Without the normal F2F socialization process, virtual team members are forced to formulate trust expectations by relying on past experiences and expectations, a form of trust characterized as swift trust. Research established that swift trust is fragile and will be adjusted upward or downward, and be modified positively or negatively soon after a virtual team starts working. Nevertheless, it is not clear what precisely replaces this initial swift trust. Deficits in virtual team trust are known to result in high stress for individual team members, low satisfaction, low relationship commitment, and a perception of low task performance. However, further research is needed to establish exactly what happens when swift trust is modified positively, and conversely, what happens when swift trust is modified negatively.

The process of building virtual team trust starts at the firm level. This presents special challenges for organizations that are functional or divisional in organizational form, because the decision-making autonomy that virtual teams often require is not a normal part of the corporate culture. It was hypothesized that virtual teams flourish in a matrix or networked organizational form. However, more research is needed in order to determine what specific type of organizational structure, and what specific attributes of that structure, will best support virtual teams and trust in virtual teams.

Trust is typically viewed from two broad perspectives. The majority of researchers examined the topic using a "rational choice" model. Adherents of this model view trust as a function of an individual's self-interest. Trust then simply becomes a matter of protecting one's self-interest. In a high-trust environment, it is perceived that less self-protection against the actions of others is needed, and this allows individuals to take more risk. The second perspective of trust uses a "social model," in which trust is a function of the strength of allegiance between an organization and its members. Implicit in the social model is the idea that trust is often based on a sense of moral duty. Virtual team trust research to date is almost entirely based on the rational approach, which is only part of the picture. Trust in virtual teams needs to be researched and studied from both the social and the rational perspectives, especially at the organizational level. Such an approach would be similar to the "combined" approach recently taken by Ishaya and Macaulay (1999). They hypothesized that trust in virtual teams is based on team members' self-interest as well as team members' sense of moral or social obligation to the team or to the organization(s) that the team represents. Under this hypothesis, a virtual team member may periodically suspend self-interest in favor of furthering the team's goals.

The attitudes and personal characteristics of individual team leaders and individual team members are the key to trust in virtual teams. We learned from the study of virtual teams that, in order to maintain high trust, individual team members and team leaders need to be acutely aware of the importance of good communication skills and commitment to the team and the project, and of the need to be sensitive to opinions and ideas of other team members. On the other hand, we also know that individuals with a high propensity to trust are more likely to perceive fellow team members as being trustworthy.

Beyond propensity to trust, are there certain skills and background training that make for a more trusting virtual team member? Are MIS-trained employees more trusting virtual team members than members with little formal computer or software training? Do some people work better in a virtual team environment than others? If so, what are their characteristics? In addition, because the cultural dimensions of virtual teams have a direct influence on trust, we need to more clearly understand the special requirements necessary for multicultural virtual teams to operate at high trust levels.

Trust is certainly an important part of virtual team success, and as Jarvenpaa and Shaw (1998) pointed out, "Only trust can prevent geographical and organizational distances of team members from turning into unmanageable psychological distances" (p. 47). Discussed in this chapter are some of the dynamics of trust in virtual teams and some ways of building and maintaining that trust. However, many unanswered questions continue to exist in this very important developing research area.

REFERENCES

Bell, B., & Kozlowski, S. (2002). *Group & Organization Management, 27*(1), 14–49.

Bos, N., Olson, J., Gergle, D., Olson, G., & Wright, Z. (2002). Effects of four computer-mediated communications channels on trust development. *Chi Letters, 4*(1), 135–140.

Bradley, W., Haines, R., & Vozikis, G. (2002). Trust in virtual teams: The use of a directive sentence in the script of the thinklet. In N. Mastorakis, & V. Mldenov (Eds.), *Recent advances in computers, computing and communications* (pp. 122–127). Athens, Greece: WSEAS Press.

Costa, A., Roe, R., & Taillieu, T. (2001). Trust within teams: The relation with performance effectiveness. *European Journal of Work and Organizational Psychology, 10*(3), 225–244.

Creed, W., & Miles, R. (1996). Trust in organizations: A conceptual framework linking organizational forms, managerial philosophies, and the opportunity costs of controls. In R. Kramer, & T. Tyler (Eds.), *Trust in organizations: Frontiers of theory and research* (pp. 16–38). Thousand Oaks, CA: Sage Publications.

Cummings, L., & Bromiley, P. (1996). The organizational trust inventory (OTI): Development and validation. In R. Kramer, & T. Tyler (Eds.), *Trust in organizations: Frontiers of theory and research* (pp. 302–330). Thousand Oaks, CA: Sage Publications.

Duarte, D., & Snyder, N. (2001). *Mastering virtual teams: Strategies, tools, and techniques that succeed.* San Francisco: Jossey-Bass.

Galvin, J., Ahuja, M., & Agarwal, R. (2002). *Dispositional and situational influences of trust behavior in virtual teams.* Working paper, Indiana University.

Glaser, R. (1997). Paving the road to trust. *HR Focus, 74*(1), 5.

Handy, C. (1995). Trust and the virtual organization. *Harvard Business Review, 73*(3), 40–50.

Hofstede, G. (1984). *Culture's consequences, international differences in work-related values,* 5. Beverly Hills: Sage Publications.

Ishaya, T., & Macaulay, L. (1999). The role of trust in virtual teams. In P. Sieber, & J. Greise (Eds.), *Organizational virtualness and electronic commerce* (pp. 135–152). Bern: Simowa Verlag (VoNET).

Jarvenpaa, S., & Leidner, D. (1999). Communication and trust in global virtual teams. *Organization Science, 10*(6), 791–815.

Jarvenpaa, S., & Shaw, T. (1998). Global virtual teams: Integrating models of trust. In P. Sieber, & J. Greise (Eds.), *Organizational virtualness* (pp. 35–51). Bern: Simova Verlag (VoNET).

Jarvenpaa, S., Knoll, K., & Leidner, D. (1998). Is anybody out there? Antecedents of trust in global virtual teams. *Journal of Management Information Systems, 14*(4), 29–64.

Kaeser, S., & Kaeser, R. (1997). The influence of task type and designated leaders on developmental patterns in groups. *Small Group Research*, *28*(1), 94–117.

Kasper-Fuehrer, E., & Ashkanasy, N. (2001). Communicating trustworthiness and building trust in interorganizational virtual organizations. *Journal of Management*, *27*, 235–254.

Kayworth, T., & Leidner, D. (2002). Leadership effectiveness in global virtual teams. *Journal of Management Information Systems*, *18*(3), 7–40.

Komorita, S. (1994). *Social dilemmas*. Madison, WI: Brown & Benchmark.

Lipnack, J., & Stamps, J. (1997). *Virtual teams: Reaching across space, time, and organization with technology*. New York: John Wiley.

Madhaven, R., & Grover, R. (1998). From embedded knowledge to embodied knowledge: New product development as knowledge management. *Journal of Marketing*, *62*(4), 1–29.

Mayer, R., Davis, J., & Schoorman, F. (1995). An integrative model of organizational trust. *Academy of Management Review*, *20*(3), 709–734.

Meyerson, D., Weick, K., & Kramer, R. (1996). Swift trust and temporary groups. In R. Kramer, & T. Tyler (Eds.), *Trust in organizations: Frontiers of theory and research* (pp. 166–195). Thousand Oaks, CA: Sage.

O'Hara-Devereaux, M., & Johansen, B. (1994). *Global work: Bridging distance, culture, and time*. San Francisco: Jossey-Bass.

Piccoli, G., & Ives, B. (2000). *Virtual teams: Managerial behavior control's impact on team effectiveness*. Proceedings of the 21st International Conference on Information Systems, 2000 (pp. 575-580). Brisbane, Queensland, Australia.

Platt, L. (1999). Virtual teaming: Where is everyone? *The Journal for Quality and Participation*, *22*(5), 41–44.

Powell, W. (1990). Neither market nor hierarchy: Network forms of organization. In B. Staw, & L. Cummings (Eds.), *Research in organizational behavior*, 12 (pp. 295–336). Greenwich, CT: JAI.

Quaddus, M., & Tung, L. (2002). Explaining cultural differences in decision conferencing. *Communications of the ACM*, *45*(8), 93–98.

Scott, J., & Gable, G. (1997). *Goal congruence, trust, and organizational culture: Strengthening knowledge links*. Proceedings of the 18th International Conference on Information Systems, 1997 (pp. 107–119). Atlanta, GA.

Sheppard, B., & Tuchinsky, M. (1996). Micro-OB and the network organization. In R. Kramer, & T. Tyler (Eds.), *Trusts in organizations; Frontiers of theory and research* (pp. 140–165). Thousand Oaks, CA: Sage Publications.

Townsend, A., DeMarie, S., & Hendrickson, A. (1998). Virtual teams: Technology and the workplace of the future. *Academy of Management Executive*, *12*(3), 17–29.

Warkentin, M., & Beranek, P. (1999). Training to improve virtual team communication. *Information Systems Journal*, *9*, 271–289.

SECTION III:

COMMUNICATION IN VIRTUAL TEAMS

Chapter VII

Newcomer Assimilation in Virtual Team Socialization

Gaelle Picherit-Duthler, University of North Carolina at Charlotte, USA

Shawn D. Long, University of North Carolina at Charlotte, USA

Gary F. Kohut, University of North Carolina at Charlotte, USA

ABSTRACT

Socialization of newcomers in traditional organizations has been given considerable attention in the literature. However, little attention has been paid to how individuals are socialized in virtual teams. Examined in this chapter is the critical stage of organizational assimilation for newcomers in virtual teams and how this stage differs for traditional organizational socialization. Specifically, we address newcomer relationship development and virtual team metamorphosis. Recommendations for effective virtual team socialization are offered as well as areas for future research.

INTRODUCTION

The sophistication of communication technology and the globalization of organizations greatly accelerated the growth and importance of virtual teams in the workplace. Teleworking and virtual teams are becoming more commonplace for several reasons — often it is more efficient, less expensive, and less technologically difficult to organize geographically dispersed workers. When employees work in teams and communicate only via technology rather than face to face, the socialization process may be altered because of the technological mediation of communication.

It is well known that communication is important to socialization into teams. For example, early in a job, newcomers concentrate on gathering information, learning about the tasks necessary for the job, and clarifying their roles in the team. To acquire information and learn about the new setting, newcomers frequently rely on a variety of sources within the team, such as peers, supervisors, and mentors (Miller & Jablin, 1991; Schein, 1988).

How well an individual is socialized into a team can determine his or her success within it and, ultimately, the team's success in achieving goals and objectives. Team socialization and the communication practices associated with that socialization have been researched extensively since Jablin (1982) first explored the intricate process. Socialization occurs when a member of a team acquires the knowledge, behavior, and attitude needed to participate fully as a member of that team. Jablin (1987) described the stages of socialization that occur as one enters an organization as anticipatory socialization, organizational assimilation (encounter and metamorphosis), and organizational exit. Unlike the abundance of research in traditional team socialization, research in the area of virtual team socialization is only now beginning to emerge (Ahuja & Galvin, 2003). The focus of this chapter is to explore how information technologies mediate communication in virtual teams, and, as a result, impact socialization processes.

A virtual team is defined as a group of geographically and organizationally dispersed workers brought together across time and space through information and communication technologies (DeSanctis & Poole, 1997; Jarvenpaa & Leidner, 1999; Lipnack & Stamps, 1997). The challenge for virtual team socialization lies with the fact that team members communicate primarily via electronic mail, telephone, and videoconferencing or computer conferencing. Because most of the communication in virtual teams is mediated, the processes involved in socialization of virtual teams may be different from traditional face-to-face (F2F) teams. However, organizations seldom differentiate between building virtual and traditional teams, assuming that the stages of socialization for colocated teams are the same as those for virtual teams.

Mediated communication is different than F2F communication. For example, interaction in mediated groups appears more impersonal, task-oriented, less friendly, and more businesslike (Rice & Love, 1987; Sproull & Kiesler, 1986). In addition, communication technologies can limit and complicate the process of developing virtual teams. For example, Mark (2001) stated that communication delays and awkwardness in turn taking can impact the communication process of team building. However, rather than viewing computer-mediated communication as limiting, Walther (1996) suggested that technologies can facilitate communication by providing opportunities for anonymity, 24-hour access, and archiving. Thus, the communication technologies transform the critical role that interpersonal communication plays in the socialization of virtual teams.

Socialization studies in virtual teams tend to focus on the ways in which employees gain knowledge about their work environments. In particular, Ahuja and Galvin (2003) explored how virtual team members sought or provided information to facilitate the socialization process. They found that newcomers engaged in information-seeking behaviors, while established members engaged in information-providing behaviors. Currently, however, no research exists in terms of the different stages of virtual team socialization.

Addressed in this chapter will be the challenges of virtual team socialization by reviewing the relevant literature on socialization and virtual teams with regard to the second stage of newcomer socialization: encounter and metamorphosis. The authors will identify the processes embedded in the assimilation stage in virtual teams. Finally, suggestions will be proposed for successfully assimilating newcomers into virtual teams.

ASSIMILATION IN VIRTUAL TEAMS

Organizational assimilation is possibly most important stage of virtual team socialization. Such assimilation concerns the processes by which individuals become integrated into the culture of an organization (Jablin, 1982). Jablin (1987) suggested that organizational assimilation is composed of two interrelated processes: planned as well as unintentional efforts by the organization to "socialize" employees, and the attempts of organizational members to "individualize" or change their roles and work environments to better satisfy their values, attitudes, and needs. Scholars viewed the two interrelated and reciprocal processes as central components of the organizational "role-making" process (Graen, 1976; Jablin, 1982), because it is "through the proactive and reactive communication of expectations to and from an individual by members of his or her 'role set' that organizational roles are negotiated and individuals share in the socially created 'reality' of organizations" (Jablin, 1987, p. 694).

Virtual Team Encounter

Schein (1988) suggested that for most newcomers, the organizational encounter is a time for learning "pivotal" behaviors, values, and beliefs associated with their jobs and organizations. Van Maanen (1976) further suggested that it is a time for learning what insiders consider to be "normal" patterns of thinking and behaving and, in particular, what things mean to members of the organization. As a result of entering a new situation, a key concern of newcomers is to clarify their situational identity through their work roles (Berlew & Hall, 1966; Feldman, 1976), or through securing the approval of others (Graen & Ginsburgh, 1977; Katz, 1978; Wanous, 1980). To reduce uncertainty, newcomers search for information that allows them to adjust by defining the expectations of others and orienting their behaviors to the behaviors of others. Relationship building is critical for understanding who is really important, the rules and norms of behaviors, and how to get things done.

Thus, it is vital for newcomers to establish and develop relationships with others in the work setting, especially with supervisors, leaders, and peers (Jablin, 2001). Organizational relationships are similar in traditional and virtual teams but are not identical. They are similar in that trust, openness, supportiveness, interaction context and relationship state, hierarchical position, group social context (cooperative–competitive), and perceived effectiveness in relationship maintenance are salient issues (Jablin, 2001). However, what makes these issues different is that much of the relationship building takes place through technologically mediated communication and generally over a shorter period of time.

Among other things, organizational relationships provide newcomers with support that facilitates the learning process and reduces stress and uncertainty associated with adjusting to a new work environment (Jablin, 2001). Much of the research on relationship development in the organizational encounter stage focuses on information seeking and information giving (e.g., Boyd & Taylor, 1998), learning behaviors and attitudes through exchange activities (e.g., Comer, 1991), technical or social information (Comer, 1991; Morrison, 1995), and regulative and normative information (e.g., Galvin & Ahuja, 2001). Evidence suggests that formal and informal socialization practices may affect the level of organizational commitment (Berlew & Hall, 1966; Buchanan, 1974), longevity in the organization (Katz, 1978; Wanous, 1980), and satisfaction and feelings of personal worth (Feldman, 1976).

Although a concern of virtual team socialization is these salient socialization issues, little attention was given to how these concepts impede or enable communication in this unique organizational structure. It is equally important to note that the research on how virtual team relationships are formed and maintained is insufficient. However, the study of information exchanges, both technical and social, provides the most important indicator of effective versus ineffective socialization of virtual team members. Examined in the next section are three central areas for relationship building in virtual teams: peer relation-ships, supervisory relationships, and mentoring relationships. Traditional team socialization provides the comparative backdrop for this examination.

Peer Relationships

In traditional organizations, most newcomers have numerous peers in their work groups but typically just one immediate supervisor. Peers may help newcomers integrate what may appear to be disjointed pieces of information (Van Maanen, 1984) and may communicate subtle values and norms that may not be well understood by supervisors. Newcomers tend to have more contact with coworkers, and, as a consequence, more opportunities to share information with them and develop relationships (Jablin, 2001; e.g., Comer, 1991; Teboul, 1994). Sias and Cahill (1998) proposed that a variety of contextual factors, including shared tasks and group cohesion (e.g., Fine, 1986), physical proximity (e.g., Griffin & Sparks, 1990), lack of supervisor consideration (Odden & Sias, 1997), and life events outside the workplace, as well as individual factors, such as perceived similarity in attitudes and beliefs as well as demographic similarity (Adkins, Ravlin, & Meglino, 1996; Duck, 1994; Glaman, Jones, & Rozelle, 1996; Kirchmeyer, 1995), may affect the development of relationships with peers. If these factors, especially physical proximity, life events outside of the workplace, and similarity in attitudes and beliefs are compromised because of the inherent structure of virtual teams, this creates a dilemma in socializing members to virtual teams. Silas and Cahill (1998) posited:

> *Relationships developed into close friendships usually because of important personal or work-related problems, although perceived similarity and extra-organizational socializing continued to impact relational development. At this point, the coworker became a trusted source of support with communication becoming increasingly more intimate and less cautious. (p. 289)*

As stated above, trust is a key factor in developing close relationships. However, due to the lack of physical proximity and the reliance on communication technologies, our understanding of trust in virtual teams is different from the trust in traditional teams. Meyerson, Weick, and Kramer (1996) coined the term "swift trust" to describe how virtual teams develop a different type of trust than that in traditional teams. Due to the highly interdependent task orientation of the team, newcomers develop trust more quickly. Team members are able to develop trust in the relationship on the basis of a shared task rather than on the basis of similar demographics or physical proximity (Jarvenpaa & Leidner, 1999).

However, swift trust is not enough to develop close peer relationships. Team members face numerous challenges, including technological mistrust by newcomers and established members, intuitive fear of the misuse of archived communication (e.g., e-mail trails), and the difficulty of sharing personal or non-work-related issues. Thus, virtual newcomers may be unable or unwilling to take advantage of the informal organizational development that appears central to organizational socialization in traditional teams. This clearly inhibits the development of close peer relationships in virtual teams, which in turn, may inhibit constructive team cohesion. Similarly, opportunities to understand organizational politics are reduced. Unless the communication among team members is open, power bases form, allowing certain behaviors to take place, such as social loafing, domination, and the formation of cliques. Groups or individuals may be alienated by these behaviors and may differ in their responses based on location or functional role, but the outcome is the same-limited effectiveness of the team, low commitment, low loyalty, and mistrust. Other sources of information, such as supervisors and mentors, may prove more helpful in recognizing and adapting to political nuances.

Supervisory Relationships

Supervisors are important for assimilating newcomers to organizations by helping build a shared interpretive system that is reflective of assimilation (Berlew & Hall, 1966; Feldman, 1976; Graen, 1976; Kozlowski & Doherty, 1989; Ostroff & Kozlowski, 1992; Schein, 1988). The supervisor frequently communicates with the newcomer, may serve as a role model, filters and interprets formal downward-directed management messages, has positional power to administer rewards and punishments, is a central source of information related to job and organizational expectations as well as feedback on task performance, and is pivotal in the newcomer's ability to negotiate his or her role, among other things (Ben-Yoav & Hartman, 1988; Jablin, 2001). The supervisor–subordinate relationship may be even more important in virtual teams than in traditional teams because of the dislocated nature of the virtual structure. The relationship is complicated by the absence of a physical communication context that characterizes most traditional teams. The supervisor's coordination of virtual team activities may be more difficult because of the distinct nature of technological feedback, the lack of robust spontaneous information exchange between supervisor–subordinate, and the obvious reduction of F2F verbal and nonverbal communication cues.

It is important for newcomers to develop professional relationships with supervisors, but, because virtual teams operate within a more limited time frame than traditional teams, close relationships leading to friendships become more difficult. Newcomer socialization in virtual teams differs in the amount of time newcomers are allowed to build strong supervisor–subordinate relationships and enact their virtual team roles. Access to historical artifacts to better socialize newcomers may be one indicator of an effective supervisor–subordinate relationship.

Regardless of whether the supervisor is part of the team or not, the effective supervisor–subordinate relationship will depend in large part on whether the organization uses a traditional approach to managing the virtual team. In traditional teams, supervisor–subordinate relationships are often characterized by hierarchical embedded roles in responsibilities, with more formalized rules, procedures, and structures (McPhee & Poole, 2001). On the other hand, in virtual teams, there is a loosening of the rules and responsibilities in the supervisor–subordinate relationship. The virtual setting reduces tangible cues that would distinguish the status and hierarchy of the team members. Thus, the supervisor–subordinate relationships in a virtual team may rely more on co-orientation, focusing on facilitating and supporting the socialization process. Such activities are also comprised in mentoring relationships, which were recognized as important to newcomers in adjusting to socialization efforts.

Mentoring Relationships

When discussing relationship building as part of the assimilation process, one would be remiss not to acknowledge the power of mentoring relationships. Mentors help facilitate newcomer adjustment to situations by offering advice, support, and if appropriate, coaching behaviors to accomplish goals. Wigand and Boster (1991) suggested that "mentoring speeds up socialization into the work role, encourages social interaction, provides an opportunity for high-quality interpersonal interactions, and enhances identification with and commitment to the organization" (p. 16). Any discussion divorcing organizational socialization from mentoring is incomplete. Mentoring is also particularly valuable in a virtual team setting. For example, Kayworth and Leidner (2002) discovered that highly effective virtual team leaders act in a mentoring role and exhibit a high degree of empathy toward other team members. In this section, we attempt to explore the roles of formal and informal mentoring in the assimilation process and the implications for virtual team socialization.

Formal mentoring is not a haphazard, unscripted organizational event that naturally develops between an established organizational member and a newcomer. Instead, it is a "deliberative pairing of a more skilled or experienced person with a lesser skilled or experienced one, with the agreed upon goal of having the lesser skilled or experienced person grow and develop specific competencies" (Murray & Owen, 1991, p. xiv). In essence, formal mentoring relationships are strategically orchestrated by the organization to achieve specific professional, social, or organizational goals. Generally, formal mentoring programs seek to "groom" newcomers for advancement or to better acclimate newcomers to their new organizational situations.

Several scholars (e.g., Allen, McManus, & Russell, 1999; Heimann & Pittenger, 1996; Seibert, 1999) acknowledged that newcomers who participate in formal mentoring relationships in traditional organizations realize greater benefits than those who do not have formal mentoring. Specifically, participation in formal mentoring increases the newcomer's understanding of various organizational issues and increases the newcomer's level of organizational and job satisfaction.

Informal mentoring, on the other hand, is not as deliberate or calculated as formal mentoring. Informal mentoring relationships develop naturally at the discretion of the mentor and protégé and persist as long as the parties involved experience sufficient positive outcomes (Jablin, 2001). As opposed to formal mentoring relationships, newcomers who participate in informal mentoring relationships are privileged to information not directly associated with the job roles or organizational tasks. These indirect issues include organizational power and politics, more career-related support, "inside" information about various organizational issues and its members that exists on the "grapevine," and increased social interaction outside of the job.

Research showed that newcomers involved in informal mentoring relationships differ from those who participate in formal mentoring programs. This difference primarily occurs in their communication behaviors. Those who have informal mentors use more direct and less regulative and contractual communication tactics to maintain relational stability than their formal mentored peers (Burke, McKenna, & McKeen, 1991; Tepper, 1995). Because virtual teams have fewer opportunities to observe and interact, members may initially be more reliant on formal rather than informal mentoring.

Recognizing the value of formal and informal mentoring relationships leads us to suggest that virtual teams would benefit from such arrangements. Acknowledging the positive impact mentoring has on the assimilation process of newcomers in traditional organizations leads us to assume that mentoring will have the same positive impact on virtual team assimilation. Because of the challenges of the virtual team structure (temporality, limited physical presence, little informal interaction, little or no prior social experience), organizations should embrace formal and informal mentoring programs according to their respective needs as a tool to socialize newcomers to virtual teams. Because of the temporal nature of some virtual teams, formal mentoring may be appropriate. However, long-term virtual teams may be more amenable to informal mentoring relationships. Mentoring programs offer organizations an opportunity to tangibly guide virtual team members to accomplish organizational goals.

As trust, commitment, and identification with the virtual team develops for the newcomer and more experienced workers, informal mentoring will naturally occur. Virtual teams benefit when barriers to communication are dismantled. This is especially true for newcomers who are uncertain about their roles and the norms of their virtual teams. By establishing formal mentoring programs within the context of the virtual team, newcomers will become more comfortable in their new organizational environments. By creating an open climate, where nonverbal cues may be nonexistent or physical presence greatly limited, virtual teams have a greater likelihood of effectively assimilating newcomers.

Virtual Team Metamorphosis

Metamorphosis is the second component of the organizational assimilation process. This is the part where the new organizational member moves from being an outsider to becoming an insider. According to Jablin and Krone (1987), "During this stage the recruit begins to become an accepted, participating member of the organization by learning new behaviors and attitudes and/or modifying existing ones" (p. 713). In virtual teams, the team member is induced to bring his or her values and ways of doing things closer to those of the team by internalizing the team's goals and values, thus leading to commitment and loyalty. However, due to the nature of virtual teams, certain factors affect membership status and member commitment and loyalty to the team. These factors include the duration of the team (fixed team versus shifting team membership), the formation of the team (within the same organization or from outside the organization), the commitment to the team, and the reporting relationships.

Duration of the Team

Some members of the virtual team might see their status as temporary, and thus, their loyalties may reside with another work group or the organization, not the virtual team. Jarvenpaa and Leidner (1999) pointed out that the permanence of a team affects the history that team members have with one another, as well as their future expectations of interaction. They found that short-term virtual teams that achieve high levels of trust are characterized by having the following: initial communication, which is highly social; ongoing communication on task and social information; proactive orientation; positive tone; task goal clarity; role division and specificity; time management; substantial feedback on work; and frequent communication with prompt responses. Overall, members of teams that reported high cohesiveness and trust were found to be more involved and more responsive to communication with peers and supervisors.

Whether the team membership is relatively stable (e.g., an established sales team) or changes on a regular basis (e.g., project teams) will have a dramatic impact on the socialization process of the virtual team. Organizations have to create ways for team members to experience membership by being explicit about the team's norms, roles, and purposes. They also need to make it easy for members to enter the team, find out the expectations, and feel welcomed and integrated into the team fast, thus facilitating the metamorphosis stage.

Formation of the Team

Virtual teams include members that come from a single organization or from different organizations. When team members are drawn from different organizations or different organizational areas, team members may have little familiarity with other's capabilities, and they may be less likely to identify strongly with the team (Duarte & Snyder, 1999). Little knowledge of other team members' capabilities stemming from mutual work history, a limited shared organizational identity, and little investment in future interactions, all have implications for communication and trust issues within the team. One implication may be that team members are less willing to initiate conversations and volunteer information.

In addition, drawing individuals from different functional areas within the same organization may create conflicting goals with intraorganizational cultures. When members from different parts of the organization join the virtual team, the integration of norms, cultures, and goals makes communication and collaboration challenging. One consequence may be confusing loyalties within virtual teams.

Commitment to the Team

Thomsett (1998) stated that one key difference between traditional and virtual teams is the nature of the commitment of the members to the team. With virtual teams, there is "an arms length commitment," because many members are "assigned" to teams and have more of a commitment to themselves or to their parent companies. Some virtual team members may place their commitments to their "home" groups or companies above their commitments to the team members. When this occurs, team loyalty is secondary to the self-interests of the individual team member.

To remedy this diminished loyalty and commitment to the team, members need to spend time socializing. Such activity is an important aspect to developing common goals and to maintaining cohesion and commitment to the team task. Several social activities are needed (both online and F2F) to build trust, support, loyalty, and commitment. Another way to increase commitment and trust is to develop a training program. Warkentin and Beranek (1999) found that virtual team members, who underwent training in team dynamics, electronic communication drawbacks, and rules of netiquette, increased their levels of openness, trust, and commitment.

Reporting Relationships

One of the basic tenets of management is one of control: control of employees, control of resources, and control of the environment. Piccoli and Ives (2000) applied Ouchi's three mechanisms of managerial control to virtual teams: outcome control, behavior control, and clan control. Outcome control, as stated in Piccoli and Ives (2000), "stems from the ability to accurately quantify output and it can be implemented when the organization can rely on 'objective' output measures" (p. 577). Behavior control refers to the extent that managers can monitor and evaluate team members' behaviors. Clan control is a form of informal control that necessitates extensive socialization, rituals, and ceremonials. Some researchers recommend that behavior control would contribute the most to team effectiveness (Piccoli & Ives, 2000; Townsend, DeMarie, & Hendrickson, 1998). However, clan control creates an environment in which individuals internalize the values of the organization that are essential to commitment and loyalty. Although behavioral control is the easiest form of control for managers, clan control offers more advantages for managers of virtual teams by building stronger commitment to the team.

Virtual teams differ from traditional teams in that they may not have to subject themselves to formal structures and traditional reporting requirements. Many researchers and practitioners are focusing on finding the best way to "manage" virtual teams (Joinson, 2002; Piccoli & Ives, 2000; Townsend, DeMarie, & Hendrickson, 1998). However, our argument is that "managing" teams is not a question of management but one of facilitation. Such facilitation of virtual teams would focus on the communication, human, and social processes that would lead to the team members internalizing norms, values, and roles.

IMPLICATIONS

Virtual teams face many challenges and issues. Often, in order to understand virtual teams, researchers and professionals apply concepts and techniques from traditional teams to virtual teams. However, studies indicate that virtual teams are different from traditional teams in many ways; not that they are not as effective, but that they are unique due to the virtualization. Because they are created via mediated communication, the communication processes involved in virtual teams are unique and need to be approached as such. Virtual teams possess distinctive characteristics that many organizations misunderstand. Organizations cannot expect team members to "recreate" the way work is done or the interpersonal interactions that exist in traditional teams. Organizations may try to manage virtual teams in similar ways as traditional teams are managed. However, organizations cannot recreate the essence of traditional teams in virtual teams.

The socialization process of team members, which is an essential component of organizational life, becomes an enigma when building virtual teams. What can the organization do to support the socialization process in order to build effective and productive teams? What is the role of the supervisor when dealing with a virtual team member? What can team members do to learn the unwritten codes, norms, and rules when faced with distances and short deadlines? The authors recommend three specific approaches to facilitating virtual team socialization, and they help to answer the preceding questions.

First, because of varying lifespans of virtual teams, organizations need appropriate mentoring programs to meet their needs. Galvin and Ahuja (2001) recognized that newcomers sought information from established members, thus easing the socialization process. They suggested that organizations should pair senior members with newcomers to increase involvement and provide support. In the long run, this helps to build relationships, which is the foundation for effective teams. A formal mentoring program would operate by officially pairing a newcomer (protégé) with an established member (mentor). An informal program would allow for the pairing to naturally develop. A mentor in a virtual team would model or suggest appropriate and desirable behaviors that would help the new virtual team members better understand the processes they are learning. In addition, this relationship provides each new member with focused feedback from individuals who have an ongoing understanding of and possibly an involvement in their team. The newcomer would benefit from learning the norms and the expectations of the team. This, in turn, would help him or her develop a sense of belonging. In the long term, the mentoring program would be critical to instill in virtual team members a sense of commitment to the team.

Second, supervisors need to assume the role of team facilitator instead of team manager. Research by Kayworth and Leidner (2002) indicated that more effective leaders display a wider degree of behavioral repertoires, as evidenced by activities related to tasks and relationships. That is, effective leaders simultaneously demonstrate the ability to be assertive and authoritative, while remain empathetic toward team members. Supervisor relationships are essential to the socialization process. In addition to developing professional relationships, supervisors of virtual teams also need to focus on helping to facilitate the building of personal relationships. This should be one of the most important goals for supervisors and organizations. Research points to the importance of a person who coordinates and supports the socialization process (Galvin & Ahuja, 2001).

Supervisors also need to focus on facilitation rather than traditional managerial command and control. Some researchers suggested that supervisors should use the communication technologies' capacities for archiving data and communications to monitor the team (Townsend, DeMarie, & Hendrickson, 1998). However, this approach may actually decrease the interactions and involvement levels of team members, thus hindering the socialization process. Team members who are being monitored may avoid "small talk," which is important for developing relationships. Monitoring may also have the unintended consequence of creating guarded communication among team members, which may lead to reduced trust. Instead, supervisors should encourage participation and open communication and provide resources necessary for the team (financial, human, training, technology, etc.). They should also recognize the need for virtual team members to take the time to get to know each other and develop relationships.

Finally, individuals being socialized in virtual teams must reconsider their roles in the socialization process. In traditional team socialization, newcomers assume a passive role in the assimilation process. There is an assumption that the only parties responsible for the socialization of the newcomer to the team are the organization, the immediate supervisor, and veterans of the organization. The virtual team structure cannot afford for the newcomer to play such a passive role. The virtual nature of the team demands that individuals become active participants in their own assimilation processes, from the initial stage of anticipatory socialization. This active participation may take the form of strategic information seeking, pursuing formal and informal mentoring opportunities, and creating more communication opportunities with supervisors and coworkers.

The virtual team structure is less linear than traditional teams. The lines of responsibility, authority, and even seniority are less apparent in virtual teams than in their traditional team counterparts. Competence and the swift acquisition of skills and information appear more salient to virtual team socialization than time on the job. Because of this new demand for speed in productivity and information processing, newcomers must be more proactive in assuming their new roles within the virtual team. In other words, the quicker newcomers learn their new roles within virtual teams, the quicker they will become fully active members of the virtual team. To remain a passive participant in ones' socialization may lead to rapid virtual team disengagement or termination from the team.

CONCLUSION

Virtual teams are the future for most organizations. Virtual teams are not the current organizational fad that is in fashion today and out of season tomorrow. Instead, virtual teams are here to stay. Organizations are turning to virtual teams as a way to remain competitive in the new century's turbulent environment that is characterized by globalization, mergers, and dependence on information technologies. This new organizational landscape is accompanied by the expectation that organizational members must be productive and effective immediately. This immediacy calls for new thinking on how to better organize and communicate. While great attention has been given to how to provide adequate virtual team infrastructure (e.g., hardware and software), little attention has been paid by academicians, practitioners, and organizational leaders to the "human-structure." We assert that how newcomers are socialized in virtual teams is just as important as what software is chosen as appropriate in order to accomplish work. The problem arises when organizations do not consider socialization as a vital aspect in virtual team development, or even worse, when organizations attempt to apply traditional organizational socialization to the unique virtual team structure.

Although we acknowledge that some aspects of virtual team socialization are the same as traditional organizational socialization, they are not identical. In reality, little is known of the process of building effective virtual teams. The importance of communication and relationships makes virtual teams a challenge for organizations that want to focus more on the outcome rather than on the process of producing effective teams. Organizations need to focus more on factors related to the internal team process rather than on outcome assessments, such as cost, productivity, and effectiveness.

If done correctly, virtual team socialization may lead to a strong sense of loyalty and commitment to the team and the organization, which in turn, may lead to greater productivity. By eradicating the perceptions by researchers and organizational leaders that socialization is a "soft" aspect of virtual team development, greater potential for virtual team member identification and productivity can be realized. However, this can only be achieved by recognizing the importance of these issues (e.g., relationship development, virtual team structure) and the potential impact on the bottom line. All virtual team stakeholders are responsible for effective virtual team assimilation. The responsibility of virtual team socialization resides with the newcomer as well as the organization and the supervisor. Our recommendations of establishing a formal mentoring program, transforming the role of supervisor from manager to facilitator, and supporting a proactive behavior for the newcomer should be identified as high priorities in the development and maintenance of virtual teams. In sum, organizations appear to have a bias in resource allocation toward investing in new technologies. While these investments are necessary, organizations could obtain a greater return, such as loyalty and commitment, by focusing on newcomer assimilation in virtual team socialization.

REFERENCES

Adkins, C. L., Ravlin, E. C., & Meglinao, B. M. (1996). Value congruence between co-workers and its relationship to work outcomes. *Group & Organization Management, 21,* 439–460.

Ahuja, M. K., & Galvin, J. E. (2003). Socialization in virtual group. *Journal of Management, 29,* 161-185.

Allen, T. D., McManus, S. E., & Russell, J. E. A. (1999). Newcomer socialization and stress: Formal peer relationships as a source of support. *Journal of Vocational Behavior, 54,* 453–470.

Ben-Yoav, O., & Hartman, K. (1988). Supervisors' competence and learning of work values and behaviors during organizational entry. *Journal of Social Behavior and Personality, 13,* 23–36.

Berlew, D. E., & Hall, D. T. (1966). The socialization of managers: Effects of expectations on performance. *Administrative Science Quarterly, 11,* 207–223.

Boyd, N. G., & Taylor, R. R. (1998). A developmental approach to the examination of friendship in leader–follower relationships. *Leadership Quarterly, 9,* 1–25.

Buchanan, B. (1974). Building organizational commitment: The socialization of managers in work organizations. *Administrative Science Quarterly, 19,* 533–546.

Burke, R. J., McKenna, C. S., & McKeen, C. A. (1991). How do mentorships differ from typical supervisory relationships? *Psychological Reports, 68,* 459–466.

Comer, D. R. (1991). Organizational newcomers' acquisition of information from peers. *Management Communication Quarterly, 5,* 64–89.

DeSanctis, G., & Poole, M. S. (1997). Transitions in teamwork in new organizational forms. *Advances in Group Processes, 14,* 157–176.

Duarte, D. L., & Snyder, N. T. (1999). *Mastering virtual teams: Strategies, tools, and techniques that succeed.* San Francisco: Jossey-Bass.

Duck, S. (1994). *Meaningful relationships: Talking, sense, and relations.* Thousand Oaks, CA: Sage.

Feldman, D. C. (1976). Contingency theory of socialization. *Administrative Science Quarterly, 21,* 433–452.

Fine, G. A. (1986). Friendships in the work place. In V. J. Derlega, & B. A. Winstead (Eds.), *Friendship and social interaction* (pp. 185–206). New York: St. Martin's.

Galvin, J. E., & Ahuja, M. K. (2001). Am I doing what's expected? New member socialization in virtual groups. In L. Chidambaram, & I. Zigurs (Eds.), *Our virtual world: The transformation of work, play and life via technology* (pp. 40–55). Hershey, PA: Idea Group Publishing.

Glaman, J. M., Jones, A. P., & Rozelle, R. M. (1996). The effects of co-worker similarity on the emergence of affect in work teams. *Group & Organization Management, 21,* 192–215.

Graen, G. (1976). Role-making processes within complex organization. In M. D. Dunnette (Ed.), *Handbook of industrial/organizational psychology* (pp. 1201–1245). Chicago: Rand McNally.

Graen, G., & Ginsburgh, S. (1977). Job resignation as a function of role orientation and leader acceptance: A longitudinal investigation of organizational assimilation. *Organizational Behavior and Human Performance, 19,* 1–17.

Griffin, E., & Sparks, G. G. (1990). Friends forever: A longitudinal exploration of intimacy in same-sex pairs and platonic pairs. *Journal of Social and Personal Relationships, 7,* 29–46.

Heimann, B., & Pittenger, K. K. S. (1996). The impact of formal mentorship on socialization and commitment of newcomers. *Journal of Managerial Issues, 8,* 108–117.

Jablin, F. M. (1982). Organizational communication: An assimilation approach. In M. E. Roloff, & C. R. Berger (Eds.), *Social cognition and communication* (pp. 255–286). Thousand Oaks, CA: Sage.

Jablin, F. M. (1987). Organizational entry, assimilation and exit. In F. M. Jablin, L. L. Putnam, K. H. Roberts, & L. W. Porter. (Eds.), *Handbook of organizational communication: An interdisciplinary perspective* (pp. 679–740). Thousand Oaks, CA: Sage.

Jablin, F.M. (2001). Organizational entry, assimilation, and disengagement/exit. In F. M. Jablin, & L. L. Putnam (Eds.), *The new handbook of organiza-*

tional communication: Advances in theory, research, and methods (pp. 732–818). Thousand Oaks, CA: Sage.

Jablin, F. M., & Krone, K. J. (1987). Organizational assimilation. In C. R. Berger, & S. H. Chaffee (Eds.), *Handbook of communication science* (pp. 711–746). Thousand Oaks, CA: Sage.

Jarvenpaa, S. L., & Leidner, D. E. (1999). Communication and trust in global virtual teams. *Organization Science, 10,* 791–815.

Joinson, C. (2002, June). Managing virtual teams. *HR Magazine,* 69–73.

Katz, R. (1978). Job longevity as a situational factor in job satisfaction. *Administrative Science Quarterly, 23,* 204–223.

Kayworth, T. R., & Leidner, D. E. (2002). Leadership effectiveness in global virtual teams. *Journal of Management Information Systems, 18,* 7–40.

Kirchmeyer, C. (1995). Demographic similarity to the work group: A longitudinal study of managers at the early career stage. *Journal of Organizational Behavior, 16,* 67–83.

Kozlowski, S. W. J., & Doherty, M. L. (1989). Integration of climate and leadership: Examination of a neglected issue. *Journal of Applied Psychology, 74,* 546–553.

Lipnack, J., & Stamps, J. (1997). *Virtual teams: Reaching across space, time, and organizations with technology.* New York: John Wiley & Sons.

Mark, G. (2001). Meeting current challenges for virtually collated teams: Participation, culture, integration. In L. Chidambaram, & I. Zigurs (Eds.), *Our virtual world: The transformation of work, play and life via technology* (pp. 74–93). Hershey, PA: Idea Group Publishing.

McPhee, R. D., & Poole, M. S. (2001). Organizational structures and configurations. In F. M. Jablin, & L. L. Putnam (Eds.), *The new handbook of organizational communication: Advances in theory, research, and methods* (pp. 503–542). Thousand Oaks, CA: Sage.

Meyerson, D., Weick, K. E., & Kramer, R. M. (1996). Swift trust and temporary groups. In R. M. Kramer, & T. R. Tyler (Eds.), *Trust in organizations: Frontiers of theory and research* (pp. 166–195). Thousand Oaks, CA: Sage.

Miller, V. D., & Jablin, F. M. (1991). Information seeking during organizational entry: Influences, tactics, and a model of the process. *Academy of Management Review, 16,* 92–120.

Morrison, E. W. (1995). Information usefulness and acquisition during organizational encounter. *Management Communication Quarterly, 9,* 131–155.

Murray, M., & Owen, M. (1991). *Beyond the myths and magic of mentoring: How to facilitate an effective mentoring program.* San Francisco: Jossey-Bass.

Odden, C. M., & Sias, P. M. (1997). Peer communication relationships and psychological climate. *Communication Quarterly, 45,* 153–166.

Ostroff, C., & Kozlowski, S. W. J. (1992). Organizational socialization as a learning process: The role of information acquisition. *Personnel Psychology, 45*, 849–874.

Piccoli, G., & Ives, B. (2000). Virtual teams: Managerial behavior control's impact on team effectiveness. *Proceedings of the 21st international conference on Information Systems* (pp. 575–580). Brisbane, Queensland, Australia.

Rice, R. E., & Love, G. (1987). Electronic emotion: Socioemotional content in a computer-mediated communication network. *Communication Research, 14*, 85–108.

Schein, E. H. (1988). Organizational socialization and the profession of management. *Sloan Management Review, 30*, 53–65.

Seibert, S. (1999). The effectiveness of facilitated mentoring: A longitudinal quasi-experiment. *Journal of Vocational Behavior, 54*, 483–502.

Sias, P. M., & Cahill, D. J. (1998). From coworkers to friends: The development of peer friendships in the workplace. *Western Journal of Communication, 62*, 273–299.

Sproull, L., & Kiesler, S. (1986). Reducing social context cues: Electronic mail in organizational communication. *Management Science, 32*, 1492–1512.

Teboul, J. C. B. (1994). Facing and coping with uncertainty during organizational encounter. *Management Communication Quarterly, 8*, 190–224.

Tepper, B. J. (1995). Upward maintenance tactics in supervisory mentoring and nonmentoring relationships. *Academy of Management Journal, 38*, 1191–1205.

Thomsett, R. (1998, October). *The team is dead...Long live the virtual team.* Retrieved November 22, 2002, from the World Wide Web: http://members.ozemail.com.au/~thomsett/main/ articles/virtual_team7.htm

Townsend, A. M., DeMarie, S. M., & Hendrickson, A. R. (1998). Virtual teams: Technology and the workplace of the future. *Academy of Management Executive, 12*, 17–29.

Van Maanen, J. (1976). Breaking in: Socialization to work. In R. Dubin (Ed.), *The handbook of work, organization, and society* (pp. 67–129). Chicago: Rand McNally.

Van Maanen, J. (1984). Doing new things in old ways: The chains of socialization. In J. L. Bess (Ed.), *College and university organizations* (pp. 211–247). New York: New York University Press.

Walther, J. B. (1996). Computer-mediated communication: Impersonal, interpersonal, and hyperpersonal interaction. *Communication Research, 23*, 3–43.

Wanous, J. P. (1980). *Organization entry: Recruitment, selection, and socialization of newcomers.* Reading, MA: Addison-Wesley.

Warkentin, M., & Beranek, P. M. (1999). Training to improve virtual team communication. *Information Systems Journal, 9,* 271–289.

Wigand, R. T., & Boster, F. S. (1991). Mentoring, social interaction, and commitment: An empirical analysis of a mentoring program. *Communications, 16,* 15–31.

Chapter VIII

Negotiating Meaning in Virtual Teams:
Context, Roles and Computer Mediated Communication in College Classrooms

Janel Anderson Crider, University of Minnesota, USA

Shiv Ganesh, University of Montana, USA

ABSTRACT

In this chapter is a study of the communication practices of students and their instructors collaborating on virtual team projects as part of small group and team communication classes at three universities — two in the United States, and one in the Philippines. Presented are three themes from student and instructor discourse that emerged as crucial in the development of the teams as they completed the project: negotiation of context, negotiation of roles, and negotiation of technology. The authors hope that attentiveness to these themes by other faculty facilitating virtual team projects in their courses will better equip students to effectively work in virtual teams and lead to greater student learning of the role communication plays in virtual teams. Attentiveness to these themes may also be of use in corporate applied instructional and training situations.

INTRODUCTION

Over the last decade, a number of universities, especially those in the United States, have begun to experiment with distance learning, with students and instructors based in multiple locations (Contractor, Stohl, Monge, Flanagin, & Fulk, 2000; Yakimovicz & Murphy, 1995). The functional premium placed on virtual teamwork and the increasing popularity of distance-learning-based models of education led to an increased emphasis upon virtual teams in university-level college classrooms. In particular, in an effort to stay current with the operational norms of contemporary organizations, some instructors of small group communication and organizational communication courses are including units on virtual collaboration and organizing virtual team assignments for their students in their courses (Jarvenpaa & Leidner, 1998; Monge, O'Keefe, Stohl, Yammine, & Contractor, 1999).

The increased emphasis upon virtual teams in the workplace and in the university has not gone without its share of criticism. Virtual team-based models of work were criticized for their poorer communication environments and increased potential for miscommunication (Handy, 1995). Distance learning was criticized for the reduced pedagogical opportunities it provides students, as well as its excessive reliance on corporate and entrepreneurial approaches to education (Noble, 2001). Given the increased popularity of virtual teams and distance learning, these attendant critiques make close examinations of virtual team communication crucial, particularly in pedagogical contexts.

Our pedagogical interest in this issue led us toward a research question: What themes in virtual team communication emerge as critical to students' ability to complete virtual team projects in university classrooms? In answering this question, we used data from our own and our students' experiences in small group communication classes, where students and instructors from diverse backgrounds and in diverse locations collaborated on course projects. Three themes in our data emerged as crucial in the development of the teams as they completed the project: negotiation of context, negotiation of roles, and negotiation of technology.

We use Bormann's symbolic convergence theory to understand the importance of these themes, while also drawing on Weick's work on sense making and organizing to explain team members' negotiation of roles, and the meanings they assigned to technology. First, we offer a review of the literature related to the themes we identified and the theoretical perspectives that we adopted for this essay. Second, we outline the methodology used in developing this project. Third, we provide an analysis of student and instructor talk from the virtual teams we studied. Finally, we offer recommendations for other instructors who use or are planning to use a virtual team project in the instructional design of their courses.

BACKGROUND

Our rendition of symbolic convergence tenets is broad, rather than disciplinary. That is, rather than examine symbolic convergence with reference to its traditional constructs, such as fantasy themes (Putnam, Hoeven, & Bullis, 1991) or chaining (Bormann, Cragan, & Shields, 1994), we locate the concept with reference to a general interpretive approach toward communication (Putnam, 1983). We maintain that symbolic convergence is usefully conceived of as a central concept within the interpretive tradition, rather than as a stand-alone theory. Accordingly, we see a close correspondence between symbolic convergence and such concepts as sense making, equivocality, consensual validation and enactment, and selection and retention (Weick, 1979, 1995).

Context

Symbolic convergence theory suggests that symbols — stories, vocabularies, jokes, and the like — develop and converge during small group communication; in fact, the symbolic nature of such communication is held to be constitutive of small groups (Bormann, 1986). Such convergence is tantamount to the assemblage of social context and meaning and is, therefore, crucial to "getting the job done" in team settings. Symbolic convergence theory helps explain how team members share symbols that create and sustain a shared consciousness and lead to team cohesiveness (Bormann, 1983).

Shared history is an important part of the social context of groups and teams (Georgoudi & Rosnow, 1985). As Fulk, Schmitz, and Schwarz (1992) noted, historical events are an important source of understanding among participants engaging in computer-mediated communication (CMC). Prior context influences a wide variety of group norms, including how group members expect to be treated by each other, mechanisms for socioemotional support, and patterns of group interaction (Levine & Moreland, 1990). It is especially significant in determining how teams develop a variety of roles and negotiate a range of technologies with which to communicate.

Roles

The concept of "role" can be defined in multiple ways — to delineate specific interpersonal relationships, to define an individual's position in a social network, or to describe behavior expected of a particular position (Stohl, 1995). Some scholars conceive of roles in general terms and divide them into task-related activity, relationship-related activity, and self-related activity (Ketrow, 1991). Within this framework, one can detect a range of more specific roles, such as task leader, social-emotional leader (McGrath & Altman, 1966), active listener (Nichols, 1995), tension releaser, information provider, central negative, questioner, silent observer, and recorder (Cragan & Wright, 1999). Symbolic convergence standpoints maintain that attention should be paid to the interaction between actual role behavior and collective perceptions about the roles that specific individuals play in the group. Bormann (1990) maintained that symbolic convergence in groups enables members to make sense of others' roles within the groups. However, such convergent perspectives on individual roles allow members to lose sight of the fact that roles are dynamic, and that individuals in groups take on multiple roles, sometimes simultaneously. The simultaneous performance of roles could be accentuated in CMC, because, as Kolb (1995) suggests, computer-mediated discourse is more interruptible and branches more quickly than "real-life" discourse. Consequently, participants in a CMC discussion might, by virtue of the fact that they pay attention to multiple conversational strands, perform multiple tasks and therefore multiple roles.

Technology

Surprisingly little research was conducted on communication technology from the symbolic convergence perspective. However, Weickian perspectives paid a fair amount of attention to the ways in which group members interpret and make sense of technology. For example, Weick (1990) identified three properties of new technologies that are of particular importance at a microlevel. First, new technologies are characterized by high degrees of uncertainty for their users; they have "stochastic" or undeterminable and random effects. Second, they are characterized by an upswing in continuous events or an emphasis on flexibility, automation, transactions, and reliability. Third, they are characterized by abstract events and involve the development of sophisticated mental maps in order to function competently (Weick, 1990). In many ways, it has become harder, not easier, for individuals to understand CMC, and individuals deal with such uncertainty by effectuating, or learning by pushing events into action; triangulating, or obtaining material from several different sources in order to figure out the reliability of an event; affiliating, or comparing what they see with someone else's version and negotiating an acceptable middle ground; deliberating, or learning through careful reasoning; and consolidating, or attempting to put an event into context (Weick, 1985). Accordingly, it is important to ask questions about the frames that group members develop about technology, because these frames serve as content and ground for symbolic convergence about the technology the group employs.

Using symbolic convergence theory as an interpretive approach to understanding small group communication, this project set out to discover themes in virtual team communication that emerge as critical to students' abilities to complete virtual team projects in classroom settings. The themes that emerged and our method of discovering them are discussed in the following sections.

METHODOLOGY

We conducted this study in an exploratory and evolutionary mode rather than a predictive one; consequently, a qualitative approach was appropriate (Ragin, 1994). Data were collected electronically in Spring 2001 by capturing student interaction on a WebCT 3.0 system, a platform for online instruction. Participating in the study were 65 students. Twenty-two were from a university in the Philippines, 21 from a university in the Midwestern United States, and 22 from a university in the Northwestern United States. Twenty-five students were male and 30 female. Most students were between 18 and 21 years of age, but several students were older and "nontraditional." Eleven teams were comprised of students representing each of the three universities. Ten teams had six members (two students from each of the three institutions), and one team had five members (two students from two institutions and one student from the remaining institution). Students were randomly selected for the teams, resulting in a mix of male and female students in all the teams but one, which was all female.

Students participated in the study as part of a project that they completed during semester-long classes on small group communication. The online project asked students to collectively identify a public communication need common to all three locales and design a campaign aimed at meeting that need. This project was conducted over a period of two months. We obtained informed consent from students in two ways. First, students were given a handout and accompanying consent form explaining the project, the voluntary nature of their participation, and their ability to withdraw from the research study without any penalty. We also displayed, on the WebCT platform, a reminder that information was being recorded. In our study, we maintained confidentiality by using pseudonyms. Students were instructed to use CMC as their only means of team communication. During that time, the instructors met online weekly and held two telephone conferences. All three instructors shared prior context; they were formerly graduate students in a large Midwestern U.S. university.

The data used for this analysis were culled specifically from chat room conversations. Using a combination of grounded and thematic approaches, 910 pages of data were analyzed. Themes were identified in the data using a loose rendition of Glaser and Strauss's constant comparative method, via intensive reading as well as keyword searches (1967). Themes were chosen for this study according to Owen's (1984) criteria of recurrence and repetition. The unit of analysis was a single chat sequence. The data set was comprised of 68 chat sequences.

ANALYSIS

Following from the literature review, we explore how students achieved convergence in three main areas: context, roles, and technology. In each section, we provide samples from discussion transcripts in order to make our arguments more lucid and tangible.

Context

There are four major observations we wish to make concerning the importance and establishment of context among the teams. First, one of the initial actions the teams took was to establish a shared context in which to complete the work of the team. Given that the students were from different home institutions, different academic majors in many cases, and different parts of the world, they had no historical or social context on which to draw. Rather, students developed shared consciousness and context through their computer-mediated conversations. Students used the modality of the chat room to negotiate and build context by developing a pool of common meaning through dialogue.

Our analysis of the chat transcripts reveals that students built context through discussion of relatively common student topics such as movies, television, music, living arrangements, alcohol use, and sexual behavior. Such common ground enabled team members to draw on familiar sets of experience to establish shared consciousness and social context in which to get the business of their team done.

In the excerpt below, Kim, Patrick, and Sharon discussed the average age of students at their respective universities. Kim missed part of the conversation and explains her absence:

Kim>>   Yeah, they're doing the Fab 5 at 5 on the radio station—they play 5 songs and you have to guesswhat they have in common
Patrick >> i love that
Patrick >> fun fun
Sharon>> oh! uma and i are graduating this april...hopefully! but at the rate we're going, it seems we'll be staying one more term!!!
Sharon>> oh! kinda like triple play in mtv?
Kim>>   I don't know— I don't watch much MTV
Sharon>> i'm really bad at that! i can never guess it right!
Sharon>> so, what movies are showing there right now?
Patrick>> just saw traffic
Patrick>> it was good

The radio promotion is an example of symbolic convergence, as both Patrick and Sharon's responses indicate their familiarity with such games. Sharon, in acknowledging the promotional game, links it to something similar that does not get taken up by her counterparts, MTV. The conversation continues as Sharon admits her lack of skill in the game, and seeing that her reference to MTV did not get taken up, moves the conversation to a new topic, movies, as the three continue to search for points of convergence.

Nearly the entire conversation serves to build a social context. The conversation ran for 58 minutes and was comprised of 213 turns. In the final turns of the conversation, shown below, a brief reference to the team project is made, followed by leave-taking turns. (Patrick already left the chatroom.) In total, only five turns were made relating to task during the near hour during which members were communicating:

Kim>>   I have a hair appt in a half hour
Sharon>> oh ok! you're getting a haircut?
Kim>>   Highlights
Sharon>> i see! ok! i'll let you go so you can go to your appointment :o)
Kim>>   OK did we decide how we
Kim>>   dangit! are going to go about doing our project?
Sharon>> not yet...if you want, let's just follow the schedule...
Sharon>> let's chat again sometime in the next couple of days to talk about
              the project...:o)
Kim>>   Ok, Pat and I will work on it from our end and hpoefully everything
              will come together. ok I'm free in the evenings any day
Sharon>> ok! bye now! it was nice talking to you! :o)
Kim>>   You too, have a nice day!
Sharon>> you 2! tc!
Kim>>   Bye!

The second observation we wish to make pertains to the students' negotiation of task and social talk within their limited context. Given that they had no prior social interaction and were operating only with an emerging context, it is understandable that student team members were relatively hesitant in their negotiation of task and social talk. Developing such a context often monopolized student chat conversations. As conversation turned to social topics, and students began to develop context, it frequently took many turns in the conversation to return to task topics. When attempts were made to transition to task topics, student team members were tentative about initiating a change in direction. Shifts to task talk were cautious and tempered by hesitancy. In the example below, Sara suggests a shift back to task:

Jenna>> Is it true you guys get drunk, really drunk when you turn 21? Here
            in the Phils. we can drink as young as 13, I think, not legally of
            course
Jenna>> ZIP: Oh, well, I guess where you live - like a dorm? or an
            apartment? and do your guys REALLY work for support yourselves
            all the way through college?

Sara>>   Yeah I'd say that's true. Probably not everybody. I'm turning 21 in about a month. I'll have to fill you in.

Latisha>> what is the legal age??

Sara>>   To change the subject just a little bit, does anybody have any ideas about a web page?

Sara's move to get the team back to task is not taken up directly. Rather, 10 subsequent turns are taken, still focusing on social topics. At this point Sara enters back into the discussion on a social level, abandoning her efforts to get the group back to task and asks:

Sara>>   Do you guys live in apartments or dorms?

Two turns later another member takes up the task subject Sara raised earlier, but the conversation continues on living arrangements and moves to cultural norms concerning the age at which people get married in the Philippines. An additional 17 turns are taken on marriage and living arrangements before the topic turns back to the task of the Web page.

The third observation we make is that shared context is evident in teams' dialogue. Interaction between the instructors is a useful point of comparison for understanding the development of context among the student teams. Context is evident in the dialogue of the instructors' chat room transcripts. The instructors had a prior context of being colleagues in graduate school. As such, they had established friendships with one another, had mutual acquaintances, and had a shared institutional history. Accordingly, their talk ranged from their prior context, covering topics such as personal relationships and institutional gossip, to topics related to the administration of the virtual team project, and their students' progress on the project. The instructors traversed freely between social and task talk and were able to carry simultaneous conversations in the chat session — one on a social level and the other on task. In the example below, Instructor S takes up a social topic that was raised 78 turns earlier, when Instructor A mentioned she would have to leave the chat room in one hour to go to an appointment with her doctor:

Instructor A>>   i thought everyone was excited about the proj

Instructor J>>   A, your students seem to be really on the ball

Instructor S>>   a lot of them are; some of them aren't, just going by the fact that a few of them were yet to post until yesterday

Instructor S>>   anyway... next subject

Instructor J>>   this whole 5 point thing seems to be motivating them

Instructor S>>   BTW, Instructor A, are you okay? It's not a serious visit to the doc, I hope

Instructor J>>   next item up, is proposal format
Instructor S>>   Yeah, I like the five point system
Instructor A>>   no, the univ.is "forcing" me to go, been dragging my feet

This example demonstrates the ease with which the instructors move between task and social talk. Instructor S alternates between task and social talk as he serves first to maintain the discussion of the task by moving the conversation on to the "next subject" and then directly takes a social turn, inquiring about Instructor A's health and the visit to the doctor. His next turn is a task turn, and the two separate threads of conversation — one task and one social — continue until the instructors' conversation is interrupted by a group of students who arrive in the same chat room to discuss their project.

In the following example, the instructors again communicate at task and social levels, discussing one instructor's child and the completion of paperwork necessary to obtain approval for the collection of data from one university's institutional review board (IRB):

Instructor A>>   How's your son?
Instructor A>>   I got your emails re IRB
Instructor J>>   He's cool - growing up so fast, getting so independent.
Instructor S>>   I have a document to send you guys
Instructor J>>   is it group assignments?
Instructor S>>   Is his hair brown?
Instructor A>>   How cute!
Instructor S>>   No, the document is something that I'd like you to sign and fax back to me

These examples are typical of the remainder of the instructors' chat room transcripts. The instructors were able to move back and forth readily between social and task topics and carry on simultaneous task and social conversations, drawing from their shared prior context. As such, common ground is already well established, and the instructors do not spend time in the conversation searching for points of convergence.

The fourth observation concerns the negotiation of task and social talk and its relation to a shared prior context. As the instructors negotiated task and social talk, they shifted freely between the two arenas, and they employed few explicit indicators suggesting a change in focus. Rather, they often switched focus with no reference to the change in direction of the conversation. However, on occasions when an explicit reference was made to change the direction of the discourse, it was always to move back to a task-related topic and the reference was direct. In the example below, the conversation moves freely between task and social topics with no reference to the change in direction:

Instructor S>>	Instructor A, do your kids have a spring break or is that an American thing?
Instructor A>>	submission of grades is April 10 so April 2 sounds okay
Instructor S>>	If so, you'll have to make a point of asking your students to insist that their team mates explain what happens on spring break to them ;-)
Instructor A>>	spring break=American
Instructor A>>	no spring here, perpetual summer
Instructor S>>	Yay!!! April 2 is a go then?
Instructor A>>	ok
Instructor S>>	They don't believe in ploughing streets here in [City]. It's not too cold, but its not easy to walk anywhere
Instructor J>>	but will April 2 give us time to evaluate/grade and have enough time for them to adjust +/- 5 points?
Instructor J>>	that could take a while - all of that
Instructor A>>	we could ask them to adjust points ahead of time

The conversation moves freely between the social topics of spring break and related weather and the task topics of due dates and evaluation of the students' projects. The conversation is managed implicitly with each participant balancing their task and social turns with no active conversation management moves.

On occasion, the instructors made explicit moves to manage the conversation, abruptly moving from social talk to task talk. In the next example, Instructor J specifies that the conversation turn to task-related talk; eight of the preceding nine turns were about her son. Her colleagues directly take up this abrupt change in direction of the conversation. Thus, the conversation about her son is over, and they move on to dividing the students into teams:

Instructor J>>	On a task-related note, I was going to start creating groups on webct
Instructor J>>	and adding my students to them
Instructor J>>	Instructor A, how many students do you have?
Instructor A>>	We're almost all logged on over here—I have 22
Instructor J>>	I have 21, Instructor S has 22

Whereas the chat room transcripts showed newly formed teams using tentative language to shift the conversation from social to task, the instructors with an existing context and established relationships are considerably more direct in their management of the conversation topic. Moreover, their efforts to manage the conversation by moving it to task talk are unilaterally taken up. All of the instructors' 17 turns to move the conversation back to task talk were taken up within four or fewer turns. Eleven of the 17 explicit turns back to task were taken up directly with the next turn.

Roles

We wish to make three observations about group roles as they emerged through interaction in the chat rooms. First, traditional group roles such as task leadership, social–emotional leadership, and active listening were played often. Take the following excerpt:

Andrea>>   Tom, can you post a discussion on the bulletin board the final contract. Our professor will ask us to log in later at 430pm my time here. So, when we open it, Rina and I, it's ready for her viewing.
Chris>>   I have the contract as well.
Tom>>   the same one as before?
Chris>>   The weekend thing will work for both Nick and I
Chris>>   yep.
Tom >>   Great
Chris>>   we can add the weekend part to it.
Heidi >>   Either Sat. or Sun.?
Andrea>>   Yep Tom. Just add that thing about the back-up chat session for emergency purpose.
Chris>>   I actually have to run so Tom do you have it availble now?

Andrea is engaging in task leadership behavior by allocating assignment-related work to other members and engaging in procedural communication about meetings and deadlines. The other members are clearly responding to her cues. Social–emotional leadership was also evident in a number of instances in the form of supportive messages, especially when the group was immersed in social talk. Take the following passage:

Maryann>>   Shannon I like to drink but sometimes I don;t like myself when I do
Jeff>>   I don't have to go now, its not until 8:00
Maryann>>   SO i haven';t in awhile
Maryann>>   So you do want to talk to us
Shannon>>   Quit leading us on, damn it!!!
Maryann>>   SHannon men are so out of it aren't they
Maryann>>   no offense jeff\
Shannon>>   Mar, I totally understand. That feeling made me quit partying.
Shannon>>   Men are strange, Mar. Are you dating anyone Mar?

Maryann>> I can be a total different person that isn't always fun to be with.
I get really sappy or I get u know touchy
Jeff>>   Alcohol is definatly a love/hate relationship

In this discussion about alcohol and partying, the two women in the excerpt engaged in supportive communication by empathizing about their experiences with men. Shannon, in particular, engaged in emotional support by expressing empathy for Maryann's feelings about drinking.

The second major observation pertains to the role of secretary/recorder. The assumption that recording is automatic in CMC situations because members are typing in text is belied by the fact that some members had to engage in more active "recording" in order to push the group toward a consensus. In such instances, task leadership specifically involved serving as a secretary/recorder. Take the passage below:

Michael>> i was thinking this (long message to follow):
Lydia>>   alrighty.
Michael>> we try to chat once a week, in this room, at a specific time
unless we change it; we check the bulletins at least three times per
week; dealines are critical; and the punishment/reward system
comes at the end of the project, when we collectively decide who
gets given/taken points
Lydia>>   ok. so what time are we suppose to meet here?
Michael>> well, that really has to be decided as a whole group, right? let's
go for suggestions on the bulliten
Michael>> i'm all for this time, actually
Michael>> u?
Lydia>>   me too. but i think we have to decide on it right now coz we have
to meet a certain deadline right?
Michael>> right . . . okay, if this works for you, let's post it as a possible
suggestion, and unless we hear otherwise in the next 12 hours or
so, that'll be it

In this passage, Michael is clearly playing the role of task leader, figuring out meeting times, pushing the group toward decisions about how often they check bulletin board announcements, etc. In addition, he is ensuring that the decision currently being made is "recorded" in a more permanent context — that of the bulletin board.

The third observation we make has to do with the emergence of what appears to be a nontraditional role, which we labeled "accounter." Members who played this role explicitly constructed reasons and justifications for the role played by a teammate from their own institution. In 10 out of 11 teams, there were two members per location. Some groups tended to treat members who were in the same physical location as sharing a special relationship, even though in many cases members in the same location did not actually meet each other in real life beyond limited discussions in the classroom; in fact, some members in the same physical location did not communicate using any other medium than WebCT and e-mail. At least three groups used the term "school partner" to refer to the dyads in each group, and one team actively conceived of itself as having "groups within a group." We identified 13 "accounter" pairs out of a total of 32 possible pairs. In the analysis of the accounter role that follows, we selected excerpts from the communication of one team in particular, in order to provide a richer sense of the communication issues involved when virtual team members are involved in accounting for other members. Two specific observations about the accounter role are in order. First, sometimes (this happened with two groups), both members from a group were together at the same computer, and the accounter simply communicated on behalf of the other person. For example:

Tom>>   HEY CHRIS
Chris>>   Hellooo
Andrea>> that's a good thing. at least you guys are willing to make
                sacrifices for each other.
Andrea>> Hello Chris!!!
Tom>>   wow...The internet is kinda cool!!!!
Chris>>   I have Nick with me here too.
*+**** Heidi— entered groupcom_Room_1. Time:Thu Feb 15 09:18:19
                2001
Tom>>   hello Nick, good to get ya part of the group bud
Andrea>> Hey Nick!
Andrea>> Hi Heidi!!!
Chris>>   So this is everybody
Chris>>   Nick says hello all.
Tom>>   is Rina coming to this
Tom>>   Thank you everyone for being on time

Here, the group acknowledges that Chris and Nick are "speaking in one voice," and members signal their acceptance by greeting both Nick and Chris. More frequent than such ventriloquism were situations where "school partners" were called upon to provide explanations or justifications for the absence of the other member in their location. For example:

Carol>>   anymore, since he hasn't shown up to any of the chats and hasn't
                posted any messages to the discussion board
Carol>>   i feel he isn't doing anything to try

Jessica>> That's not what we want - is there something else he can do to make it up?

Jessica>> If he wasn't in our group?

Carol>> he has a full time job so he said he might not be able to make it to the chats- but he hasn't tried to set a diffeent time or at least post a message to keep us updated at to what he has done if anyhing

Jessica>> Yeah - he sent an e-mail but hasn't gotten much beyond that.

Carol>> i would like him to be in our group because otherwise i have to do the whole [state] part on my own- but he hasn't even been in class for me to at least assign him something to catch up

Jessica>> I honestly don't know what he'd do...our research portion is almost over, and we have to have every thing done in another week

Jessica>> He's have to jump right in - but it doesn't sound like he can make the time for that.

Here, Carol acknowledges her frustration with her uncommunicative teammate, but also voices her own dependency on him vis-à-vis her insecurity about having to do the "state" part on her own. Accounters not only were willing to excuse irresponsible behavior on the part of teammates, they also tended to make more active decisions in the group in general. Take the following example, again from the case of Chris and Nick. As before, they are seated together, and Chris is technically speaking on Nick's behalf. The group is trying to decide their next meeting time, and several members expressed their inability to meet on Sunday:

Heidi>> I can not make it to Sunday, I will post my information.. I landed a huge catering job for the [State] Orchestra.great money.. I will be up to date with the board..Andrea Sat sounds good1

Tom>> i will be vacationing in florida, but will make it on sunday

Heidi>> How long are you going for Tom?

Chris>> ok then I will (TOM you are spoiled) we will talk to you all on Sunday

Tom>> so i should get my info on the surveys and get my research and e-mail it all to rina

(Two other members then expressed concern about the Sunday meeting time).

Chris>> so no chat on Sunday?

(other members agree)

Chris>> ok. no chat on Sunday!

During this process, Chris did not mention Nick's name a single time. It is possible that she consulted with him, because he was sitting next to her. However, she used the first person throughout the discussion ("ok, then I will") and the rest of the group did not ask what Nick thought of the decision. This sort of incident did not occur very often, but it is illustrative of the larger process, whereby accounters, by virtue of their presence at more chats, ended up (willingly or not) making more decisions than the people they were accounting for.

We also observed miscommunication between the accounter and the person being accounted for. For example, there were several times when Chris promised to update Nick:

Chris>> hey did you guys see that message from Nick?
Chris>> hi :)
Heidi>> Yes
Chris>> I feel so bad for him!
Heidi>> What happened?
Chris>> he doesn't spend much time on the computer, so I'm sure he doesn't know how to fix it.
Chris>> it's okay though. I will update him.

However, in the very next chat, when Nick was logged in as an active chatter, he demonstrated a lack of awareness of the very decision he was to be informed about:

Nick>>   got any ideas for the project
*+**** Vickie— entered groupcom_Room_1. Time:Mon Feb 26 09:14:58 2001
Tanya>> i think andrea's proposal is good
*-**** Vickie— left groupcom_Room_1. Time: Mon Feb 26 09:15:16 2001
Tanya>> that has something to do with the virtual teams...
Tanya>> how about you?
Nick>>   I am a little confused about what exactly we are suppose to do.....
Tanya>> i think webct is interesting...
Heidi>> How would we collect data on webct?
Nick>>   could someone summarize the webct interactionproject....
Heidi>> I will start looking for information and asking around to see how many people are familiar with virtual teams.
Nick>>   Do you guys have the list of objectives that we have to turn into the instructor by tommorrow?
Tanya>> we can touch on the benefits of working with virtual teams in the work setting and try to compare that to having virtual teams in the school curriculum
Andrea>>nick, it is in the handout already. we basically need to submit the project schedule.

Here, the group does not actively respond to his requests for clarification. Toward the end, there is a somewhat impatient comment from Andrea indicating that the answers to the questions he was asking were available in handouts that were distributed to each class.

Technology

There are two major observations and arguments that we wish to make about the way in which members discussed and negotiated technology in the chat rooms. First, when members expressed frustration with the technology, commiseration was the dominant response. For example:

Tom>>   this computer is really slow so bear with me
Heidi>> My computer is slow today too.
Tom>>   i am @ work
Tanya>> i've seen chris's postings...
Nick>> tom ican feel your pain
Heidi>> Me too.

Here, one can see Tom's frustration at the technology being echoed by Nick. Interestingly enough, this was one of the few times that Nick offered any form of support (social–emotional or informational) to his teammates. Problems with technology tended to be a way in which students bonded and created additional context for their communication. In fact, support was evident even when students were not actively expressing frustration. For example:

Andrew>> This is the first time I have every been on a chat line
Danita>>   Oh, good. me too. As soon as I saw there were more than one, I didn't know what to do.
Andrew>> I can't believe how slow it takes to reply to someone
Danita>>   At least this is faster than ICQ.
Andrew>>
Andrew>> What is ICQ?.. I have never heard of it till today

Above, it is evident that Danita and Andrew are identifying and, therefore, tacitly supporting each other by establishing/declaring their lack of familiarity with the technology. However, there were a few odd situations in which members did not commiserate or support an expression of frustration. In the following excerpt, Bob types out a sentence that makes no sense, and the other group members are clearly perplexed:

Bob>>   ellsmokerLLbI 'IoAe e :kerkg aboutc. myd welcomesaid commuion earlierI tiwwith my habitccation
Danita>>   What?
Andrew>> Whoa Bob what was that?

Cassandra>> huh???
Elizabeth>> did you guys get my e-mail from edsamail.com.ph?
Vickie>> what?
Cassandra>> spanish?? french??

What follows is Bob's protest that there was something wrong with the keyboard, but no one in the group responded. This may have had something to do with the team's dissatisfaction with Bob's contributions, and they may have been more inclined to explain his behavior dispositionally than situationally.

The second major observation that we wish to make about technology pertains to member observations about other forms of technology that they were using to communicate with each other: e-mail and bulletin boards. E-mail was used as a means of communicating detail and personal information. In the following excerpt, Carol and Tabitha are negotiating details involved in their schedules:

Carol>> I only have about 25 minutes to chat until i hvae to go to school
Tabitha>> i see... can u give us your schedule?
Carol>> Are you and Vi really good friends, and are both of you there right now?
Tabitha>> yes we are good friends, but she's not here now
Carol>> If you give me your e-mail adress i will e-mail you my class schedule
Tabitha>> i think she's at home, she forgot to go online
Tabitha>> alryt, its tabbi@pacific.net.ph

Sometimes, members tended to see e-mail as a more "trustworthy" medium, even when it was not necessarily so. Take the following excerpt:

Andrew>> Sounds good to me..Do you have my number?
Danita>> Is it in the phone book? If you type it over this, anyone can find it. You could e-mail me.
Andrew>> It's in the book...But, I could give a crap less if everyone knows...Random people call me everday!
Danita>> I'll call then. Hopefully we can schedule a special group chat this weekend.
Andrew>> Sounds good..Hang on one more minute I'm going to check other rooms to see if anyone else has logged on there.
*-**** Andrew— left groupcom_Room_2. Time: Fri Feb 23 09:48:50 2001
*+**** Andrew— entered groupcom_Room_2. Time:Fri Feb 23 09:49:06 2001
Danita>> Sounds like a good idea.
Andrew>> It doesn't look like anyone else is going to show..I'll E-mail you with my number just in case

This is interesting for at least two reasons. First, participants are negotiating a mutually acceptable view of the security or lack thereof in the chat room. Second, the participants in question were actually from the same institution and met three times a week in class. That they chose to use technology rather than face-to-face communication points to their increasing facility with the medium, despite their protestations to the contrary in an earlier example.

The other technology that students made frequent reference to was the bulletin board. This technology was framed as a means to communicate task and chat deadlines and status reports. For example:

Patrick >>   and i just searched the internet for awhile
Sandra>>   i searched the internet too
Patrick>>   hey kim.how was the rest of class?
Kim>>   I just read the bulletin board and for some reason Uma and Nifer were under the impression that the chat time was at 7am their time and they were the ones that initially said 8am. That was an hour ago so I don't think they are going to be here.
Patrick>>   i realized that too earlier
Kim>>   We just worked on that group problem solving thing and talked about it
Patrick>>   oh

Here, the group obviously made use of the bulletin board as a place for posting announcements, using it as a means to solidify deadlines and meeting times. Students coordinated the tricky issue of chat times (VanRyssen & Godar, 2000) by using bulletin boards as a medium to communicate chat deadlines. This was most commonly achieved in groups when members posted their schedules on the bulletin board, calculated time differences, and figured out times that they could chat.

Interestingly, students seemed to prefer to use bulletin boards for this rather than e-mail. In fact, when members appeared to be in a hurry, they made reference to the bulletin board as a place to put more "permanent" information:

Sharon>>   let's agree on a chat time na coz i have to leave in 5 mins
Umara>>   yah that's why i said we're only free in the evening
Umara>>   gotta go!
Kim>>   let's just post info to each other for now and figure it out later
Umara>>   anyway i'll check the discussion board later
Umara>>   BYE!!!

The idea that bulletin boards were more permanent sources of data or information can be seen from the fact that some groups actually posted transcripts of their chat discussions on the bulletin boards for members to review:

Chris>> are you there?
Tanya>> hello!!!
Tanya>> did everybody leave already?
Chris>> Erin, Andrea and I met an hour ago...they had to go, but I am
posting everything on the discussion board
Tanya>> i'm really sorry i just read your postings today
Tanya>> i was out of town yesterday..

In sum, the students' use of technology demonstrated that as the project progressed, they made sense of and achieved a measure of convergence about the meaning and use of each technology, sharing frustrations and successes en route, and ascribing particular functions to particular technologies.

CONCLUSION

In discussing the implications of this study, we focus upon pedagogical contexts in particular, rather than other contexts for virtual team communication, such as for-profit, public, or nonprofit contexts. Too many recommendations for business and professional practices have come from research drawn from the experiences of the average U.S. undergraduate student. The last two decades of research in organizational and group communication complicated easy assumptions about effective small group communication and demonstrated the importance of contextualizing recommendations for "real-world" practice based upon research conducted in similar or analogous situations (Cheney, Christensen, Zorn, & Ganesh, 2003). Consequently, we believe that our recommendations are best generalized to issues of pedagogy and instruction in undergraduate settings. However, they could also be applicable to other more applied instructional and training situations.

The results from this study have several pedagogical implications. First, in order to effectively facilitate student virtual teams, instructors collaborating on such projects should enter into the arrangement with a shared context or actively develop social and task context prior to the beginning of the course. Certainly, the recommendation that instructors develop a shared context is cumbersome, but we suggest this for two reasons. First, because there is a fair amount of task negotiation among the collaborating instructors, faculty who enter into virtual team projects with a prior context will be better equipped to effectively negotiate tasks related to the student assignment, such as project objectives, deadlines, and evaluation criteria. The more clarity such issues have from a student perspective, the better the learning opportunities for the students. Our second reason for making this recommendation is pragmatic. Our data suggest that students (assuming no prior context) spend considerable amounts of time establishing a context. Instructors who elect to include a virtual team project in their curriculum will incur a sizeable amount of additional work simply by adding the virtual team project to the course. The additional time associated with creating a relationship and associated context would likely make the project too taxing on one's schedule.

Second, we recommend that instructors assign virtual teams context-building exercises early in the project. Ideally, such exercises would have direct linkages to the objectives of the virtual team project. For example, if students need to select a topic as part of the team assignment (related to a decision-making objective), they may be asked to interview each other in chat rooms to learn about the social norms, demographics, climate, and campus issues of their teammates. Such an exercise would begin to establish a context and would aid in the discovery of points of convergence that may lead naturally to decision making regarding project topics.

Third, we recommend that when implementing virtual team projects in their courses, faculty take time in class to discuss with students the impact that technologies may have on their work in virtual teams. Specifically, we suggest that the discussion cover the wide range of experience their teammates may have with various technologies, the negotiation of roles that may take place within their discussions, and the pragmatic use of those roles to effectively negotiate task and social talk. Discussing these topics will raise students' awareness of the importance of their own communication in teams and provide a vocabulary for students to use to engage in ongoing dialogue about their experiences communicating in virtual teams. Likewise, trainers, managers, and others supervising or involved with the development of virtual teams in nonaca-demic settings may positively influence the outcomes of virtual teams by sensitizing them to such issues and by coaching new teams through context-building activities as the teams commence.

We believe that when the themes discussed in this chapter — context, roles, and frames of technology — are attended to by faculty facilitating virtual team projects in their classrooms, both in their own communication and in sensitizing students to these themes, the virtual team project can provide an effective pedagogical opportunity for students to experience teamwork much as it exists in the workplace today. Attentiveness to these themes has both pragmatic and pedagogical potential: pragmatic in that students will be better equipped to get the work of the project done, and pedagogical in that students will be more apt to be aware of and learn through their communicative behavior as members of a virtual team.

ACKNOWLEDGMENTS

The authors would like to thank the editors, Prof. Sue Godar and Prof. Pixy Ferris, for their input and help with this article, as well as the two anonymous reviewers for their careful suggestions. In addition, we would like to thank the students of the classes in Small Group Communication for participating enthusiastically and fully in our research study. Finally, our special thanks and acknowledgments are due to Dr. Angeli Diaz, without whom our experiences analyses and reflections would be much the poorer.

REFERENCES

Bormann, E. (1983). The symbolic convergence theory of communication and the creation, raising and sustaining of public consciousness. In J. I. Sisco (Ed.), *The Jensen lectures: Contemporary communication studies* (pp. 71–90). Tampa, FL: University of South Florida, Department of Communication.

Bormann, E. (1986). Symbolic convergence theory and communication in group decision-making. In R. Y. Hirokawa & M. S. Poole (Eds.), *Communication and group decision making* (pp. 219–236). Thousand Oaks, CA: Sage.

Bormann, E. (1990). *Small group communication: Theory and practice.* New York: Harper & Row.

Bormann, E., Cragan, J. F., & Shields, D. C. (1994). In defense of Symbolic Convergence theory: A look at the theory and its criticisms after two decades. *Communication Theory, 4*(4), 259–294.

Cheney, G., Christensen, L., Zorn, T. E., and Ganesh, S. (2003). *Organizational communication in an era of globalization: Issues, reflections, practices.* Prospect Heights, IL: Waveland Press.

Contractor, N., Stohl, C., Monge, P., Flanagin, A., & Fulk, J. (2000). *Communication in the global workplace: Advanced E-Quad collaboration tools to support multi-university cooperative learning and teaching.* Unpublished Manuscript, University of Illinois, Urbana-Champaign.

Cragan, J., & Wright, D. (1999). *Communicating in small groups: Theory, process, skills.* Belmont, CA: Wadsworth.

Fulk, J., Schmitz, J. A., & Schwarz, D. (1992). The dynamics of context–behavior interactions in computer-mediated communication. In M. Lea (Ed.), *Contexts of computer-mediated communication* (pp. 7–29). New York: Harvester Wheatsheaf.

Georgoudi, M., & Rosnow, R. L. (1985). The emergence of contextualism. *Journal of Communication, 35*(1), 76–88.

Glaser, B. G., & Strauss, A. L. (1967). *The discovery of grounded theory: Strategies for qualitative research.* Chicago: Aldine.

Handy, C. (1995). Trust and the virtual organization. *Harvard Business Review, 73*(3), 40–50.

Jarvenpaa, S. L., & Leidner, D. E. (1998). Communication and trust in global virtual teams, [Internet]. *Special Issue of Organization Science and the Journal of Computer-Mediated Communication on Virtual Organizations*. Retrieved October 7, 1998 from the World Wide Web: http://www.ascusc.org/jcmc/vol3/issue4/jarvenpaa.html

Ketrow, S. M. (1991). Communication role specializations and perceptions of leadership. *Small Group Research, 22*(2), 234–254.

Kolb, D. (1995). Discourse across Links. In C. Ess (Ed.), *Philosophical perspectives on computer-mediated communication* (pp. 15–26). Albany, NY: SUNY Press.

Levine, J. M., & Moreland, R. L. (1990). Progress in small group research. *Annual Review of Psychology, 41*, 585–634.

McGrath, J. E., & Altman, J. (1966). *Small group research: A synthesis and critique of the field.* New York: Holt, Rinehard & Winston.

Monge, P. R., O'Keefe, B. J., Stohl, C., Yammine, P., & Contractor, N. (1999). *Advanced collaboration tools to support multi-university distributed learning in organizational communication.* Paper presented at the Panel discussion presented at the National Communication Association Annual Meeting, Chicago, IL.

Nichols, M. P. (1995). *The lost art of listening.* New York: Guildford.

Noble, D. F. (2001). *Digital diploma mills: The automation of higher education.* New York: Monthly Review Press.

Owen, W. F. (1984). Interpretive themes in relational communication. *Quarterly Journal of Speech, 70*, 274–287.

Putnam, L., Hoeven, S. V., & Bullis, C. (1991). The role of rituals and fantasy themes in teachers' bargaining. *Western Journal of Communication, 55*(1), 85–103.

Putnam, L. L. (1983). The interpretive perspective: An alternative to functionalism. In L. Putnam & M. Pacanowsky (Eds.), *Organizational communication: Interpretive Approaches* (pp. 46–57). Thousand Oaks, CA: Sage.

Ragin, C. (1994). *Constructing social research.* Thousand Oaks, CA: Pine Forge Press.

Stohl, C. (1995). *Organizational communication: Connectedness in action.* Thousand Oaks, CA: Sage.

VanRyssen & Godar, S. (2000). Going international without going international. *Journal of International Management, 69*(1): 49–60.

Weick, K. (1979). *The social psychology of organizing.* Reading, MA: Addison-Wesley.

Weick, K. (1985). Cosmos vs. chaos: Sense and nonsense in electronic contexts. *Organizational Dynamics, 14*(2), 51–64.

Weick, K. (1990). Technology as equivoce. In P. S. Goodman, & L. S. Sproull & Associates (Eds.), *Technology and organizations.* San Francisco, CA: Jossey-Bass.

Weick, K. E. (1995). What theory is not, theorizing is. *Administrative Science Quarterly, 40*, 385–390.

Yakimovicz, A. D., & Murphy, K. L. (1995). Constructivism and collaboration on the Internet: Case study of a graduate class experience. *Computers and Education, 24*(3), 203–209.

Chapter IX

The Strategic Use of "Distance" Among Virtual Team Members:
A Multi-Dimensional Communication Model

Paul M. Leonardi, Stanford University, USA

Michele Jackson, University of Colorado at Boulder, USA

Natalie Marsh, University of Colorado at Boulder, USA

ABSTRACT

Distance, in the context of virtual teams, has traditionally been treated as an unproblematic, in fact positive, by-product of work practices mediated by information and communication technologies. Research has largely overlooked the notion of distance and its relationship to virtual team work practices and digital telecommunications technologies. Explored in this chapter is the nature of distance by investigating perceptions of "distance" among teleworkers and addressing how virtual team members strategically use the distance enabled by telecommunications technologies to manage a variety of organizational practices. Interviews with 46 distance workers across 10 industries, making up 17 virtual teams, found that members conceptualize distance across three important dimensions: distance and emotion, distance and identity, and distance and communication strategies. We discuss each of these dimensions and propose moving from a notion of distance as a mere outcome of the use of information and communication technologies, to a reconceptualization of it as a multidimensional construct created and maintained through communication practices.

INTRODUCTION

One quality of information and communication technologies (ICTs) that has been taken as straightforward is their ability to support working at a distance. The concept of distance has been understood, in a fairly unproblematic way, to mean physical distance: The ability to work from some *place* other than the office. ICTs were argued to allow increased physical distance by decreasing "functional" distance — that is, workers can access information and communicate with colleagues more easily and more quickly than without the use of such technologies (Heaton, 1998; O'Mahony & Barley, 1999; Waisbord, 1998). Accordingly, our typical understanding of virtual teams revolves primarily around the notion of distance work; members do not have to be physically copresent in order to accomplish shared tasks. Yet, this view centers primarily on the capabilities of the technology to transmit information. Intuitively, we know that distance is a richer concept than what is presented in this conceptualization. In an important sense, distance is perceived more than it is objectively measured. We "feel" more or less distant from others or from our places of work. Thus, distance is tied to the issue of "connection." As such, distance is an important organizational and management concern.

Distance, in the context of virtual teams, was traditionally treated as an unproblematic, in fact, positive, by-product of work practices mediated by ICTs (DeSanctis & Monge, 1998). Accordingly, the notion of distance and its relationship to work practices and digital telecommunications technologies was largely overlooked by researchers of virtual teams as a fundamental concept for teamwork (O'Mahony & Barley, 1999). Explored in this chapter is the nature of distance by investigating perceptions of "distance" among teleworkers and addressing how virtual team members strategically use the distance enabled by telecommunications technologies to manage a variety of organizational practices.

DISTANCE WORK AND TECHNOLOGY

Fluid organizational forms emerging over the past decade ushered in new arrangements and expectations for work (DeSanctis & Fulk, 1999; DeSanctis & Monge, 1998; Keen, 1990; McPhee & Poole, 2001). A "new economy" evolved in which "postentrepreneurial" professionals adopt "boundaryless careers"

(Arthur & Rousseau, 1996). Distance work and telecommunications were always linked. The combination of high gasoline prices and new capabilities for data communication allowed for the creation of distance work in the 1970s, which allowed people to work at home while still maintaining contact with those at the office (Nilles, 1975). Since then, the use of telecommunications technology has been a staple in nearly every definition of distance work (or its variants, such as telework, telecommuting, virtual work, and mobile work) (O'Mahoney & Barley, 1999). Regardless of the nomenclature, with each of these terms, an attempt was made to capture the fact that individuals can work together without being together physically. Technology, in this arrangement, has been understood to create a virtual space for teamwork to take place, while eliminating the constraints of physical distance between team members (Belanger, 1999; Jarvenpaa & Leidner, 1998).

Research on distance work centered largely on an enduring theme in studies of communication technology: The ability of technologies to eliminate or to transcend barriers of space and time (Bailey & Kurland, 2002; DeSanctis & Monge, 1998). Though usually not framed in this manner, these are also recurring interests in studies of virtual teams. For example, in investigating perceived advantages and disadvantages of telework, Teo and Lim (1998) suggested that factors of telecommuting distance and quality of work life are issues of overcoming space, and factors of commuting and child care are issues of managing time. For the traditional worker, an office provides constraints related to space, including the geographical location of the office building, and the positioning of the worker within that building, and the positioning of workers to each other. Similarly, time constrains the traditional worker in the following ways: through the length of the traditional workday, through set times for lunch and breaks, and through the ability to have one's time interrupted (Perlow, 1997).

One of the most prominent themes in literature on distance work concerns the social effects of technology on virtual team members, especially upon family and workplace structure. Individual mental health issues, i.e., stress, isolation, and loneliness are also consistently addressed as a crucial element in all virtual work situations (Bailey & Kurland, 2002). Unilaterally, scholars focusing on communication in virtual organizations focused on the concept of distance as a by-product of particular technologies (Contractor & Eisenberg, 1990; Fulk & Boyd, 1991; Haythornthwaite & Wellman, 1998; Trevino, Daft, & Lengel, 1990). In an attempt to explain how distance workers use telecommunications technologies, scholars crafted several theories that predict media choice. These theories predict that when individuals choose a medium for electronic communication, they seek out technology that provides a medium as similar as possible to face-to-face (F2F) communication, thus reducing perceived distance (Korzenny, 1978).

Two theories of media choice are especially influential. The first, social presence (Short, Williams, & Christie, 1976), asserts that communications media differ in their degree of social presence, and in this way, become a key factor that molds interaction. In short, social presence is the degree to which individuals perceive a medium to replicate the physical presence of another communicator. Second, media richness (Daft & Lengel, 1986) predicts that when individuals have to communicate delicate or complex information, they will choose the richest media possible. A medium's richness, or fidelity, can be measured by how well it transmits information normally encountered in F2F communication, such as immediate feedback, multiple cues, and language variety. Further, researchers posited that social presence and information richness involve two important physical dimensions, bandwidth (the ability to exchange information from all human senses) and synchrony (when people can communicate at the same time) (Hinds & Kiesler, 1995). Many empirical studies of computer-mediated communication (CMC) supported the propositions of these theories (c.f., Kayany & Yelsma, 2000; Korzenny & Bauer, 1981; Trevino et al., 1990). As Ware (2000) summarized:

1.   Social presence is essential for intense and relational CMC.
2.   Richer media facilitate more accurate and meaningful transmission of ideas.
3.   Individuals prefer to solve collaborative, equivocal tasks through a medium that is able to sustain relationships and facilitate spontaneous, interactive communication.

Media richness models, which are based on organizational information-processing theory, have become prominent in the choice of communication media in organizations The outcome of such research, however, has largely positioned distance as an evil that must be overcome by the choice of rich media that restore social presence. Seldom is the distance inherent in virtual work seen as something positive. Research on new organizational forms (DeSanctis & Fulk, 1999) shows that the relationship between organization and technology is anything but predictable and is, in fact, an emergent process (Dutton, 1999; Fulk & DeSanctis, 1999; Poole & DeSanctis, 1990) in which the users of technology play a critical role in shaping the alignment between technology and communication practices. Adopting an emergent perspective compels us to question the assumption that the distance virtual team members experience in their work arrangements must always be negative and leads us to the research question of this study:

Do virtual team members use the technologies available to them to strategically manipulate the distance inherent in their work arrangements in order to accomplish certain individual work objectives?

METHODOLOGY

Participants

This study included the participation of 46 virtual team members or distance workers, representing 10 industries and 20 companies, and working in seven states in the United States (with one respondent from the United Kingdom). Seventeen virtual teams are represented across a variety of industries, including public relations, computer manufacturing, publishing, paper processing, and telecommunications. Participants in this study were recruited by snowball method and by cold calls made to various organizations that were known to utilize virtual teams and to allow distance work. Bailey and Kurland (2002) were careful to point out that though much of the current research about people who work at a distance focuses on workers who rarely meet with others, most organizational members who work in virtual teams often participate in F2F meetings as well. In order to advance research on the latter population, our sample consists largely of virtual team members who maintain regular-interval physical contact with other team members. All participants self-identified as working at a distance, although they used many different names to illustrate this work arrangement, including telecommuters, teleworkers, virtual teamers, virtual office employees, and quite often, simply, employees.

Procedure

A standard protocol was used for all interviews, yielding data points of rough equivalence and, therefore, allowing systematic comparison across respondents. Interviews ranged from 20–45 minutes, averaging approximately 30 minutes in length. The protocol asked respondents to describe not only their use of technology but also the nature of their work and their relationships to their organizations, their managers, and their coworkers. We asked them to identify aspects they were satisfied with, as well as what they wished to see changed or improved. Participants were asked a series of questions about their work practices before and after they began working remotely, their uses of technology to do their work, their relationships with team members and organizations, their perceptions of themselves as distant, and the strategies they used to either increase or decrease feelings of distance. All three researchers then reviewed transcriptions of the interviews' references to distance; given the exploratory nature of this study, we explicitly sought to be inclusive rather than exclusive in identifying these references. Our analysis then focused on these references. Because we were interested in how respondents conceptualized distance, we allowed patterns and themes to emerge inductively through discussions among the researchers. From this analysis emerged a set of three dimensions. Finally, each dimension was assigned to one member of the research team, who then analyzed the data again using a procedure of constant comparison to develop each dimension in more detail.

FINDINGS

Our findings show that virtual team members frequently used various communication strategies in order to increase and decrease perceptions of distance between themselves and virtual team members. Through the use of such strategies, participants conceptualized perceptions of distance across two dimensions — emotion, and identity. Participants in this study actively engaged in the distance they experienced as distance workers and manipulated it through the use of communication technologies and through their own work practices.

Distance and Communication Strategies

Communication and information are often central components of distance work. Despite their physical separation from the office, workers are expected to remain connected to the organization. The most obvious manifestation of this connection is through communication. As a result, workers employ various communication strategies to manipulate the strength of this connection and to maintain control over their environments. However, the strategies differ according to how "distance" is conceptualized. Few of our respondents conceptualized distance as equal to the number of miles away from an office where one works. And, even those who referred to what we might call "actual distance," did not indicate that their communication strategies changed as this distance changed. Several respondents indicated that the nature of their work did not depend on their physical location; their work would not change if they worked at home instead of in an office, for example. One respondent stated the following:

> It's kind of hard to say just because this is such a weird job. I mean, if I was in an office outside of the home, I'd still be just as remote in one sense, because my work is outside of any office, because it's traveling to schools or that sort of thing. So, whether my office was here or somewhere else, I don't think it makes a difference.

Another respondent commented as follows:

> I sat at my computer all day long and talked on the phone and went to visit clients and sat with them, and then came home and sat on the phone some more. I did essentially exactly the same thing I would have done when I was in the office except for I tended to work longer...

This is not necessarily a surprise to the distance worker, "I think we could pretty much do our job from wherever. I mean, it's not brain surgery. We don't have to touch anyone physically."

Communication strategies of distance workers reflect and respond to the ways in which they conceptualize distance. This section presents two such conceptualizations: distance as a feeling of connection to a group of other individuals, and distance as one's "presence" in a location. In these conceptualizations, distance becomes something that is perceived rather than measured. As such, communication strategies may act to either increase or decrease the extent to which individuals perceive themselves to be working "at a distance."

Distance as connection

The most common perception of distance is that of connection to others. For most respondents, frequent conversation was critical to establishing and maintaining a feeling of connection. Respondents varied, however, in whether they saw distance work as necessarily decreasing opportunities for conversation. Sometimes, individuals saw working at a distance as removing them from the occasions of talk:

> I have a really good friend who I work with. She only lives in Walnut Creek (half hour car trip) but we never talk. It seems like so much effort to call her up just to chat. There's no yelling over the cubicle, that kind of stuff that keeps you connected.

Other respondents referred to missing out on "water cooler talk" or talk being easier when colleagues are "just being a few offices down." For these respondents, F2F interactions were crucial to connection, "And [in virtual teams] you don't get that *true interaction* as if that person were right at your desk and you were asking him something." Many respondents indicated that some types of relationships could not develop without F2F interaction, particularly mentoring, client development, or customer service, and instruction or training.

To compensate for this perceived lack of connection, respondents advocated a number of communication strategies. The most common was to create special occasions for coworkers to come together for conversation and interaction in a F2F context. One occasion is the launch of a new team:

> I think before the virtual teamer gets integrated onto the team, you need to invest in some form of face to face contact with the rest of the team. So, when you first bring them on, fly them out to your office, get to meet them face to face, spend a day with them, get to know them as people, and then the working relationship is better moving forward.

Another occasion is annual meetings:

> I just came back from the meeting in San Diego and the meeting itself was pretty much a waste of time, ... but it's strange, because you see these people once or twice a year and you feel like they're really your good friend and you know them so well...

For some, such meetings seem to provide relationship development in a concentrated form:

The one thing that helps me stay connected or feel connected? That's a really hard question. Well, the things that, I mean, I know this sounds nuts but like our annual meetings are crazy. They are so much fun. People live for them. I mean, they're like big class reunions. And, that helps a tremendous amount.

A second strategy was to use technology to maintain or increase one's level of conversation with others. In a sense, by increasing connection, workers actually decrease distance:

Because my very best friends in the company are located in San Diego, Omaha, St. Louis and Honolulu. You know, I can't just go see them, I can't say like, hey, let's go get coffee. ... But, with email and voicemail, we probably talk anywhere from three to 20 times a week. And, we really keep in touch that way and it really helps to keep you from feeling so isolated in a job that could get really lonely.

Or, as one respondent commented, dismissing the idea that distance worker would feel less connected, "Well, when people are calling you all day long, it's hard to disappear."

A final communication strategy for increasing connection was to plan or schedule interaction. This ranged from being more conscientious about planning meetings, to arranging social engagements such as lunch dates. As one respondent remarked, "If you want to be around people, you have to plan it." Communication becomes strategic, rather than taken for granted:

For one thing, you have to put yourself out. You can't expect people to come to you. You can't go to meetings and sit there and hope that everybody comes over and introduces themselves to you. I mean, you have to go out and introduce yourself to them.

In this perspective, communication is intentional, and individuals are reflective about what mode of communication is necessary, "Look at the task that needs to be accomplished, and map it to the interface that is necessary to complete the task."

Distance as "presence"

A second conception of distance is tied to a sense of place or location. Distance becomes the perceived proximity to that place, or to the kind of social environment that one would be immersed in at that place. It is in this conception that the idea of the "office" becomes most salient:

Yeah, I guess it would have to, because, if you were not the kind of person that could work in this situation, and you needed to be in the same place every day, and to have people, and be in an office, and that kind of environment, you couldn't do this job. Because, this job can get lonely.

For some, an office environment is not desirable:
I could not stand having to go to the same building, and sit in the same office, and do the same thing, in the same place, with the same people, every single day. I would go insane.

Yet, others miss the office environment,
I think it's harder, because sometimes you want that immediate gratification. And you want a quick answer ... I have my GM located in San Jose, and she's not always available, so I have schedule time to meet with her to discuss certain issues when had she been in the office I could know what she was up to and then maybe just pop in and get my question answered really quickly, so I find it at times frustrating ...

In this conceptualization, distance can mean, on the one hand, independence and increased control over one's own work that comes from being freed from the expectations of office life. For example, office workers may be expected to always be available; distance workers appreciated having fewer interruptions. In particular, respondents valued the ability to avoid the informal social interactions that for them characterized office work:
Like being in an office, when I was in the school, and I hadn't always been a teacher, I had worked in different business offices before, but a lot of time gets wasted with just people chitchatting. And, the same thing happens in school, and I was never really able to get any substantial work done.

The view of another respondent is similar:
But I know I do work smarter. You don't realize how much of your day is spent socializing when you're at the office. When I go in I get annoyed that people talk so much and don't even work.

On the other hand, distance from an office can also mean missing out on the advantages that come from being involved with coworkers, such as learning from one another's experiences, resources, and knowledge. A number of respondents recognized this and responded with communication strategies that recreated the sense of an office, virtually, for example, through electronic lists or online newsletters. For our respondents, these virtual offices decrease the sense of distance, while avoiding what they perceive as the shortcomings of a physical office:

> *One of the things that they [the organization] did do is they provided an email list. And, I think that the thing that made it so attractive to so many of us was that now we could talk to each other. You know, not only could we communicate with our corporate office and our printing plant, but now we could email each other. And, that was fabulous.*

Our findings show clearly that distance is manipulated strategically through communication strategies, such that distance is created, conveyed, and managed communicatively. In other words, distance workers constitute distance through communication.

Distance and Emotion

One consequence of the social constitution of distance is that it reconfigures the *emotional* relationship distance workers have with coworkers, the organization, and the task at hand. Models of media richness and social presence describe a type of distance that is felt more than one that is observed. Individuals cannot easily measure the distance between themselves and coworkers, but they can *feel* a certain amount of distance from one another. The findings presented here show that distance workers have distinct emotional responses to and relationships with various aspects of their job, precisely because they feel a certain amount of distance from the typical trapping of work office life.

Distance workers in this study largely felt that the distance between themselves and their coworkers was positive for a number of reasons. Participants said repeatedly that they felt more productive and relaxed when working at a distance from coworkers. They did not have to "waste time" worrying about office dynamics and other problems that occur in normal office settings. As suggested above, they instead could focus intently on the work and improve their own productivity.

In this way, participants viewed an increased feeling of distance from the office and from coworkers as an advantage of distance work. As members of virtual teams, participants noted that they did not have to make small talk with the people they did not care for and did not have to worry about appearances, dressing appropriately, of being uncomfortable in the office. Feeling distanced from their job helped participants to feel more relaxed and energized about and committed to their work.

Although perceiving more distance from their job was good for participants in terms of their productivity and overall morale, increased distance could increase anxiety if, as one participant noted about her work, "you're just still going or you work a lot on the weekends and things like that just because it's there. You're not as distanced from it." So, while distance workers might feel more distant from the pressures put on them by coworkers, they may also feel more stress from a more intimate relationship with their work.

Distance workers who participated in this study experienced a critical emotional conflict that placed them in a paradox: They were happy to be distanced from coworkers so that they could focus more on their own work, but lack of interaction with those same coworkers made them feel overly anxious about their work. In order to assuage this tension, participants enlisted several strategies. One key move distance workers in this study made in order to move their focus off their work alone was to reclaim informal communication. However, participants did so by taking advantage of the distance that they already enjoyed for allowing them to avoid much of what they perceived to be the senseless talk that occurs in the office. One participant recounted a move that her team members made in this direction:

> *Well, actually, one of the things that a lot of us have now is we have formed our own like, Yahoo's users group thing, and there's about 10 of us, and so, it's really neat. Because, if you have a problem or question, you can email and everybody gets it and they can respond if they choose, that kind of thing.*

Participants observed that rather than calling others or arranging F2F meetings, they often engaged in asynchronous forms of communication when they wanted to talk informally. By doing so, they could respond to the comments they wanted to and could also participate only when they wanted distraction or help. However, not all of the communications activities arranged by distance workers in this study were asynchronous. Participants explained that they would often take advantage of times when they were able to talk live with coworkers to serve a dual purpose: (a) to be able to spend a few minutes concentrating on something other than the work, and (b) to maintain working relationships by interjecting planned brief social interactions. As an example, many participants acknowledged that they would call a coworker on the telephone three or four minutes before a scheduled client call so that they could talk socially. The distance at which they worked, however, allowed them to plan the amount of time they wished to talk, thus helping to reduce their work anxiety, while simultaneously restricting the annoyance of too much social time. As one participant commented:

> *If I call [our sales rep], I always ask her how she's doing, what did you do over the weekend, you know, she took a few days off, well, what did you guys do, did you go on a bike ride, you know, how's your Mom doing... it takes the focus off of work for a while.*

The distance from coworkers and workplace experienced by participants in this study created distinct and often conflicting emotions. Participants were aware that distance functioned to attract or distract them from their job and work tasks in a variety of ways. Participants were clearly aware that they could also use their feeling of distance to their advantage by enlisting strategies that would help to control it, and thus help them to obtain optimal emotional connections with their coworkers and their work.

Distance and Identity

The traditional understanding of identity creation posits that an individual observes and adopts the values, attitudes, and behaviors exhibited by others. Essentially, this is the process of identification that is not only continuous but also assumes F2F interaction as a necessity. The traditional understanding of the process of identification is challenged by the emergence of the distance worker. It would seem working at a distance would hinder the process of organizational identification due to the lack of F2F interaction. However, the process of identification evolved for distance workers, as technologies such as voicemail, e-mail, corporate chat rooms, and video phones provided mediated interaction. For the majority of individuals in this study, the process of identification was not hindered by physical distance, but in fact, it was enhanced by the ability to use technology to apply "quality control" to their interactions, eliminating unnecessary "water cooler" gossip and focusing on talk that accomplishes tasks and establishes trusting relationships. What emerges from this study is the evolution of the process of identification as mediated interaction. Distance workers characterize their distance work processes as the same as the office work processes and further associate these behaviors with their identities as professionals of their organizations.

One of the first findings presented above is that participants described distance work as no different from working from the office. This finding is crucial to understanding the identification processes of distance workers. On one level, the perception is that it makes no difference to their work. But on a more important level, distance work makes no difference to their *identity*. One participant emphasized that she was no different from other organizational members when stating the organization understands her "not as Sarah, Telecommuter, but Sarah, Global Communications Professional." Distance workers emphasized their work as simply taking place remotely, but the values and behaviors associated with their identities as organizational members could not be differentiated due to working at a distance.

This finding accentuates a new conceptualization of identification and distance. Physical distance did not prohibit interaction for the process of identification; rather, distance workers utilized mediated communication as a means of developing and maintaining professional identities. Workers used various strategies, depending on their communicative preferences: sustaining constant contact with others through telephone conversations, engaging in informal social talk, or being able to be reached at any time. The particular strategy is not as important here as is the observation that distance workers actively managed their identities in a way that would occur "naturally" if they did not work at a distance. The socialization of organizational values and expected behaviors occurred through mediated interaction.

A further finding is a possible professional identity of the "distance worker." Participants described the particular personality traits and behaviors that distance workers possessed. For example, all participants described how the distance worker actually extends the workday and works longer and harder than those at the office. Although remote work routines may parallel the office routines, distance workers identified with the values of working longer and harder than those at the office. Thus, the identity of the distance worker begins to emerge as not simply a member of a particular organization but one who works harder than those at the office. Distance here did not mean that the individual was less a part of the organization but was actually more committed and more dedicated. For example, as a participant said:

...My tendency was to always work longer... you're always tempted to go and just say, oh did that email come in, or is there something else I need to do, can I tweak that paragraph. It's pretty hard to draw the line.

Participants described working remotely as corresponding to the values of working hard and producing for the organization that provided the opportunity to work at a distance. Technology for the distance worker reconceptualizes the meaning of distance. Physical distance does not alter the sense of work practices and it does not alter the loyalty and dedication of organizational members. Rather, technology provides an "always-on" connection as well as mediated socialization of how to be a distance worker.

The process of identification has not altered for distance workers in the sense that interaction is necessary in order to observe and adopt the traits, values, and behaviors expected in organizations. What evolved are the types of interaction and the means for interaction. Identification for distance workers is to connect with organizational members through technologies. Through e-mail, telephone, chat rooms, and so forth, the distance worker connects to and interacts with other members, who provide socialization on how to be not only a member of the organization but also a distance worker for the organization. To fully exemplify this, one participant stated the following:

It [distance work] definitely takes a kind of personality. It also takes a sort of commitment and sort of a belief in the organization (and I hate to sound corny), but [its] philosophy...And to feel connected, you sort of have to believe in that. And, I obviously believe in it, but the people that work here, I think do as well. And, to feel connected, you sort of have to buy into that idea...you're just the kind of person that you work [here].

CONCLUSION

The findings presented in this chapter lead to implications for theory and practice about the conceptualization of distance among virtual team members. As revealed in distance workers' observations of their work arrangements, distance is much more than a mere outcome of the use of ICTs; it is rather a tool virtual team members can use to manage their relationships with their coworkers and their organizations. Media choice theories such as social presence theory and media richness theory paid attention to the ways in which individuals attempt to reduce distance through the selection of an appropriate medium. While such theories were instrumental in directing attention to how distance can be perceived to be reduced, they have not addressed how distance can be used strategically to benefit distance workers. Our findings urge a reconceptualization of distance as a multidimensional construct created and maintained through communication practices and not only through physical location. Although we have only scratched the surface in this chapter, we began to show several ways in which distance workers use distance strategically to create communication practices that work to relate them to their jobs in specific ways, ways that were not possible in traditional office work arrangements.

Beyond social presence and media richness, there is evidence that technology is central to the perception and creation of distance, but this is not so much a product of media characteristics. Instead, workers actively engage to control and shape perceptions of distance. The use of technology is one part of a larger strategy for adapting to distance work. The use of multiple technologies, in particular, appears among our respondents as critical to avoiding problems and maximizing the potential of distance.

A second key finding is the relevance of the kind of work to the nature of distance. What to some is anxiety-producing isolation from coworkers is to others a way to become more connected with clients. When working at a distance, participants in this study were cognizant that the space that separated them from their virtual team members was both positive and negative in terms of their own well-being at work. When focusing on the task-based functions of their jobs, most participants felt that working at a distance enhanced their productivity and efficiency on the job. Accordingly, participants used a variety of communication strategies in order to maintain a certain amount of distance from their coworkers in order to take advantage of this increased work ability.

When musing on the maintenance-based functions of their job, however, many participants observed that distance created isolation. In order to combat this, participants enacted several communication practices to mitigate the perceived distance in their work arrangements.

Third, our study reinforces the findings of earlier studies regarding the critical link between distance and time. Distance work is often adopted in order to control one's time and schedule; virtual teaming requires conscientious planning and scheduling of time. Distance workers must not let their work bleed over into personal time. Most participants in this study perceived an orthogonal relationship between distance and time. First, as distance from virtual team members increased, so did the amount of time participants felt that they could spend on work tasks. Second, as participants spent more time interacting with one another via different communication media, they felt that the distance between them decreased. It is important to keep in mind that both of these relationships are perceptual and not necessarily related to any objective measure of distance. For participants in this study, time was often the independent variable that influenced participants' perceptions of distance.

These insights suggest practical strategies for managers and team members to use to understand how distance — and feelings of connection — are created, and how this might improve work practices and team dynamics. Overall, these findings may challenge the idea of distance, as a stable construct for understanding this type of work in comparison to traditional office-based work. Distance is fundamentally relative. Any objective sense of distance is possible only if we start with a single location as representing the heart of an organization and its work. Yet, what this study demonstrates are the possibilities for organizations to mirror what workers have already done, and use distance strategically. For example, by giving workers laptops, work is disengaged from an office, and distance is measured by a worker's access to a hard drive and modem. Locating workers at client sites may make them physically distant from the office but may also heighten their identification as members of the organization by actively representing it to others.

In sum, paying attention to distance as an *opportunity* directs our attention to the way it is strategically manipulated through communication practices. Distance workers have clearly begun to challenge our traditional notions of distance and prompted us to examine its role in the creation and maintenance of virtual teams.

REFERENCES

Arthur, M. B., & Rousseau, D. M. (1996). *The boundaryless career: A new employment principle for a new organizational era.* New York: Oxford University Press.

Bailey, D. E., & Kurland, N. B. (2002). A review of telework research: Findings, new directions, and lessons for the study of modern work. *Journal of Organizational Behavior, 23*(4), 383–400.

Belanger, F. (1999). Communication patterns in distributed work groups: A network analysis. *IEEE Transactions on Professional Communication, 42*, 261–275.

Contractor, N. S., & Eisenberg, E. M. (1990). Communication networks and new media in organizations. In J. Fulk, & C. Steinfield (Eds.), *Organizations and communication technology* (pp. 143–172). Thousand Oaks, CA: Sage.

Daft, R. L., & Lengel, R. (1986). Organizational information requirements, media richness, and structural design. *Management Science, 32*(5), 554–571.

DeSanctis, G., & Fulk, J. (1999). *Shaping organization form: Communication, connection, and community.* Thousand Oaks, CA: Sage.

DeSanctis, G., & Monge, P. (1998). Communication processes for virtual organizations. *Journal of Computer Mediated Communication, 3*(4), Retrieved December 4, 2001 from the World Wide Web: http://www.ascusc.org/jcmc/vol2003/issue2004/desanctis.html

Dutton, W. H. (1999). The virtual organization: Tele-access in business and industry. In G. DeSanctis, & J. Fulk (Eds.), *Shaping organization form: Communication, connection, and community* (pp. 473–495). Thousand Oaks, CA: Sage.

Fulk, J., & Boyd, B. (1991). Emerging theories of communication in organizations. *Journal of Management, 17*(2), 407–447.

Fulk, J., & DeSanctis, G. (1999). Articulation of communication technology and organizational form. In G. DeSanctis, & J. Fulk (Eds.), *Shaping organization form: Communication, connection, and community* (pp. 5–32). Thousand Oaks, CA: Sage.

Haythornthwaite, C., & Wellman, B. (1998). Work, friendship, and media use for information exchange in a networked organization. *Journal of the American Society for Information Science, 49*(12), 1101–1114.

Heaton, L. (1998). Preserving communication context: Virtual workspace and interpersonal space in Japanese CSCW. *Electronic Journal of Communication, 8*(3/4). Retrieved September 20, 2002 from the World Wide Web: http://www.cios.org/getfile/Heaton_V2008N2398

Hinds, P., & Kiesler, S. (1995). Communication across boundaries: Work, structure, and use of communication technologies in a large organization. *Organization Science, 6*(4), 373–393.

Jarvenpaa, S. L., & Leidner, D. E. (1998). Communication and trust in global virtual teams. *Journal of Computer Mediated Communication, 3*(4).

Retrieved December 4, 2001 from the World Wide Web: http://www.ascusc.org/jcmc/vol2003/issue2004/jarvenpaa.html

Kayany, J. M., & Yelsma, P. (2000). Displacement effects of online media in the socio-technical contexts of households. *Journal of Broadcasting & Electronic Media, 44*(2), 215–229.

Keen, P. G. W. (1990). Telecommunications and organizational choice. In J. Fulk, & C. Steinfield (Eds.), *Organizations and communication technology* (pp. 295–312). Thousand Oaks, CA: Sage.

Korzenny, F. (1978). A theory of electronic propinquity: Mediated communication in organizations. *Communication Research, 5*(1), 3–24.

Korzenny, F., & Bauer, C. (1981). Testing the theory of electronic propinquity: Organizational teleconferencing. *Communication Research, 8*(4), 479–498.

McPhee, R. D., & Poole, M. S. (2001). Organizational structures and configurations. In F. M. Jablin, & L. L. Putnam (Eds.), *The new handbook of organizational communication* (pp. 503–543). Thousand Oaks, CA: Sage.

Nilles, J. M. (1975). Telecommunications and organizational decentralization. *IEEE Transactions on Communication, 23*, 1142–1147.

O'Mahony, S., & Barley, S. R. (1999). Do telecommunications technologies affect work and organizations? The state of our knowledge. In B. Staw, & R. Sutton (Eds.), *Research in organizational behavior* (Vol. 21, pp. 125–161). Greenwich, CT: JAI Press.

Perlow, L. A. (1997). *Finding time: How corporations, individuals, and families can benefit from new work practices.* Ithaca, NY: ILR Press.

Poole, M. S., & DeSanctis, G. (1990). Understanding the use of group decision support systems: The theory of adaptive structuration. In J. Fulk, & C. Steinfield (Eds.), *Organizations and communication technology* (pp. 173–193). Thousand Oaks, CA: Sage.

Short, J., Williams, E., & Christie, B. (1976). *The social psychology of telecommunications.* London: Wiley.

Teo, T. S. H., & Lim, V. K. G. (1998). An empirical study of attitudes towards teleworking among information technology (IT) personnel. *International Journal of Information Management, 18*, 329–343.

Trevino, L. K., Daft, R. L., & Lengel, R. H. (1990). Understanding managers' media choices: A symbolic interactionist perspective. In J. Fulk, & C. Steinfield (Eds.), *Organizations and communication technology* (pp. 71–94). Thousand Oaks, CA: Sage.

Waisbord, S. (1998). When the cart of media is before the horse of identity: A critique of technology-centered views on globalization. *Communication Research, 25*(4), 377–398.

Ware, S. (2000). Communication theory and the design of live online reference services. *Proceedings of the 2nd Annual Digital Reference Conference.*

Chapter X

How Hard Can It Be to Communicate?

Communication Mode and Performance in Collaborative R&D Projects

William H. A. Johnson, Bentley College, USA

ABSTRACT

Survey data and case studies of collaborative R&D projects are used to analyze the relative usage of communication modes [e.g., face-to-face (F2F), categorized as soft modes, versus written, categorized as hard modes]. Incremental (versus radical) innovation projects tended to use more written communication, as did those in which project managers defined the significant problems. Those with high ambiguity or equivocality did not rely more on F2F, but predictably, conflict and goal changes negatively impacted communication and performance. Despite managers' insistence that F2F communication is critical, only the use of written communication was associated with project success. Soft communication modes (F2F) may be needed to set direction in projects involving radical innovation, or any other project in which goals are unclear and not well agreed upon. However, when the innovation is incremental, and goals are understood and accepted, the use of hard communication modes (written) is no deterrent to success.

INTRODUCTION

Does the fact that virtual, geographically dispersed research and development (R&D) teams have to depend more heavily on computer-mediated and written forms of communication, designated "hard" modes in this chapter, have an effect on project success? Specifically, as might be predicted from intuitive thinking about communication modes, does this put them at a disadvantage?

Described in this chapter is research that examines these general questions. It begins with a succinct discussion of past research on communication, colocation, and project performance, which focuses on the relative effect of communication modes, described along a continuum ranging from hard to soft modes, on project communication and performance characteristics.

Hard modes are tangible channels of communication, such as documents and computer-mediated communication (CMC), that rely on "hard" technologies. Soft modes utilize social interaction, or "soft" technologies, archetypically through face-to-face (F2F) contact. Virtual teams and geographically dispersed collaborative projects, by definition, must rely to a greater extent on hard modes of communication than do nonvirtual, colocated teams. Does that put such projects at a disadvantage in terms of achieving success, as extant research and theory on communication modes suggests it might? The conclusion of the literature review is mixed, and it is suggested that this is due to significant variables of the function of communication within project management that were neglected in past research.

Several hypotheses were developed and tested using a survey of collaborative R&D projects sponsored by a private consortium engaged in funding research on intelligent systems and robotics technologies, called PRECARN. The sample ($n = 25$ projects) constituted 80% of all the projects sponsored by PRECARN. While most of the hypotheses were confirmed, there was one interesting finding. While managers insist that soft communication modes were the most important for project success, the data did not provide strong support for that claim.

The fact that hard modes were significantly and positively associated with project success suggests that virtual teams may not be at a disadvantage after all, due to their more heavy use of harder modes of communication, provided that certain criteria are met. The chief criterion appears to be the lack of conflict or equivocality and a solid agreement among project participants as to the goals of the project. The chapter concludes with a discussion of the situations in which soft modes may be necessary, based on normative theory and case analyses from the larger research project. From the analysis, several suggestions for management are made regarding the situations in which virtual teams may effectively rely to a large extent on hard modes only.

BACKGROUND

A substantial amount of research was conducted on the role of communications and information sourcing in R&D projects and other teams designed for
innovation. Seminal work was conducted by Allen (1977) and resulted in a
number of related works (e.g., Nagpaul & Pruthi, 1979; Pasquale, Triscari, &
Wallace, 1985; Ritchie, 1977). Much of this early research dealt with the flow
of information and suggested that colocation of individuals led to greater informal
contact and eventually greater communication flow. For example, a 10 meter
increase in distance was found to result in a 70% decrease in probability of
informal contact (Allen, 1977). All of this data suggested the importance of the
likelihood of F2F contact to information flow (Allen & Fusfield, 1975; Hough,
1972; Rothwell & Robertson, 1973; Tomlin, 1981).

F2F contact can be categorized as a soft mode of communication, which
requires social interaction skills and is synchronous (i.e., taking place in real
time). Hard modes involve communication across geographic distances and may
be asynchronous (McDonough & Kahn, 1996), utilizing digital and artificial
technologies for communication purposes. Hard and soft modes can be visual-
ized as anchor points along a continuum of communication technologies or
channels, as illustrated in Figure 1. While the designation of mode is equivalent
in many ways to the well-established categories of media richness theory, the
terms of designating mode are used here for a number of reasons. One reason
stems from the notion that each mode implies the primary use of either soft or
hard technologies (McDonough & Kahn, 1996). Furthermore, the term "richness" implies a judgment that hard modes of communication, such as written
documents and e-mail messaging systems, are somehow less powerful or worthy
(rich) media than F2F communication as modes of communication in general. For
example, information flows in some F2F situations may actually be as constrained, or more so, as compared with the case of written documents, and thus
no richer as a medium of communication in decreasing equivocality (Schmidt,
Montoya-Weiss, & Massey, 2001). A final reason stems from the intuitive usage
of the terms "hard" and "soft" in real project management situations. Soft modes,
as designated here, are often thought to require soft skills by managers for
effective communication. A hard mode in the form of a written document is often
referred to as a "hard copy." Along the continuum of usage depicted in Figure 1,
project managers often refer to e-mail messages as "soft copies," distinguishing
them from the hard copy mentioned earlier and implying that the communication
technology fits where it was placed in the schematic of Figure 1.

Two major categories can be used to distinguish hard modes from soft
modes. The first category is time. Harder modes tend to be "timeless" in their
communication power, because they exist outside the immediate interaction
between sender and receiver and, therefore, allow for asynchronous communi-

Figure 1: Communication modes, their characteristics and similarity to information richness.

Communication Technologies	Continuum of Modes	Time & Colocation	Information Richness Similarity
Face-to-face meetings	Soft	Synchronous & Colocated	High Media Richness
Personal telephone calls			
Virtual conferences			
Email			
Fax	Hard	Asynchronous & Dispersed	Low Media Richness
Letters			

Source: Based on Daft and Lengel, 1984.

cation. For example, a written document may be stored in a file for years and then be reexamined as if it were new. The second category is geographic space or distance. Hard modes, as they may be disembodied from the sender, can also be useful in communicating over great distances. Soft modes, particularly the archetypal mode of F2F communication, require synchronous colocation. Thus, the softer a communication mode becomes (or more toward the soft mode end of the continuum of Figure 1), the more constrained the communication is in terms of time and location. Of course, this points out that the designation of hard versus soft along the continuum is a matter of degree, such that communication technologies need to be compared to see their relative positions along the continuum of Figure 1 in designating the softness or hardness of the mode. A new communication technology, such as the virtual F2F meeting, for example, involves a mixture of hard and soft technologies, but in comparison to a real, colocated F2F meeting, it is considered a harder mode of communication. In the research described here, the archetypal forms of mode (i.e., F2F communication for soft modes and written documents for hard modes) were used.

Recently, researchers looked at the different roles that each communication mode plays in the R&D processes taking place across organizational boundaries. This is pertinent, because the R&D processes within and between many organizations are increasingly dispersed geographically (Gassmann & von Zedtwitz, 1998, 1999; Gerybadze & Reger, 1999) and thus require harder modes of communication in interpersonal interaction. An empirical question arises as to whether this requirement in utilizing hard modes of communication puts these types of geographically dispersed virtual projects at a disadvantage. For example, a recent study of virtual teams at Sabre, Inc. indicated that the major challenges for managing virtual work groups were building trust, cohesion, and team identity, and overcoming isolation among team members (Kirkman, Rosen,

Gibson, Tesluk, & McPherson, 2002). In general, it is often believed that there is a requirement for the presence of at least some soft modes for project success, at least at the beginning of projects (Boutellier, Gassmann, Macho, & Roux 1998). It was even stated (Handy, 1995) that "paradoxically, the more virtual an organization becomes, the more its people need to meet in person" in relation to trust building.

A review of the literature, however, suggests that there are mixed results regarding the effectiveness of soft modes on project performance. Some studies suggest the primacy of soft modes to project success (Allen, 1977; Boutellier, Gassmann, Macho, & Roux, 1998; Daft & Lengel, 1984, 1986; De Meyer, 1985; Lewis, 1998; McDonough & Kahn, 1996; Pinto, Pinto, & Prescott, 1993). Other studies suggest no relationship, implying that hard modes suffice for success in virtual projects (Ocker, Hiltz, Turoff, & Fjermestad, 1996; van Engelen, Kiewiet, & Terlouw, 2001; Yoo & Kanawattanachai, 2001). In other studies, conflicting evidence was found (Hauptman, 1986; Hedlund, Ilgen, & Hollenbeck, 1998; Kivimaki, Lansisalmi, Elovainio, et al., 2000; Patti, Gilbert, & Hartman, 1997; Schmidt, Montoya-Weiss, & Massey, 2001).

THEORETICAL PREDICTIONS

The theoretical literature suggests an explanation for these contradictory findings. The information tasks performed via communication may be a moderating variable. The analysis concerning the information tasks performed by communication modes, which is briefly described in the next few paragraphs, is summarized in Table 1. It stems from Daft and Lengel's (1984, 1986) influential media richness theory combined with the principles of process management. Normative theory suggests that soft modes, which in media richness theory are known as a "rich communication medium," will be needed at different times during a project to build a shared understanding among project participants or reduce equivocality, defined (Daft & Lengel, 1986) as "the existence of multiple and conflicting interpretations" (p. 556) of a situation. This will be most often needed at the project's beginning (Boutellier, Gassmann, Macho, & Roux, 1998). Hard modes, typically seen as "lean media" channels of communication, are most useful for the integration of data and information used for decreasing uncertainty. Hard modes help decrease uncertainty, which is, by definition, a lack of information, by providing more information on a specific but highly uncertain problem. The resulting artifact of hard mode communication (e.g., piece of paper or e-mail message) can be extensively examined and referred to in decision making over time, whereas decision making in soft mode communication may be more ephemeral (videotaping the soft mode interaction may help in utilizing the communication over time by allowing for reexamination and reinterpretation; but, note that the resulting videotape would then be categorized as a harder mode of

Table 1: Theoretical analysis of communication mode.

Framework	Hard Modes	Soft Modes
Technologies/Techniques Utilized	Information and communication technologies (ICTs) 'Written Documents'	Social- Face to Face Contact 'FtF Meetings'
Media Richness Theory	Decreases Uncertainty	Decreases Equivocality
Process Management Perspective	Manages ROUTINE Processes	Manages NON-ROUTINE Processes
Direction of Technological Innovation	Incremental	Radical
Needed when?	Uncertainty is high and more information is needed to solve problem	Shared understanding of problem is lacking or non-existent

communication). Ironically, despite their power in promoting real-time social interaction, soft modes can be confounded by social influence (Nemeth & Staw, 1989; Schmidt, Montoya-Weiss, & Massey, 2001). Under conditions of real-time social interaction, new information may be ignored (Stasser & Titus, 1987), and, because reducing uncertainty requires more information, soft modes will not be as useful in decreasing uncertainty. Thus, a theoretical analysis suggests that hard modes will be more associated with uncertainty reduction than soft modes.

Analysis of the information tasks performed by each communication mode also suggests that communication processes in incremental technological innovation, which would be expected to have lower equivocality associated with them than more radical projects, will take place primarily via hard modes. It is thus predicted that incremental innovation projects will use hard modes to a greater extent than will radical innovation projects. According to the framework summarized in Table 1, such a project will also be associated with uncertainty reduction. At first glance, it might seem that radical innovation projects also need uncertainty reduction. Eventually in the development of a new technology this may be true; however, it is argued that whereas incremental innovation requires reduction in uncertainty, radical innovation, by its very nature, tends toward utilizing uncertainty for innovative purposes. That is, uncertainty reduction does not necessarily lead to success in radical innovation until the innovation is better known — but by then, it may be considered an incremental innovation. As such, radical innovation may require taking many uncertain paths to lead to success, but incremental innovation requires project participants to stay closer to the original incremental objectives. Thus, an incremental innovations project should utilize hard modes more extensively.

Research findings by Zack (1994) into the use of electronic messaging in an ongoing work group that performed cooperative tasks comply with the predictions made in Table 1. For example, he found that communication was more effective: when F2F meetings were used to build a shared interpretative context when it was deficient; when electronic messaging was used to communicate only within an existing shared interpretative context; and when communicators complied with communication procedure by choosing the expected mode of communication. Another case study of one distributed R&D community found soft modes related to equivocality reduction and suggested that as the complexity of the group tasks increased, so should media richness (Lewis, 1998).

With the above arguments and observations in mind, the following hypotheses were made:

Hypothesis 1: Project managers' perceptions are that both soft and hard communication modes are equally important to project performance.
Hypothesis 2: Both soft and hard communication modes are equally important to project performance.
Hypothesis 3: Greater total frequency of communication is associated with greater project performance.

These first three hypotheses are general and concern the effect communication is believed to have and actually does have on project performance. The first two can be seen as null hypotheses regarding differences in communication modes. The former tests the perception of management, and the latter tests the actual relationship utilizing data from the research described next in the methodology section. The communications literature suggests that communication in general and both types of modes are important to the process of project management, but that some will be more or less important than others at particular times during the project (e.g., Boutellier, Gassmann, Macho, & Roux, 1998). Longitudinal effects were not tested with the data here. However, given the cross-sectional nature of the research, the overall perception of managers should reveal that both are important to the project in general. The next hypotheses are contingent hypotheses looking specifically at types of tasks and project innovations and their associated communication modes.

Hypothesis 4: The more incremental the technological innovation of the R&D project, the greater the use of hard modes of communication in general.
Hypothesis 5: The more centrally defined the problems (i.e., when goals are determined by project management and not participants) of the project, the greater the use of hard rather than soft modes of communication.

These two hypotheses relate to the argument made above concerning hard modes, which theory suggests are useful for uncertainty reduction when equivocality is not a problem. A reduction in equivocality is operationalized as centrally defined problems and goals. Hypothesis 5 specifically looks at the ratio of hard to soft modes, suggesting that although soft modes may actually be utilized in cases of well-defined incremental projects, their relative utilization will be less than that for hard modes.

Hypothesis 6: The greater the change in a project's goals during the project, the greater the use of soft modes of communication.

Hypothesis 7: The greater the conflict over a project's goals, the greater the use of soft modes of communication.

These last two hypotheses relate to the argument made above concerning soft modes, which theory suggests are useful for equivocality reduction. Changing project goals is an indication of increasing equivocality, and conflict is ultimately manifested as equivocality. Normative theory suggests that the use of soft modes of communication should be used to counteract equivocality.

Of course, it must be kept in mind that media richness theory and the analysis made here are based on normative arguments. Just because a project has a great deal of equivocality does not mean it will utilize soft modes but only that it should utilize soft modes. This should be the case in well-performing projects, so the hypotheses above can be used to test this normative behavior when also looking at performance. The reason that projects should utilize soft modes under increasing equivocality is because of their positive effects on performance under such conditions. Or, put another way, utilizing soft modes under increasing equivocality will help in avoiding the negative performance effects associated with conflict. As discussed later, evidence suggested that misalignment with the predictions of the normative theory was associated with low performance. Briefly described in the next section are the data used to test these hypotheses.

METHODOLOGY

The data reported here were obtained from a survey of 25 collaborative R&D projects involving at least three different types of organizational participants. Each project utilized a combination of soft and hard modes. All projects involved various participants who were geographically dispersed, such that much communication and work was done virtually, although top project management met F2F periodically and during emergencies throughout any particular project. The actual ratio of soft to hard modes depended upon the particular needs and management styles of individual projects. The collaborative R&D projects were part of 32 projects (of which 30 were potential respondents due to time and memory issues) that to that date were all sponsored by PRECARN, a private consortium engaged in funding research on intelligent systems and robotics technologies (examples are a digital microscope capable of analyzing a living sample utilizing multiple spectroscopic tests and a lumber grading system based on noninvasive measuring techniques). The research was part of a larger study that examined the factors and processes of technical knowledge creation in such projects. In that larger study, six of the projects were examined in more depth using a case study methodology (Yin, 1989). Data pertaining to the issue of communication modes in the project is reported here from the survey and the case studies.

In both cases, data were obtained from the senior management of each project. In the case studies, this meant interviewing the senior manager or participant from each of the organizations involved in the collaborative R&D project. Twenty-one people were interviewed from six projects. Most of these interviews took place around the time of project completion, so that memory bias was not thought to be problematic. In the surveys, project leaders and, in some cases, other senior managers provided responses to a self-report survey. Forty-two responses were obtained for the 25 projects, with 11 projects having multiple respondents. This was utilized in triangulating responses and testing for internal consistency of the items used. The research was conducted at the project level, so each response within the same project was expected to be somewhat similar. In fact, the inter-rater reliability (using Cronbachs alpha) for the projects with multiple informants averaged 0.76 (s.d. = 0.09; range = 0.62-0.90) for the survey questions used. Samples of the items examined in this chapter are displayed in the appendix. The achievement of technical objectives was determined from a two-item scale (± = 0.72), and it signified project success for purposes of the research. All survey items were measured using a Likert seven-point scale.

RESULTS

Displayed in Table 2 are the results of the survey item "How effective were the following communication modes in advancing the technological objectives of

Table 2:   Perception of the effectiveness of communication modes.

Communication Mode Items	Project Survey	
How effective were the following communication modes in advancing the technological objectives of the project?	Mean Response	Std. Dev.
Face-to-face meetings among project members.	6.4 *	0.8
Telephone conferences among project members.	4.8	1.3
Telephone calls between individual project members.	5.2	1.1
Email and faxes among project members.	5.3	1.3
Written correspondences among project members.	5.0	1.3

* Item's mean is significantly different from all other items' means at p<.01

Table 3: Spearman rank correlations.

	μ	s.d.	1	2	3	4	5	6	7	8
1) Tech Objectives	5.5	1.1								
2) Total Com.	5.2	0.8	0.527**							
3) Soft Com.	5.7	0.7	0.206	0.694**						
4) Hard Com.	4.5	1.2	0.626**	0.905**	0.425*					
5) Hard Ratio	0.4	0.1	0.512**	0.545**	-0.064	0.810**				
6) Problems Defined	4.0	1.5	0.109	0.337	0.179	0.399*	0.455*			
7) Incremental Tech.	6.0	1.0	0.413*	0.447*	0.178	0.494*	0.344	0.090		
8) Goal Change	2.3	1.2	-0.308	-0.572**	-0.682**	-0.418*	-0.127	-0.280	-0.097	
9) Goal Conflict	2.6	1.3	-0.501*	-0.577**	-0.573**	-0.481*	-0.297	-0.145	-0.472*	0.538**

** Correlation is significant at the 0.01 level (2-tailed).
* Correlation is significant at the 0.05 level (2-tailed).

Table 4: Regressions on achievement of technical objectives.

Variable	Model 1	Model 2	Model 3	Model 4	Model 5
Total Com.	0.81*				
Soft Com.		0.46			-0.08
Hard Com.			0.63**		0.66**
Hard Ratio				12.05**	
R^2	0.34	0.09	0.47	0.43	0.47
Adjusted R^2	0.31	0.05	0.45	0.41	0.43
F-statistic	11.830	2.317	20.580	17.580	9.924
Null Probability	0.02	0.14	0.00	0.00	0.00

$N = 25$ Projects; $\dagger p < .10$; $*p < .05$; $**p < .01$; $***p < .001$

the project?" While hard modes were perceived by management as important to project performance (e.g., averages of greater than five on the seven-point scale), the average of 6.4 for the archetypal soft mode was found to be significantly higher than the other averages at a 99% confidence level. As such, Hypothesis 1 was only partially supported. The evidence (i.e., mean responses to survey items) suggests that managers thought that softer modes, in particular, F2F meetings, were most important to project performance, even though response means were high for the harder modes as well.

However, when the actual association between communication mode and performance in terms of achieving technical objectives is examined, only hard modes, and not soft modes, are significant. This is seen in the correlations of Table 3 and the regression analysis of Table 4. Thus, Hypothesis 2 is not entirely supported. The evidence suggests that only hard communication modes were significantly associated with the achievement of technological objectives.

Hypothesis 3 was supported. The scale of total communication regressed on achievement of technological objectives, as well as the correlation data, was positive and significant.

Displayed in Table 5 is the regression analysis for the hypotheses concerning hard modes. The evidence suggests that hard communication modes were associated with incremental innovation, and thus, Hypothesis 4 is supported. The evidence also suggests that hard, but not soft, communication modes were associated with more defined problems, and thus, Hypothesis 5 was supported. Shown in Table 7 is regression analysis using a scale of the ratio of hard modes to total communication. This is an indication of the relative usage of each archetypal mode in a project, and the results from this analysis, as shown in Table 7, parallel those found for the modes when looked at independently.

Table 5: Regressions on hard-mode scale.

Variable	Model 1	Model 2	Model 3
Problems Defined	0.36*		0.31*
Incremental Technological Development		0.56*	0.50*
R^2	0.19	0.21	0.35
Adjusted R^2	0.15	0.17	0.29
F-statistic	5.267	6.014	5.838
Null Probability	0.03	0.02	0.009

N= 25 Projects; $\dagger p < .10$; $*p < .05$; $**p < .01$; $***p < .001$

Table 6: Regressions on soft-mode scale.

Variable	Model 1	Model 2	Model 3	Model 4
Goal Change	-0.39**			-0.35**
Goal Conflict		-0.24*	-1.36	-0.08
Goal Conflict (Quadratic)			0.20	
R^2	0.43	0.19	0.35	0.45
Adjusted R^2	0.41	0.17		0.40
F-statistic	17.486	5.430	5.990	8.920
Null Probability	0.00	0.03	0.008	0.00

N= 25 Projects; $\dagger p < .10$; $*p < .05$; $**p < .01$; $***p < .001$

Table 7: Regressions on ratio of hard-mode-to-total-communication scale.

Variable	Model 1	Model 2	Model 3	Model 4	Model 5	Model 6	Model 7	Model 8
Problems Defined	0.02*	0.08					0.02*	0.02*
Problems Defined (Quadratic)		-0.01						
Incremental Tech.			0.03*				0.03*	0.02†
Goal Change				-0.01				0.01
Goal Conflict					-0.02†	0.06		-0.01
Goal Conflict (Quadratic)						-0.01		
R^2	0.20	0.26	0.21	0.01	0.13	0.23	0.37	0.41
Adjusted R^2	0.17		0.18	-0.03	0.10		0.31	0.29
F-statistic	5.813	3.86	6.263	0.312	3.520	3.320	6.356	3.440
Null Probability	0.02	0.04	0.02	0.58	0.07	0.06	0.007	0.03

N= 25 Projects; $\dagger p < .10$; $*p < .05$; $**p < .01$; $***p < .001$

Table 8: Regressions on total communication scale.

Variable	Model 1	Model 2	Model 3	Model 4
Goal Change	-0.41**			-0.31*
Goal Conflict		-0.33**	-0.89	-0.19†
Goal Conflict (Quadratic)			0.10	
R^2	0.40	0.31	0.34	0.47
Adjusted R^2	0.37	0.28		0.43
F-statistic	15.133	10.136	5.63	9.865
Null Probability	0.00	0.00	0.01	0.00

N= 25 Projects; †p < .10; *p < .05; **p < .01; ***p < .001

Table 9: Regressions on achievement of technical objectives.

Variable	Model 1	Model 2	Model 3	Model 4
Problems Defined	0.23			
Incremental Tech.		0.62**		
Goal Change			-0.38*	
Goal Conflict				-0.49**
R^2	0.09	0.29	0.18	0.34
Adjusted R^2	0.05	0.26	0.14	0.31
F-statistic	2.188	4.972	9.571	11.898
Null Probability	0.15	0.005	0.04	0.00

N= 25 Projects; †p < .10; *p < .05; **p < .01; ***p < .001

Shown in Tables 6 and 7 are results contradicting the theoretical predictions made earlier. Hypothesis 6 was not supported. In fact, projects in which the main goals changed were negatively, and strongly, associated with all the scales of hard, soft, and total communications. This suggests that projects with changed goals may have resulted in, or been the result of, negative and destructive influences that resulted in, or were the result of, less communication among team participants. Although this study does not and cannot make judgments regarding causation (e.g., does low communication cause poor performance or vice versa?), the results in Table 8 confirm that goal change and total communication within projects were, in fact, negatively related.

Hypothesis 7 was also only partially supported. As seen in Tables 8 and 9, projects in which there were significant conflicts over goals were negatively and significantly related to the use of hard and soft modes, and in this case, goal conflict also had a significant negative relationship with project success. (Again, causation is speculative. It is impossible to tell in this study whether conflict caused poor performance or vice versa.) Conflict over goals in these types of multiorganizational projects often resulted in retreating to one's own organization. This parallels a significant finding from the analysis on knowledge creation factors that demonstrated that tension or chaos in collaborative R&D projects is often destructive and rarely "creative" (Johnson, 2002).

DISCUSSION

The results of the analysis suggest that there are moderating variables that may have the power to explain the varying relationship between communication modes and project performance. The findings lead to some practical implications to managerial practice in managing communication processes in virtual and collaborative R&D projects.

First, the results suggest that project managers need not worry too much about the utilization of expensive soft modes if and when the project's goals are agreed upon and the problems to be solved by the project team are clearly defined by management. The less that these conditions are met, the more likely soft modes need to be utilized to ensure the project is successful. In a number of cases, soft modes may not be needed. The development of the open source code for the operating system, Linux, is a case in point. This development was the result of a network of volunteer programmers acting as a true virtual team. One reason for the success of such a constructionist undertaking was the simultaneous existence of standard and variant versions, where the selected definition of the next generation was centrally controlled (Axelrod & Cohen, 1999). That is, when a problem in the operating system was defined (most often by the users of the system), decentralized "volunteer" programmers (also users of the system) worked on fixing the bug, but for the final adoption of the software, Linux's central management held the power to decide whether to keep the solutions generated. As such, problems were concretely defined by the programmer-users, but the ultimate goals (via adoption of the solutions) were made by central management.

A second major implication of the study points to the importance of the management of conflict and the changing of goals, which needs careful attention by project managers. The data from the study suggest that conflict within collaborative R&D project teams is associated with less overall communication among participants, not more, although it is difficult to determine what causes what. Shown in Table 8 is the relatively strong negative relationship. Conflict either resulted in less communication, or less communication resulted in more conflict. Anecdotal evidence from case studies of the projects examined suggests that both directions of causation may apply. It is easy to understand, however, that conflict cannot be resolved without communication and, in particular, without soft modes that allow for the expression of reconciliation in collaborative projects. Reconciliation may be difficult to convey via hard modes, especially when disagreement already exists between parties.

For example, in one of the projects studied, which was developing technology toward a multimodal microscope system, the sections of the initial project proposal were written separately by two major participants and were then spliced together. The resulting zeitgeist of the project environment was that the main goals differed substantially for various project members. The lead researchers for the project, which were at prestigious Canadian and U.S. universities, felt that the commercial partner would not commercialize the technology, because its expertise was in satellite optics engineering and not microscopy. Communication started off poor and remained languid for the entire life of the project. One potential project member dropped out early because of lack of communication. Interproject conflicts inevitably developed, and communication, when it took place, was often via hard modes. A typical example was a letter from a participant's lawyer regarding intellectual property issues and potential legal action. All in all, communication was poor. The overall result was that the project was suspended for 6 months, while the main financial sponsor, PRECARN, intervened and helped facilitate negotiation sessions on the future of the technology developed in the project. In the end, there was some measure of success, because the technological development was sound, and the intervention of PRECARN management helped to facilitate reconciliation. However, with better management and communication, the entire project may have been more successful and completed earlier, thus saving time, money, and aggravation in general.

While the results reported here bode well for the utilization of hard modes in virtual projects, a more interesting finding was the lack of association between soft modes and project success. While the specific hypotheses made were rejected, the findings fit with the theory developed. The lack of soft mode communication in projects with conflict and the associated poor performance are exactly what one would expect from the normative theory. Unfortunately, the small "n" makes multivariate analysis impossible, but the independent relationships between conflict, communication, and performance fit theoretical predictions. Of course, another reason for the lack of evidence for Hypotheses 6 and 7 may be that goal changes and conflict did not affect most of the projects examined in this research (e.g., the means for the goal changing and conflict items were only 2.3 and 2.6 on seven-point Likert scales). However, what appears to support the normative theory is that for those limited number of projects that were affected by conflict, the effects were most often adverse, as the one case study above indicates. Theory and practice suggests that in such situations, more communication, particularly utilizing soft modes, and perhaps a communications facilitator, as in the case example above, is necessary to realign project participants' commitment and shared understanding of the main problems to be solved. Further research is necessary to see if it is possible to overcome such barriers in communication purely through harder modes of communication. Already, however, the research of Schmidt, Montoya-Weiss, and Massey (2001) shows evidence of the superiority of virtual team decision making over F2F in some situations, and van Engelen, Kiewiet, and Terlouw (2001) described a methodology based on hard modes that improves new product development team performance via managing polarity, a concept related to conflicting interpretations of a situation or equivocality.

Overall, the findings of this research show that virtual collaborative R&D projects may not be at a disadvantage due their necessarily greater reliance on the use of hard modes of communication. What appears to be of utmost importance to the utilization of hard modes is the type of technological innovation and establishment of well-defined centralized goals associated with the project. The first may be beyond management's control, but the second is definitely something that management can utilize by making sure that project goals are well defined and actively managed by project managers. In terms of media richness theory, the findings suggest that low equivocality projects can utilize hard modes extensively, without adverse performance effects. Under these ideal conditions, hard modes can suffice for project success. However, if and when these projects undergo extensive goal changes or conflicts arise among project participants, then communication takes on greater importance, and specifically, the utilization of soft modes needs greater and more careful scrutiny. The general reaction upon the introduction of conflict is often to decrease communication in general and, ironically, soft communication modes specifically. This is the wrong thing to do in such cases. While conflict may be a good thing in generating new ideas for solving the problems faced by the project, the combination of conflict and lack of communication is a recipe for project failure. Soft modes in these types of situations will be more effective than hard modes because of the need to reestablish a shared understanding of the conflicting issues. Of course, in many situations of conflict, communications take the form of hard modes because of the unease that conflicting participants may feel in soft mode situations, like F2F meetings. In situations of deep conflict, the use of a facilitator or moderator to help in F2F meetings is suggested, based on the success of PRECARN's intervention in the case mentioned above. Of course, before a facilitator is approached, project management must recognize the conflict and the need for greater, not less, soft-mode communication.

As with all research, there are limitations to the generalizability of the findings. The biggest threat to generalizability concerning the recommendation to use primarily hard modes for virtual projects is that the types of projects examined in this research were engaged in intelligent systems innovations. As such, they are well suited to the use of computer-mediated technologies by their participants, both because the technologies developed are often digital in nature (making them ideal for hard mode communication) and because the participants are highly knowledgeable and experienced with digital forms of communication.

As an interviewee in one of the projects studied stated, "That's sort of a given in our industry — everybody's life is around e-mail. It's such an effective way of communicating." Less computer-sophisticated participants may not be as well suited to utilizing primarily hard modes successfully. However, with the increasing use of e-mail messaging, this issue should become less problematic. People involved in virtual teams are most likely to be recruited with computer skills anyway. Nevertheless, more research is needed in the area of communication mode to determine the nuances involved in general practice, including the effects on other definitions of project performance. For example, the limitations of this study meant focusing only on achievement of technological objectives, which is only one of many potential criteria of project success, albeit an important one. Regardless, it is hoped that the results reported here provide a small glimpse toward how to better manage communication in these virtual, collaborative projects.

CONCLUSION

The research reported here found, as might be expected, that conflict was associated with poor communication. But the fact that geographically dispersed collaborative R&D projects, with heavy use of hard modes of communication, might be at a disadvantage was not found, as projects primarily utilizing hard modes were also associated with success in achieving their technical objectives. Instead, it seems that careful design of virtual projects can create a context in which hard modes of communication will suffice. Thus, with careful design, hard modes of communication may create a sufficient sense of relationship or media richness to prevent the breakdown of communication that is associated with project difficulties. Managers who do not have the option of using soft communication modes like F2F meetings may take comfort in the knowledge that under certain conditions, they can successfully manage the communication processes that lead to positive project performance within the virtual collaborative R&D project.

REFERENCES

Allen, T. J. (1977). Managing the flow of technology: Technology transfer and the dissemination of technological information within the R&D organization. Cambridge, MA: MIT Press.

Allen, T. J., & Fusfield, A. R. (1975). Research laboratory architecture and the structuring of communications. *R & D Management, 5*, 153–164.

Axelrod, R., & Cohen, M. D. (1999). *Harnessing complexity: Organizational implications of a scientific frontier*. New York. The Free Press.

Boutellier, R., Gassmann, O., Macho, H., & Roux, M. (1998). Management of dispersed product development teams: The role of information technologies. *R & D Management, 28*(1), 13–25.

Daft, R. L., & Lengel, R. H. (1984). Information richness: A new approach to managerial behavior and organizational design. *Research in Organizational Behavior, 6*, 191–233.

Daft, R. L., & Lengel, R. H. (1986). Organizational information requirements, media richness and structural design. *Management Science, 32*(5), 554–571.

De Meyer, A. C. L. (1985). The flow of technological innovation in an R&D department. *Research Policy, 14*(6), 315–328.

Gassmann, O., & Zedtwitz, M. V. (1998). Organization of industrial R&D on a global scale. *R & D Management, 28*(3), 147–161.

Gassmann, O., & Zedtwitz, M. V. (1999). New concepts and trends in international R&D organization. *Research Policy, 28*(2,3).

Gerybadze, A., & Reger, G. (1999). Globalization of R&D: Recent changes in the management of innovation in transnational corporations. *Research Policy, 28*(2,3), 251–274.

Handy, C. (1995). Trust and the virtual organization. *Harvard Business Review, 73*(3), 40–48.

Hauptman, O. (1986). Influence of task type on the relationship between communication and performance: The case of software development. *R & D Management, 16*(2), 127–139.

Hedlund, J., Ilgen, D. R., & Hollenbeck, J. R. (1998). Decision accuracy in computer-mediated versus face-to-face decision-making teams. *Organizational Behavior and Human Decision Processes, 76*(1), 30–47.

Hough, E. A. (1972). Communication of technical information between overseas and head office laboratories. *R & D Management, 3*, 1–5.

Johnson, W. H. A. (2002). Assessing organizational knowledge creation theory in collaborative R&D projects. *International Journal of Innovation Management, 6*(4), 387–418.

Kirkman, B. L., Rosen, B., Gibson, C. B., Tesluk, P. E., & McPherson, S. O. (2002). Five challenges to virtual team success: Lessons from Sabre, Inc. *Academy of Management Executive, 16*(3), 67–79.

Kivimaki, M., Lansisalmi, H., Elovainio, M., et al. (2000). Communication as a determinant of organizational innovation. *R & D Management, 30*(1), 33–42.

Lewis, R. (1998). Membership and management of a "virtual" team: The perspectives of a research manager. *R & D Management, 28*(1), 5–12.

McDonough, E. F., & Kahn, K. B. (1996). Using "hard" and "soft" techniques for global new product development. *R & D Management, 26*(3), 241–253.

Nagpaul, P. S., & Pruthi, S. (1979). Problem-solving and idea-generation in R&D: The role of informal communication. *R & D Management, 9*(3).

Nemeth, C., & Staw, B. (1989). The trade-offs of social control and innovation in groups and organizations. *Advances in Experimental Social Psychology, 22*, 175–210.

Ocker, R., Hiltz, S. R., Turoff, M., & Fjermestad, J. (1996). The effects of distributed group support and process structuring on software requirements development teams: Results on creativity and quality. *Journal of Management Information Systems, 12*(3), 127–153.

Pasquale, S., Triscari, T., & Wallace, W. A. (1985). Reliability of communication flow in R&D organizations. *IEEE Transactions on Engineering Management, 32*(2), 91–97.

Patti, A. L., Gilbert, J. P., & Hartman, S. (1997). Physical co-location and the success of new product development projects. *Engineering Management Journal, 9*(3), 31–37.

Pinto, M. B., Pinto, J. K., & Prescott, J. E. (1993). Antecedents and consequences of project team cross-functional teams. *Management Science, 39*(10), 1281–1297.

Ritchie, E. (1977). Communication networks: Tools for the efficient management of R&D. *R & D Management, 7*, 85–88.

Rothwell, R., & Robertson, A. B. (1973). The role of communication in technological innovation. *Research Policy, 2*, 204–225.

Schmidt, J. B., Montoya-Weiss, M. M., & Massey, A. P. (2001). New product development decision-making effectiveness: Comparing individuals, face-to-face teams, and virtual teams. *Decision Sciences, 32*(4), 575–600.

Stasser, G., & Titus, W. (1987). Effects of information load and percentage of shared information on the dissemination of unshared information during group discussion. *Journal of Personality and Social Psychology, 51*, 81–93.

Tomlin, B. (1981). Inter-location technical communication in a geographically dispersed research organization. *R & D Management, 11*(1), 19–23.

van Engelen, J. M. L., Kiewiet, D. J., & Terlouw, P. (2001). Improving performance of product development teams through managing polarity. *International Studies of Management & Organization, 31*(1), 46–63.

Yin, R. K. (1989). Case study research: Design and methods. Thousand Oaks, CA: Sage.

Yoo, Y., & Kanawattanachai, P. (2001). Developments of transactive memory systems and collective mind in virtual teams. *International Journal of Organizational Analysis, 9*(2), 187–208.

Zack, M. H. (1994). Electronic messaging and communication effectiveness in an ongoing work group. *Information & Management, 26*(4), 231–241.

APPENDIX

The items concerning managers' beliefs of the varying importance of communication modes are listed in Table 2.

Items concerning frequency of communication came from survey questions asking respondents to choose along a seven-point scale from never to often:

How often were various communication modes used (Never — Often):

- Face-to-face meetings were used as important sources of ideas.
- Face-to-face meetings were used for developing a shared understanding between members of the project.
- Face-to-face meetings helped develop shared technical skills.
- Written documents were used to express new ideas.
- Written documents were used to increase learning in the project.

Total communication was determined from a scale consisting of all of the items ($\pm = 79\%$). Soft modes were determined from a scale consisting of the first three items ($\pm = 76\%$), and hard modes from a scale consisting of the last two items ($\pm = 80\%$). Alphas are all Cronbachs alpha and are considered reasonable, given that anything between 60 and 90% is generally considered good.

Items concerning Hypotheses 4 through 7 came from survey questions asking respondents to choose along a seven-point scale from agree to disagree (i.e., *Agree — Disagree*):

1. Incremental innovation
    • The technology is a significant incremental improvement over previous technology.
2. Problem definition
    • Project management defined all the significant problems facing the project.
3. Goal change
    • The project's main goals changed during the project.
4. Goal conflict
    • There was significant conflict over the goals of the project.

The achievement of technical objectives was determined from a two-item scale ($\pm = 0.72$), where the two items were as follows:

- Overall, the project was successful in meeting most of its original goals.
- All of the original technological objectives were met.

Chapter XI

Technology and Virtual Teams

Sharmila Pixy Ferris, William Paterson University, USA

Maureen C. Minielli,
Indiana University-Purdue University at Indianapolis, USA

ABSTRACT

Explored in this chapter are available technological tools for virtual teams. Beginning with asynchronous messaging systems, the technology of e-mail, discussion lists, electronic bulletin boards, Web logs, and short message service are reviewed. Next, synchronous messaging systems, including chat, instantaneous interactive messaging, and videoconferencing are examined. Then, the chapter turns to information-exchange/data-management systems and focuses on tools like the Internet, File Transfer Protocol, Gopher, Telnet, the World Wide Web, and Internet alternatives. Commercial (proprietary) groupware packages and specialized conferencing tools conclude our exploration.

INTRODUCTION

Considered in this chapter are the software and communication technologies that enable and facilitate virtual teams. Virtual teams utilize a wide range of technological applications, primarily, but not limited to, computer, audiovisual, and phone applications. Our focus in discussing the support system technologies employed by virtual teams will be on the team member as end user rather than on the hardware, as installation, programming, and setup as considerations of hardware and programming are not in the domain of this book.

DEFINITION OF TERMS

Two broad terms are traditionally considered in a discussion of the technologies utilized by virtual teams: decision support systems and group support systems. As stated in Simon (1965), decision support systems are "heuristic programming techniques" (p. 47) that support decision making. As decision support systems are not specific to team/group work, the term "group decision support systems" is used to refer to systems that support group decision making. While the term "distributed group decision support systems" is sometimes used in reference to virtual groups, a more commonly used term in use is "group support systems." The latter has come to refer to computer software and hardware used specifically to support group functions and processes (Easterbrook et al., 1992; Miranda, 1994). While group support systems (GSS) are associated with group decision support systems (GDSS), GSS is often used as a broader term. GSS can be defined (Narayan, 1997) as a "diverse set of tools to facilitate individual activities, group process activities, and coordination related activities to be undertaken in either synchronous or asynchronous manner" (p. 1). It should be noted that GSS often comprise technologies that are not necessarily limited to computers and are often used in everyday life, such as telephones and videoconferencing. Noncomputer and computer technologies may be determined to be GSS if they possess one of the following characteristics: "it fosters collaboration between people, it fosters the sharing of information, and it enables the communication between groups of people" (Burns, 1995 in Brusic, 2003, p. 1).

A third, related, term used in the literature on virtual teams is "computer-supported collaborative (or cooperative) work." Popularized by the seminal work of Bowers and Benford (1991), the term encompasses computer systems, software, and hardware (Scrivener & Clark, 1994), in addition to such traditional methods of communication as face-to-face interaction, audio systems, and video systems (McGrath & Hollingshead, 1994).

Whatever the terminology used, the technological support systems used by virtual teams encompass a wide range of technological applications that allow individuals and teams to communicate, exchange information, interact collaboratively, and manage data, within the group and outside of the group, synchronously and asynchronously. To organize our discussion of the technologies used by teams, we will use the classification scheme of messaging/conferencing systems, information-exchange/data-management systems, and commercial groupware packages.

MESSAGING SYSTEMS

Messaging systems enable and facilitate communication among team members. Communication among team members can be one-to-one or one-to-many and synchronous or asynchronous. The earliest methods using computers and the Internet were largely asynchronous, with limited synchronous communication. The advent of the World Wide Web and wireless technology increasingly allows people to use messaging systems to communicate in real time. In this section, we will consider asynchronous messaging (e-mail, discussion lists, bulletin/message boards, Weblogs, and short message service, or SMS), synchronous messaging (chat and instantaneous interactive messaging), and conferencing.

Asynchronous Computer Messaging Systems

E-mail

E-mail is the simplest form of messaging. It involves one person composing an electronic (computer) message that can be sent to one or multiple recipients through a networked computer — that is, via electronic data-transfer networks. E-mail messages vary in form from oral or "phone-like" messages to literate or "electronic memos and letters." Although e-mail has some similarities to phone and traditional memos and letters, it differs in important ways from both. E-mail has built-in information-management features that allow for easy storage and retrieval, as well as easy editing, replying and sending attachments.

E-mail today has become about as "transparent" and easy to use as the telephone for interpersonal communication. Perhaps for this reason, e-mail is today the primary means of communication in organizations (Barnes, 2003). Wireless access to the Internet frees users from the constraints of a networked computer and allows for greater flexibility in the use of e-mail. Today, e-mail can be sent and received from means other than the traditional desktop or laptop computer. By far, the most common alternatives are handheld Personal Digital Assistants (PDAs). Newer cell phone technologies, with embedded computing and wireless access to the Internet, also provide easy alternatives to the computer.

Audio and video e-mail

Although e-mail has traditionally been text-based, evolutions in the technology increasingly facilitate vocal and visual features for e-mail. The cost of such software is currently high, but some freeware exists. One example of a freeware telephony program melding voicemail and e-mail is the Talk99 freeware from MediaRing.com (http://www.mediaring.com). Talk99 allows computer users to call others computer users for free, and it incorporates a VoizMail feature that allows users to send voicemail in the form of an e-mail message.

Web cameras provide a newer technology that takes e-mail a step beyond its "phone" and "mail functions" by providing visual and (with a microphone) verbal elements to e-mail. Although audio and video e-mails are not yet popular, the advent of cheaper technology may be the catalyst for change. Today, sending video e-mail requires the simplest of "add-on" technologies to the average user's personal computer: cameras and software. Video e-mail software today is cheap and accessible. Some examples are CyberLink's VideoLive Mail (www.cyberlink-usa.com/) and Cornell University's CU-See Me (www.cuworld.com/). Most commercial groupware (such as Lotuses' Domino® and Microsoft Windows® XP Messenger) also have embedded software that enables videomail.

Monthly subscription services are available to enable those who wish to incorporate added visual and verbal dimensions to their e-mail on a regular basis. One example is Talkway® Communication's VMailTalk Express™ (www.talkway.com), which, for a monthly fee, provides a webcam, a 12-month account, and 25 video e-mails per month. A more sophisticated commercial e-mail program is Avistar® Communications vBrief™ video e-mail (www.avistar.com) that allows users to create, manage, distribute, and track video e-mail to single recipients or to groups. Because video e-mail messages from vBrief are wrapped in a custom-designed HTML template and contain streaming video, personalized text messages, and links to Web pages and attachments, they have the advantage that no special software is required by recipients to view vBrief messages, which appear in a recipient's regular e-mail inbox (*Business Wire*, October 2002). The variety of choices and the ease of accessibility and use make e-mail, the simplest form of messaging, one of the most widely used by virtual teams.

Electronic bulletin boards

Electronic bulletin boards (BBSs) are "worldwide, posted public messages on a wide variety of subjects" (Lamb, 1999). BBS services provide bulletin boards where messages can be posted by individuals and read by groups. BBS's are often linked to particular projects or classes, providing a forum in which participants can view assignments and readers' responses. Because BBS's function in much the same manner as bulletin boards in public forums, they are of limited use to virtual teams. They are a means of providing connected or disconnected individuals with a means of sharing knowledge and information, and they help close the distance and isolation gap between individuals. As stated in O'Leary (2002), BBS's create intimate communities among people who may be dispersed around the world. They bring together those with common interests and concerns who would otherwise never connect.

Those who like the listserv or BBS formats and would like to use them on the Web can do so through links to their personal Web pages. Those who cannot, or would rather not, link team tasks to personal Web pages can use InsidetheWeb (http://www.insidetheweb.com) to post messages on a bulletin board and enable threaded discussions. Inside theWeb is a free bulletin-board service that can be used to post messages, can serve as a forum for extended discussion, and can be used to keep track of group discussions. Designers can set up parameters for where the message board is housed, posted, and responded to.

Another freeware program message board available on the Web is ngBook (www.bigfoot.com/~huangng). While largely geared toward educators, it allows for the creation of a discussion forum, as well as a BBS-style posting of comments.

Discussion lists

Discussion lists provide an asynchronous communication medium with some similarities to e-mail. Discussion lists, such as listservs and newsgroups, allow communicators to post and read messages. While neither newsgroups nor listservs are primary means of communication for teams, moderated listservs are of the most use to team members. Moderated listservs are generally subscription based and allow for threaded discussion among participants. Team members can set up discussion lists through any networked computer system with the capacity to process and store messages from list members.

Weblogs

Weblogs (or blogs) are a Web-based variation of discussion lists, with the difference that they are individually maintained journaling sites. Individuals regularly post opinions, commentary, and analysis on their blogs. Discussion is facilitated through the provision of linked e-mail addresses so that readers can engage in dialogue. Like other technological innovations, Weblogs have integrated themselves into the corporate world. Business software like Manilla™(http://manila.userland.com) and Traction® (http://www.traction software.com) now allow corporate intranet teams to converse with each other. This software serves as a "community-building and coordinating tool" (Herman, 2003). Business blogs also allow for instantaneous communication between team members, for tracking of team communication and decision making, for communication with clients and other business partners, and for serving as informational references for team members and clients to consult (Herman, 2003). Other Weblog software vendors include Blogger™ (http://www.blogger.com), Moveable Type (http://www.moveabletype.org), and phpNuke (http://www.phpnuke.org).

Short message service

At this writing, short message service (SMS) is a growing phenomenon in the United States and Canada. Already popular in Europe and Asia, SMS allows wireless individuals to exchange short (less than 160 characters) text messages with other wireless users. At 5-20 cents per message, SMS messages are growing in popularity in the business sector, for they are typically cheaper than voicemail messages (*Computer Weekly*, 2003). As one business user puts it, "SMS is a way for some to keep costs down during peak hours" (Dickinson, 2002).

Business communications specialist TOPCALL noted that many "businesses feel SMS is a highly efficient and powerful way of alerting recipients to time-specific information" (*Business Wire*, 2003). SMS is a convenient method for sending and receiving information (Denison, 2003) and is an "effective, affordable, intrusive and yet discreet communication" tool (Wilfahrt, 2002). In addition, it is a "silent" form of communication (January, 2002) that allows users to communicate with each other as well as allows users to send immediate messages to several recipients (Devi, 2003).

According to Telephony (2002), there were approximately 13.4 million SMS users in the United States, and that number is expected to increase to 95.1 million by 2006. That growth is due in part to the six major U.S. cellular companies allowing open SMS among their systems (Hamilton, 2003). Users will no longer need to belong to the same cellular network to send and receive SMS messages.

SMS offers several benefits to virtual teams. Global applications, like general staff and other internal communication, as well as specific applications, like reminders of or changes in meeting times, or quick answers to questions, are some of the advantages SMS offers (Mills, 2003). The limited character length allows for "straight-to-the-point" messages to be created (Yap, 2003), thus discouraging lengthy or superfluous messages. Communication can occur when voice calls would be inappropriate or unfeasible (Bermant, 2003), e.g., during meetings and presentations. In addition, with the advent of Multimedia Messaging Service (MMS), text messages can now be accompanied with photographs and videos (Fitzsimmons, 2003). Although slow to catch on in the United States, SMS appears to be poised to integrate into business communications along the same lines as the cellular phone and the handheld computer.

Synchronous Computer Messaging Systems

Instantaneous interactive messaging

Synchronous interactive communication programs are available in many different platforms. The name of the program depends on the platform used – in UNIX platforms "Talk" and "nTalk", on BM VM/CMS systems "Tell" and VAX systems "Send" and in the popular America Online software "Instant Messenger" or "IM." All of these systems allow for real-time text-based communication among communicators. Because communication is in real time, participants must be online at the same time. However, they are still free of the constraints of geographical presence and, with new technologies and embedded computing, as in PDAs and cellular phones, communicators are not locked into one location. To facilitate the use of Talk/Tell/Send/IM, most systems allow participants to check whether others are logged on at the same time, employing user IDs or preestablished lists.

Since its adoption by such subscription services as America Online, Yahoo, and MSN, synchronous communication using freeware has achieved great popularity, and it expanded into use in business and industry. As stated in Schwartz (2002), "According to Stamford, Conn.-based Gartner Inc, 42% of business Internet users use IM in the workplace, even though 70% of IT departments don't support it."

Members of virtual teams using synchronous interactive messaging should note that the netiquette governing the use of Talk, Tell, and Send messages in corporate and higher education environments largely does not exist on popular software platforms like AOL's IM. While it is considered inappropriate to send frivolous Talk/Tell/Send messages [a breach significant enough to cost the user their computer privileges, according to Sudweeks, Collins, and December (1995)], the same does not hold true for IM users. Team members may be better advised to refrain from using IM for task purposes.

The U.S. Navy uses Lotus® Sametime® messaging software for its ship-to-ship and submarine-to-shore communications. As Schwartz (2002) pointed out, "The Navy values having written transcripts of all orders and communiqués, which is possible using Sametime." Other software packages include QuickConference® (http://www.quickconference.com) and Ikimbo's Omniprise® (http://www.ikimbo.com).

Despite the lack of an industry standard, and the inability of different messaging systems to communicate with each other, the use of IM in businesses is growing. Schwartz (2002) states, "IDC in Framingham, Mass., predicts that worldwide, corporate IM use will shoot up from 5.5 million users in 2000 to 180 million in 2004."

Chat systems

The simplest form of online conferencing is chat, a software protocol that enables participants to interact virtually. Internet Relay Chat (IRC) is an Internet-based network that enables multiple communicators to synchronously interact in an online environment. IRC is easily undertaken by connecting to a server on the IRC network. Because of its ease of access, IRC can be a convenient and powerful meeting tool for virtual teams. However, issues of privacy arise, as IRC is a public forum and thus cannot exclude other participants. Some feel that the use to which users have put IRC — often for interaction of a sexual or fantasy nature — gives it a dubious reputation (Sudweeks, Collins, & December, 1995).

Commercial networks and proprietary groupware and course management software also have chat systems that provide cyber meeting places for real-time communication. Privacy and related issues are of significant concern on commercial networks, where chat rooms largely provide forums for frivolous social interaction. Several chat rooms designed specifically for business and industry use exist, including WebTrain (http://www.webtrain.com), Magma Communication's Chat Server (http://www1.magma.ca), ParaChat™ (http://www.parachat.com), Volano® Chat (http://www.volano.com), and divine Expressions® (http://www.divine.com).

Synchronous Conferencing Systems

While they also enable synchronous and interactive communication, conferencing systems are more specifically designed to facilitate synchronous virtual meetings than chat or IM. While many corporate and higher education facilities maintain on-site teleconference rooms (with computer-controlled audiovisual transmission between locations), the value of computer-enabled conferencing comes from allowing team members at separate geographic locations to work together in real time.

Proprietary conferencing packages

Various free proprietary software packages currently exist to facilitate computer conferencing. One example is Microsoft® Netmeeting® (http://www.microsoft.com/windows/netmeeting). This downloadable software allows users to engage in audio- and videoconferencing. In addition, NetMeeting 3.0 software also offers real-time white boards, online chats, file transfer, and program sharing.

Another example of conferencing freeware is Sun Microsystems' (freeware.thesphere.com) Java-oriented (mostly educational) software programs and iVisit (http://www.ivisit.org). At the time of this writing, Sun Microsystems has the Java® Shared Data Toolkit, Java Web Server™ and Java WorkShop™ available for download.

Videoconferencing

While similar to computer conferencing, videoconferencing uses Web cameras or other hardware to provide visual images of the communicators. Videoconferencing has the advantage of "richer" communication, as it "returns" some of the dimensions of traditional F2F communication lost in computer conferencing. Verbal and visual aspects of communication are present in videoconferences. High-end business videoconferencing vendors include First Virtual Communications (http://www.fvc.com) and Polycom iPower (formerly PictureTel) (http://www.polycom.com), which operate over private ISDN lines or private IP networks, and lower-end vendors like GrassRoots Communications' Grass Roots Live (formerly FocusFocus.com) (http://

www.grassrootscommunication.com) and SeeSaw.com by Reality Fusion (http://www.realityfusion.com) (Metz, 2001).

Videoconferencing systems can also be built around chat systems, incorporating audio and visual elements. An example of a computer program that allows users to broadcast live audio and video to others, and provides the ability for all viewers to participate interactively, is WebCast ProServer (http://bant.ms.ornl.gov). A related service is WebCast Personal ICQ® (http://www.icq.com), which is an Internet telephony software package that weds message boards, chat rooms, data conferencing, and file transfer onto the same site. Several other software programs exist that allow for real-time business collaboration, including Netopia® Timbuktu Pro (http://www.netopia.com), Genesys' Meeting Center (http://www.genesys.com), Altiris® Carbon Copy (http://www.altiris.com), and Tandberg® Management Suite (http://www.tandberg.net).

INFORMATION-EXCHANGE/ DATA-MANAGEMENT SYSTEMS

Finding, exchanging, and managing information, and sharing data and information resources are essential to the functioning of teams. While virtual teams have access to all the information resources of traditional teams, in this chapter, we will only consider information and data management resources that are technological in nature.

The Internet

The Internet as it exists today is a vast system of networked computers, reaching across the globe. The Internet originated in the 1970s with the first wide-area computer network, ARPANET, the Advanced Research Projects Agency Network, a government-sponsored experiment that linked research universities and the military. ARPANET grew to encompass other networks, including NSFNET and tens of thousands of local, regional, national, and international networks (Barnes, 2003; Sudweeks, Collins, & December, 1995). The Internet utilized packet switching and communication protocols to enable the transmission and sharing of information across the Internet (Barnes, 2003). Today, the global network that is the Internet houses and accesses enormous amounts of information and is the single largest information resource in existence.

The immense amount of information on the Internet requires shared communication protocols and necessitates software programs to search, retrieve, and manage information.

File Transfer Protocol (FTP)

File Transfer Protocol (FTP) is a program for transferring information and public domain software from one computer location to another. The host computer stores (archives) and maintains information, which can be obtained by any user using "anonymous FTP." The program ARCHIE is a useful related service that can be used to search the contents of most FTP archive sites.

Although FTP protocols were developed before the advent of the World Wide Web, post-Web iterations of FTP exist. Companies such as Netmanage (www.ftp.com) provide services for users to access host applications from a desktop or a browser; publish host screens as customized, intuitive Web pages; integrate host applications with other business systems; and transform host applications from a desktop or a browser.

Gopher

A second network information tool is Gopher, a program developed by the University of Minnesota. Gopher's usefulness comes from its ability to find information on many different computers on the Internet, including public access databases, online books, news, and phone directories. The program VERONICA works with Gopher, providing the ability to search keywords (Sudweeks, Collins, & December, 1995).

Telnet

A software program that can be used with FTP and Gopher is Telnet, a software application that connects remote computers, generally through a telnet port. That is, users "telnet in" from one networked location to another. Telnet allows users to execute commands remotely through a telnet interface (Telnet, 2003). Telnet's usefulness as an information management tool comes from its ability to obtain information from public access databases.

Internet Alternatives

To bypass the delays, slowdowns, and interruptions that networked computers on the Internet are sometimes subject to, a number of alternative networks are in development. Access to these alternatives can expedite the working of virtual teams. Some of these alternatives are Internet II, National Science Foundation's very-high-performance Barebone Network Service (vBNS), the Department of Energy's Energy Sciences network (Esnet), and NASA's Research and Education Network (NREN). The alternative network that received the most publicity is Internet II. This faster, more powerful network was set into motion in 1997 by 34 universities. The plan was to connect the universities through a new network of high-speed cables. Internet II was projected to run up to 1000 times faster than the existing Internet, with correspondingly increased capacity and potentials. Thus, not only would communication be improved but also information management features could be enhanced, as would audio and video capabilities.

World Wide Web

One aspect of the Internet demands special consideration. The World Wide Web is the largest part of the Internet today, globe spanning, still growing, and the single largest source of information in existence. The Web is an Internet medium that uses hypertextual links (Barnes, 2003), an "interconnected assortment of Internet computer servers that conform to the same network interface protocols" (p. 11). Put more simply (Cozic, 1997), it is "a collection of commercial, educational, and personal 'Web sites' that contain electronic pages of text and graphics" (p. 6). The Web brings together, to a hitherto unprecedented extent, research, history, literature, art, science, news, and entertainment, as well as commercial information and personal Web pages. The Web also provides information in multimedia form: graphics and audio and video material are easily and freely available. Through the use of search engines, virtual teams can access data, information, and records on almost any issue of interest. As of 2001, there were over 26,000,000 host sites on the Web (Barnes, 2003, p. 68).

The remarkable amount of information on the Web necessitates specialized software tools for information location and retrieval. Browsers are programs that enable the finding, interpretation, and display of documents in hypertext markup language (HTML). They provide a "point-and-click" function that facilitates the utilization of the Web as an information source. The first text-based browser evolved into today's popular Netscape® Navigator, with rival browsers such as Windows® Internet Explorer (Barnes, 2003). Miniature browsers in PDAs and cell phones make wireless access to the Web possible.

Search engines are related software tools that help users locate and retrieve information on the Web. Both search engines (such as Yahoo!® and AltaVista™) and meta-search engines (such as Google™ Dogpile®, ProFusion, WebCrawler®, MetaCrawler®, and Ask Jeeves®) exist free to all users, with some competition among providers.

Online Databases

The Internet and Web enable access to thousands of online databases, which have made collections of information available online. Library catalog systems (OPACs), specialized information (scientific, legal, medical, etc.), news services, business and academic databases, to name but a few, are all online. Library systems, like the New York Public Library (http://www.nypl.org), newspapers (see, for example, the *New York Times*, www.nytimes.com), and television news sources (such as CNN, see www.cnn.com) all provide access to archived information online. Similarly, many universities make academic

databases available to both account holders and nonaccount holders. The sheer
number of databases available today makes a detailed consideration impossible
here. One suggested resource to learn more about online databases is Radford,
Barnes, and Barr's (2002) *Web Research: Selecting, Evaluating and Citing.*

COMMERCIAL (PROPRIETARY) GROUPWARE PACKAGES

So abundant is the number of proprietary groupware systems now available,
that a detailed consideration is beyond the scope of this chapter. But the pivotal
role commercial groupware plays in the working of virtual teams calls for a
discussion, even if limited in scope. This section will, therefore, consider
representative commercial groupware from three perspectives: comprehensive
groupware packages as provided by commercial giants (Microsoft, Novell, and
Netscape), specialized (and smaller) conferencing providers (eStudio, Vermics,
and the National Center of Supercomputing Applications), and course management software (BlackBoard, eCollege, and WebCT). Additional information on
the host of other commercial software systems can be found on the Groupware
yellow pages, (http://www.csua.berkeley.edu/~mogul/groupware/), which provide links to academic and business resources, or through discussion on the
Group Support Systems List.

Comprehensive Proprietary Groupware packages

Several software giants have long-developed groupware packages, some
reaching back across three decades. In the category of software packages
developed specifically as groupware are included Lotus Notes® and Domino®
(http://www.lotus.com), Novell® GroupWise®, (http://www.novell.com/prod-
ucts/groupwise), Netscape Collabra (http://wp.netscape.com/collabra/v3.5/
index.html), Fujitsu Teamware® (http://www.teamware.com), and NCSA
Habanero® (http://www.isrl.uiuc.edu/isaac/Habanero/). Other software systems [such as Microsoft Exchange (http://www.microsoft.com/exchange/) and
Oracle® Collaboration Suite (http://www.oracle.com/ip/deploy/cs/), as well as
various Course Management Software] have larger functions but can also be
applied as collaborative tools. Here, Lotus Notes and Domino, Microsoft
Exchange, and Netscape Collabra will be considered as representative software.

Lotus Notes and Domino

The most widely used groupware system (in terms of market penetration)
is Lotus Notes, and Domino, the Web-enabled version of Notes. As stated on its
Web site (Lotus, 2003), Notes is an integrated collaborative environment that

presents "comprehensive messaging and collaborative application development capabilities in one integrated solution." Messaging through e-mail and threaded discussions, information management through shared databases, data exchange across different platforms in real time, and custom application development are possible. Web functions are enabled through Domino.

Microsoft Exchange

Lotus' major competitor is Microsoft Exchange. Although many users are familiar with Exchange for e-mail and scheduling capabilities, the software can function as a comprehensive groupware package, with messaging in the form of e-mail, instant messaging, Internet voicemail, and chat services. Information and data management as well as conferencing functions exist through the Exchange 2000 Conferencing Server that provides data-, audio-, and videoconferencing, as well as application sharing and browser access to all Web Store content with user-friendly URLs.

Netscape Collabra

Netscape Collabra is an online groupware tool. Messaging tools include e-mail and online discussions. Specific groups of users can be defined with access control. Information management tools include online information exchange, links to newsgroups, and prioritization of postings or messages.

Specialized Conferencing Tools

Far more than comprehensive groupware systems, companies providing specialized conferencing tools are rapidly growing. In this section, we will discuss three representative providers (eStudio, Vermics, and the National Center of Supercomputing Applications). Other conferencing tools include Office Clip™ s Office Clip-In-A-Box (http://www.officeclip.com), Hyperwave's eKnowledge (http://www.hyperwave.com), Flypaper™ TeamSpace (http://www.flypaper.com), and Groove Networks' Groove Workspace™ (http://www.groove.net).

A growing trend in business communication is to use Web services or application service providers (ASPs) instead of comprehensive proprietary groupware packages. Web services and ASPs use the World Wide Web to allow for project collaboration between multiple partners and organizations (*New Straits Times-Management Times*, 2002). Alwang (2001) pointed out that "web-based collaboration provides a cost-effective solution without the headaches inherent with supporting complex in-house systems." Services like Thurport's HotOffice™ (http://www.hotoffice.com), OnProject's OnProject (http://www.onproject.com), NetDocuments® Enterprise (http://www.netdocuments.com), Punch WebGroups® (http://www.punchnetworks.com), and TeamDrive (http://www.teamstream.com) all narrowly focus on document management, as do numerous other specialized services. Services like Entellium™ (http://www.entellium.com), eRoom™ (http://www.documentum.com), and BlueStep™ (http://www.bluestep.net) are broader in nature and offer several services and subservices, including communication services.

National Center of Supercomputing Applications' Habanero

As stated in Narayan (1997), this software system represents "a new generation of universally accessible collaborative environments built by developing and extending existing robust frameworks" (p. 3.). It is a Java-based system that provides applications that let the user interact with existing messaging, conferencing, and information management tools on the Web, e.g., whiteboard, "clip-n-ship," local neighborhood, Telnet, and chat (Habanero, 2003).

Vermics

A commercial software package that bridges course management software and commercial groupware is Vermics. This distance-learning distribution program has excellent applicability to teams in higher education and business settings. To some extent, Vermics provides messaging, conferencing, and information management tools. Messaging options include two-way audio and video interaction; conferencing includes interactive collaborations, interactive white boards, shared presentation control, and use of DVD, VHS, and document cameras; and information management options include guided Web browsing, access to existing Web content, and application sharing. Because the Vermics platform is based on standard Internet Protocol (IP) and PC technology, this commercial software is easily used in higher education and industry (*Business Wire*, July 2002).

e-StudioLIVE

This desktop Web-casting system provides limited messaging tools with interactive features such as surveys and text chat. Its value to virtual teams lies in its multimedia conferencing and information management tools. E-StudioLIVE software supplies live and on-demand streaming audio and video, PowerPoint® slides, guided Web tours, Web graphics, and multimedia online presentations with interactive features. This software could be useful to team members who meet virtually to present information, work on product development, and conduct some (although limited) problem solving or decision making.

Representative Course Management Software

In higher education, most of the commonly used instructional technology software packages contain features that are useful to virtual teams, as will be demonstrated here. Such software was created for educational use, primarily as course support, or as a vehicle for online courses. However, the usefulness of course management software for virtual teams goes beyond the classroom. Faculty and staff members at institutions of higher education with subscriptions to the software will find it useful for facilitating virtual team functioning. (Note that subscriptions are not necessary to use course management software, as free instructional technology software programs exist. See, for example, ThinkWave Educator, ClassBuilder, NgBook and Class Information Manager.) With student and other virtual teams in mind, groupware features of the three most used course management systems will be considered here: WebCT, Blackboard and eCollege (comparison data obtained from Edutools, 2003).

BlackBoard 6.0

BlackBoard offers virtual team options comparable to comprehensive proprietary groupware. Messaging tools include e-mail to individuals and groups, with a file attachment option. Discussion lists options exist, with posts possible in plain text, formatted text, or html, with attachments and URLs. Threaded discussions can be viewed by date and by thread. Conferencing tools are adequate. Chat and internal groups are options. Private chat rooms can be created, and all chats are archived. Internal small groups can be created, with their own whiteboards, discussion forums, and synchronous tools. Information management and data resource options include file exchange, with options to upload files to a private or shared group folder. Whiteboards also exist, with image and PowerPoint uploading and group Web browsing. Whiteboard sessions are archived.

WebCT 3.8 and Vista 1.2

While similar to the previous platform, WebCT offers more groupware features. Messaging functions are expanded: participants can e-mail individuals and groups and attach files, they can also archive files and forward messages to external e-mail accounts. E-mail is searchable by subject lines. The use of discussion lists is similar, with posts in plain text, formatted text, or html, with attachments and URLs. Discussions can be viewed by date and thread and also by topic. Conferencing is broader, as up to four simultaneous group discussions in private chat rooms are supported, with archived chats. Internal groups can be created, with separate discussion environments and shared group presentation folders. Information management and data resources are more limited here, with files uploaded to a group folder. Whiteboards are supported.

ECollege AU

While sharing many features with the two previous platforms considered here, this software offers some notable added features. Messaging tools include e-mail to individuals and groups, with a file attachment option, but e-mail can also be spell-checked and sent via a searchable address book. Discussion lists options exist, with posts possible in plain text, formatted text, or html, with attachments and URLs. Threaded discussions can be viewed not only by date and thread but also by topic. Private chat rooms can be created, and all chats are archived. Conferencing tools are a little stronger. Chat and internal groups exist, with archived private chat. Internal small groups can be created, with their own whiteboards, discussion forums, and synchronous tools, as well as assignments, activities, assessments, group e-mail lists, and journal areas. Information management and data resources are a little broader, with file exchange, options to upload files to a private or shared group folder, and archived whiteboards with image, PowerPoint uploading, group Web browsing, and polling. Another added feature here is virus protection.

CONCLUSION

With the rapidly expanding use of virtual teams, particularly after September 11, 2001, we see a greater need for suitable technology. Focusing on the end-user rather than on the hardware, we surveyed in this chapter the existing support systems technologies that are available to virtual teams. Asynchronous messaging systems like e-mail, discussion lists, bulletin/message boards, Weblogs and short message services, synchronous messaging systems like chat and instantaneous interactive messaging, and conferencing were examined. In addition, the use of information-exchange/data-management systems, like the Internet, FTP, Gopher, Telnet, the World Wide Web, and Internet alternatives were examined. Commercial (proprietary) groupware packages and specialized conferencing tools conclude our examination.

As technology advances and becomes more accessible and easier to use, we will see increasing use. Virtual teams now span continents and time zones, 24 hours a day, seven days a week. Solomon (2001) stated, "As businesses become more interconnected and more global, they must learn to make faster and smarter strategic decisions, and to take advantage of technological advancements." Virtual teams need to take advantage of all resources available to them, especially computer technology, to maximize development and growth and minimize problems and errors that can arise when working in cyberspace.

REFERENCES

Alwang, G. (2001, October 30). Web collaboration. *PC Magazine*. Available online: http://www.pcmag.com/article2/0,4149,71267,00.asp

Barnes, S. B. (2003). *Computer-mediated communication*. New York: Allyn & Bacon.

Benest, I. D., & Dukic, D. (1993). Computer supported teamwork. In D. Diaper, & C. Sanger (Eds.), *CSCW in practice* (pp. 127–150). New York: Springer-Verlag.

Bowers, J. M., & Benford, S. D. (Eds.). (1991). *Studies in computer supported cooperative work* (pp. 211–224). New York: North-Holland.

Burns, N. (1995). Groupware: Myths and realities. Cited in I. Brusic, Groupware classification schemes. *Human-Computer Interaction CS6751.*

Business Wire. (2002, July 29). Vermics breaks new ground with distance learning solution enabling onsite delivery of live, interactive, instructor-led courses. Lexis-Nexis Database.

Business Wire. (2002, October 21). Avistar launches vBrief video e-mail messaging product. Lexis-Nexis Database.

Business Wire. (2003, June 10). TOPCALL helps businesses discover the value of text; Research reveals the top ten applications that are paving the way for SMS use in critical enterprise communications. Lexis-Nexis Database.

Cashing in on the SMS phenomenon. (2003, March 20). *Computer Weekly.* Retrieved July 19, 2003 from EBSCOHost.

Cozic, C. P. (1997). Introduction. *The Future of the Internet.* San Diego, CA: Greenhaven Press.

Denison, D. C. (2003, February 3). RU ready 4 SMS? Young consumers overseas have embraced the wireless experience of short messaging service. Now more than ever U.S. cellphone users are catching on to the text-messaging craze. *Boston Globe.* Lexis-Nexis Database.

Devi, C. (2003, March 17). Trends from text messaging culture. *New StraitsTimes -Management Times.* Retrieved July 19, 2003 from EBSCOHost.

Dickinson, C. J. (2002, May 3). Wireless messaging growing in popularity. *The Central NewYork Business Journal.* Lexis-Nexis Database.

Easterbrook, S. (Ed.). (1993). *Computer supported cooperative work.* New York: Springer-Verlag.

Edutools. (2003). *Comparison of course management software.* Available online: http://www.edutools.info/course/productinfo/index.jsp

Ferris, S. P. (1995). *An investigation of a role of computer-mediated communication as a media choice in the facilitation of task performance in small groups.* Unpublished dissertation. College Park, PA: The Pennsylvania State University.

Fitzsimmons, C. (2003, May 10). The must-have that puts you in the picture. *The Australian.* Retrieved July 19, 2003 from EBSCOHost.

Habanero news release. (2003). Available online: http://www.ncsa.uiuc.edu/News/Access /Briefs/00Briefs/000328.Habanero.html

Hamilton, T. (2003, January 24). Text messaging goes continental. *Toronto Star.* Retrieved July 19, 2003 from EBSCOHost.

Herman, J. (2003, April). Blogs for business. *Business Communication Review*. Retrieved May 5, 2003 from EBSCOHost.

January, B. (2002, May 17). Growing number of cell phone users pay for capability to send text messages. *The Record* (Hackensack, NJ). Retrieved July 19, 2003 from EBSCOHost.

Jessup, L. M., & Valacich, J. S. (Eds.). (1993). *Group support systems*. New York: Macmillan.

Johansen, R., Vallee, J., & Spangler, K. (1979). *Electronic meetings: Technical alternatives and social choices*. Reading, MA: Addison-Wesley.

Lamb, S. E. (1999, October–December). E-mail and online communications. *Business and Economic Review*. Retrieved May 3, 2003 from EBSCOHost.

McGrath, J. E., & Hollingshead, A. B. (1994). *Groups interacting with technology*. Thousand Oaks, CA: Sage.

Messaging mayhem. (2002, May 6). *Telephony*. Retrieved July 19, 2003 from EBSCOHost.

Metz, C. (2001, November 27). Virtual meetings. *PC Magazine*. Available online: http://www.pcmag.com/article2/0,4149,13339,00.asp

Mills, K. (2003, February 25). 3G unlikely to deliver for business, Deloitte predicts. *The Australian*. Retrieved July 19, 2003 from EBSCOHost.

Miranda, S. M. (1994). Avoidance of groupthink: Meeting management using group support systems. *Small Group Research, 25*, 105–136.

Narayan, S., & Rana, A. (1997). *Object oriented role modeling and group support systems*. Available online: http://hsb.baylor.edu/ramsower/ais.ac.97/papers/narayan.htm

National Center of Supercomputing Applications. (2002, March 18). *New Straits Times-Management Times*. Web services gain popularity. Retrieved May 3, 2003 from EBSCOHost.

O'Leary, M. (2002, January). Supportpath.com: Bulletin board epitome. *Information Today*. Retrieved May 3, 2003 from EBSCOHost.

Pinsonneault, A., & Kraemer, K. L. (1989). The impact of technological support on groups: An assessment of empirical research. *Decision Support Systems, 5*, 197–216.

Radford, M. L., Barnes, S. B., & Barr, L. R. (2002). *Web research: Selecting, evaluating and citing*. New York: Allyn and Bacon.

Rice, R. E., & Case, D. (1983). Electronic message systems in the university: Description of use and utility. *Journal of Communication*, 131–152.

Schwarz, M. (2002, January 7). The instant messaging debate. *Computerworld*. Retrieved May 3, 2003 from EBSCOHost.

Simon, H. (1965). *The shape of automation for men and management*. New York: Harper and Row.

Solomon, C. M. (2001, June). Managing virtual teams. *Workforce*. Retrieved May 3, 2003 from EBSCOHost.

Sudweeks, F., Collins, M., & December, J. (1995). Internetwork resources. In Z. L. Berge, & M. P. Collins (Eds.) *CMC and the online classroom: Volume 3 — Distance Learning* (pp. 193–212). Cresskill, NJ: Hampton Press.

Telnet. (2003). Telnet Tech support. Retrieved April 7, 2003 from the World Wide Web: http://telnet.org

Wellens, A. R. (1993). Group situation awareness and distributed decision making. In N. J. Castellan, Jr. (Ed.), *Individual and group decision making* (pp. 267–293). Hillsdale, NJ: Lawrence Erlbaum.

Wilfahrt, G. (2002, May 6). Mobile text messaging next for wireless operators. *San Diego Business Journal.* Retrieved July 19, 2003 from EBSCOHost.

Yap, C. (2003, March 11). The SMS tease and please. *New Straits Times – Management Times* Retrieved July 19, 2003 from EBSCOHost.

Young, J. R. (1997, October 17). Demonstration gives lawmakers and researchers a taste of Internet 2. *Chronicle of Higher Education*, A28.

Section IV:

Effective Uses of Virtual Teams

Chapter XII

Virtual Teams and their Search for Creativity

Mila Gascó-Hernández, Open University of Catalonia, Spain

Teresa Torres-Coronas, Universitat Rovira i Virgili, Spain

ABSTRACT

In this chapter, we examine the differences in processes and results when creativity techniques are used in the management of traditional and virtual teams. To do this, we discuss the following three main elements: the definition of creativity and its relationship with team performance; the variables that enhance creativity in a virtual team; and the most suitable creativity techniques for a virtual environment. We draw two main conclusions. First, creativity can help virtual teams become more effective, and second, not all the methods that foster creativity in a face-to-face context are appropriate in the virtual environment.

INTRODUCTION

The transition to the so-called information society, and particularly the emergence of tools based on the new information and communication technologies, is profoundly affecting productive processes and working methods. As a consequence, numerous changes are taking place within the organizational context. For example, the number of knowledge workers is increasing, divisions between companies and departments are disappearing, networks are being created between countries, minority workers are being included, and workers' needs are being recognized.

These changes require more flexible and adaptable structures that result in new forms of organization. One of these is the establishment of virtual teams that allow employees to work outside the office and to communicate and interact effectively with other colleagues in a "virtual" way. For many businesses, survival in the new era depends on the effectiveness and creativity of these virtual teams.

Many studies already showed how a team can become more creative, and therefore more efficient, but only a few researchers focused on how a virtual team can use creativity techniques to perform better. In this chapter, therefore, we study what differences there are (both in terms of processes and in terms of results) when creativity techniques are used in the management of traditional and virtual teams. To do this, we discuss three main elements: the definition of creativity and its relationships with team performance, the variables that enhance creativity in a virtual team, and the most suitable creativity techniques for a virtual environment.

CREATIVITY AS A TOOL FOR IMPROVING TEAM PERFORMANCE IN TRADITIONAL ORGANIZATIONS AND STRUCTURES

Creativity is the shortest way to search for unconventional wisdom and produce paradigm-breaking ideas and innovation. However, as we will show in this chapter, creativity is also a tool for improving organization and team performance. To understand this, we need to address two elements. First, we will discuss the meaning of creativity. Then, after reviewing the literature, we will answer this question: "Is there a reliable relationship between creativity and performance?"

Meaning of Creativity

Most researchers believe that the key to organizational success lies in developing intellectual capital and acquiring a new set of thinking: the creativity to produce an idea and the innovation to translate the idea into a novel result (Roffe, 1999). We can say the following (Roffe, 1999):

> ...the key is to turn ideas into useful knowledge and the useful knowledge into added value. In practice, this means bringing together the creative thinkers so that they can discuss and elaborate on their ideas, even if they do not really want to. It also

means finding the resources necessary, when resources are limited, and trying to manage what is often an unpredictable, unmanageable process. (p. 1)

Explaining the meaning of creativity is not straightforward. There are more than 1000 definitions of creativity (Aleinikov, 1999, p. 840), but, from all these definitions, most researchers agree that the two elements that define creativity are *novelty* and *usefulness* (Torrance, 1966; Amabile, 1996). Creativity was also defined in terms of either a process or a product, and at times in terms of a certain kind of personality or certain kinds of environmental conditions (Torrance & Goff, 1992). As Firestien (1996) pointed out, in 1961 Mel Rhodes, who was trying to find a universal definition of creativity, described : Person, Process, Product, and Press. These Four "P"s highlight the meaning of creativity as it is today most broadly understood:

- **The Creative Person**. Highly creative people are characterized by several cognitive factors, which are components of performance, such as: fluency, flexibility, originality, and elaboration (Bleedorn, 1998). However, there is another critical factor: a strong *belief* in one's personal creativity. Dobbins and Pettman (1997) stated, "from the law of belief we know that we always behave in a manner consistent with our beliefs. If we believe we are creative, then we behave in a manner consistent with being creative" (pp. 521–522).
- **The Creative Process**. How are problems found and solved? Problems with clear solutions are solved using conventional and routine thinking approaches, and fuzzy and unclear problems ("ill-defined problems") are solved using a creative thinking approach. The Creative Problem Solving (CPS) process, first develop by Alex Osborn in 1963, is the most widely used model for dealing with ill-defined problems. Researchers, such as Parnes (1981), VanGundy (1992), Basadur (1994), and Treffinger, Isaksen, and Dorval (1994) contributed to its development.
- **The Creative Press**. The third "P" in creativity research involves the press of the environment, which facilitates creative processes and products. A suggestion for igniting the creative spark is to create an atmosphere conducive to creativity. This advice applies in two areas: physical environment and corporate attitude (Smolensky & Kleiner, 1995). As far as the organization is concerned, happy, open, optimistic, and encouraging environments foster creativity.
- **The Creative Product**. The last "P" is the result of creative work and can range from a product to a specific behavior (Richards, 1999). This creativity dimension is highly related to the other three. So, if a creative product is examined, information about the qualities of the creative person,

about the creative process used, and even about the creative environment in which the product was developed can be found (Puccio, 1994).

These Four "P"s of creativity emphasize that each of us is inherently creative, and that it is just a matter of stimulating the part of our brain that comes up with the new perspectives. There are workable techniques for bringing about the desired creativity as well as friendly designed environments.

Creativity and Team Performance

Although team-centered structures dramatically improved product and operational performance, organizations now realize that future radical improvements in performance hinge on creativity (Feurer, Chaharbaghi, & Wargin, 1996). Needless to say, organizations have not sufficiently addressed the issue of creativity, and, as a result, the potential of teams has not been completely fulfilled.

In the past few decades, team performance research has not focused on creativity. Several researchers hypothesized that variation in team performance can be explained by differences in team structure. Stewart & Barrick (2000) demonstrated that structural characteristics related to the allocation of tasks, responsibilities, and authority influence team performance. Waller (1999) showed how the frequency of information collection activities has a positive association with performance. Other studies established that levels of group efficacy vary among groups that appear to have equal skills, abilities, and resources (see Gibson, 1999). For teams to be productive, there must be a balance of skills, abilities, and personalities among the group (Belbin, 1993).

Awareness about the fact that process plays a vital role in team performance increased attention on developing theoretical models of team effectiveness, with team processes occupying a central role (Hackman, 1983). Such models view processes as mediating mechanisms linking variables such as member, team, and organizational characteristics with criteria such as performance quality and quantity. In other words (Marks, Mathieu, & Zaccaro, 2001), "teamwork processes are the vehicles that transform team inputs to both proximal and long-term outcomes" (p. 358).

These results can be related to studies on how group potency (or the collective belief of a group that it can be effective) affects group satisfaction, group effort, and team performance (Lester, Meglino, & Kosgaard, 2002). These authors found that group process factors and, specifically, charismatic leadership affect work group outcomes.

Other issues worthy of investigation are the effects of work group composition and interpersonal conflict on performance. Personal characteristic diversity (Harrison, Price, & Bell, 1998) and functional diversity (Bunderson & Sutcliffe, 2002) can affect work group processes and outcomes.

On the other hand, research on creativity directly correlated with individual, team, and organizational performance is rare. Most creativity research stresses how teams can be used to foster creativity (Mohram, Cohen, & Mohrman, 1995) or how the role of an organizational and team environment affects the creative behaviors of individuals and teams (Amabile & Conti, 1999; Taggar, 2002). These studies further demonstrate the importance of creating the appropriate social conditions [such as diversity of information, organizational values and norms, flexibility of organizational resources, and supervisory behaviors and attitudes (Baker, Winkovsky, Langmeyer, & Sweeney, 1976)] to enhance creativity.

According to the componential model of creativity and innovation in organizations (Amabile, 1983, 1988, 1998), five environmental components affect creativity (Amabile & Conti, 1999):

1. Encouragement of creativity (which encompasses open information flow and support for new ideas)
2. Autonomy or freedom (a sense of individual ownership of and control over work)
3. Resources (to perform the job)
4. Pressures (including positive challenge and negative workload pressures)
5. Organizational impediments to creativity (including conservatism and internal strife)

In Amabile's research, the work team environment is considered to exert a powerful impact on creativity by influencing the employee's intrinsic motivation. Management practices indicate that performance can be fostered by allowing freedom and autonomy to conduct one's work, matching individuals to work assignments, and building effective work teams that represent a diversity of skills and are made up of individuals who trust and communicate well with each other, challenge each other's ideas, are mutually supportive, and are committed to the work they are doing (Amabile & Gryskiewicz, 1987).

At this point, it can therefore be argued that team and creativity research are related. They both consider that environmental and structural factors are key elements of organizational and team performance. Therefore, a creativity-based management aimed at fostering team and organizational performance must manage both types of variables in order to enhance employees' internal drives to perceive every project as a new creative challenge (Andriopoulos & Lowe, 2000).

CONTEXT FOR CREATIVITY IN VIRTUAL TEAMS: DIMENSIONS THAT ENHANCE CREATIVITY IN A VIRTUAL TEAM

We will now discuss the factors that enhance creativity in a virtual team. However, as there are many barriers to creativity in a virtual context, we will also consider several controversies regarding cyberspace and team effectiveness.

Creativity Variables in a Virtual Team

Nemiro and Runco (1996) identified six factors that are necessary in a work environment to foster creativity in work groups: autonomy and freedom, challenge, clear direction, diversity/flexibility/tension, support for creativity, trust, and participative safety. These variables were also developed by other authors. However, these studies have not addressed dimensions that may be necessary when groups no longer interact in traditional structures (Nemiro, 2001). In fact, so far, the only research seriously conducted about this issue is that by Nemiro (2001).

Nemiro (2001) identified several key elements that influence creativity in virtual teams and, therefore, result in effectiveness and high levels of performance. From our point of view, the more important of these elements are as follows:[2]

- **Goal and role clarity**: Many authors, such as Bal and Teo (2001, p. 208), Lipnack and Stamps (1997), George (1996), and O'Hara-Deveraux and Johansen (1994, p. 125), have seen purpose as the essence of virtual teams. It was proven that virtual teams experience more affectiveness and task conflict[3] than do traditional teams (Hinds & Bailey, 2000) because of three direct consequences of their virtuality: mediated communication, unshared context, and nonexistence of bureaucratic rules and regulations. All of these types of conflict are associated with reduced performance on virtual teams, although the literature on creativity suggests that a low level of conflict in a team can enhance group creativity and therefore its performance (see, among others, Runco, 1994). But, as Hinds and Bailey (2000) stated:

  ...distance, coupled with a reliance on mediated communication, can create depersonalised interactions. These interactions promote inappropriate interpersonal behavior, make it difficult to share information, and block the feedback necessary to identify miscommunication. (p. 3)

Having clear goals and objectives can help virtual team members stay focused and oriented to each other and their tasks, keep in tune and aligned, avoid false assumptions and indecision, and therefore reduce conflict and achieve a high level of performance.

As well as having a high level of shared vision, goals, and rules, role clarity appears to be an important factor for successful creative virtual teams (Nemiro, 2001). Although there is a need for flexibility so as not to kill creative thinking among team members, [4] expectations about roles and responsibilities must be clarified and made explicit. Doing so will help to identify the necessary criteria for selecting or developing virtual team members, thereby assuring that different points of view and different perspectives are considered, giving rise to a creative virtual team.

- **Trust**: According to Duarte and Snyder (1999), "Trust is a critical structural and cultural characteristic that influences the teams' success, performance, and collaboration. Without trust, building a true team is almost impossible" (p. 139). Virtual teams that want to be creatively effective must learn to build trust among their members. Two explanations support this assertion. On one hand, trust and participative safety are crucial for group creativity, because these dimensions encourage participation in a nonthreatening, nonevaluative environment, which is one of the most important factors for achieving individual and group creativity. On the other hand, when there is trust within a virtual team, irrespective of the level of geographic or temporal virtuality, each team member commits to having the freedom and the responsibility to contribute his or her best.
- **Communication patterns**: Henry and Hartzler (1998) found that keeping the synergy and creativity flowing, without frequent face-to-face (F2F) interaction, is the greatest challenge to a virtual team. They also believe that communication is the main vehicle for keeping a team together and moving forward. [5] Communication and information exchange enables interaction, which helps to build relationships and create bonds. These relationships and bonds are essential for people working in virtual teams, because within cyberspace, it is easier for individuals to "disappear" or drop out of the discussion.

The findings of Nemiro (2001) highlight the importance of this third variable. He reported that in the highly creative stories, team members described situations in which they communicated regularly with one another, shared the results of their efforts, offered open and honest feedback, and updated information regularly.

Virtual team communication cannot take place as it does within a F2F team. Schein (1993) pointed out that most communication workshops emphasize active listening, which means paying attention to spoken words, body language, tone of voice, or emotional content. Virtual team members who want to communicate successfully cannot actively listen in this sense. Therefore, other tools must be explored, for example, the use of multiple media or several communication technologies (Bal & Teo, 2001). However, as Van der Smagt (2000) showed, it is crucial to ensure that dialogue is the primary form of interaction between team members:

> *In a dialogue, the difficult part is to make one's own assumptions manifest, not the exchange of insights with others. The attitude in relation to other actors is one of openness, which makes it relatively easy to get behind the position and possibilities of actors. (p. 155)*

As with F2F teams, the creative interplay of ideas in cyberspace will determine the effectiveness of the virtual team. Although the dimensions discussed in this section[6] for enhancing the creativity of virtual teams may be the same as those needed by other types of teams, they become crucial when virtuality is the main characteristic of a group. However, virtual teams may also suffer from lack of creativity and, therefore, from low performance levels. In the next section, we will highlight the main obstacles to creativity in virtual teams.

Virtual Teams' Creativity Barriers

Brynteson, Wiger, and Hardt (1998) identified three factors that may hinder creativity in a virtual team. First, it may be more difficult to achieve trust, and this may undermine the creative process. Nemiro (2001) also noted that trust may develop more slowly between virtual team members than between F2F team members. Kossler and Prestridge (1996) stated that with less visual contact, it may take longer to identify and adjust to the habits, quirks, and skills of team members. When trust is not enough, there are fewer opportunities to build relationships and establish effective communication patterns, or to clarify, negotiate, and share a common direction.

Second, technology, rather than the creative process, may become the focus of the team. Brynteson, Wiger, and Hardt (1998) believed that "fumbling with technology, or worse, a preoccupation with technology, may cause the team to use lock step, linear thinking, which forces a single, linear solution" (p. 2). Bal and Teo (2001) agreed and reminded us that the glamour or convenience of technology should not seduce teams, which can end up serving the technology rather than having the technology serving them.

Finally, some individuals may have a difficult time unlocking their creativity. Team members can be affected by the traditional barriers to creativity, such as rules and traditions (i.e., status hierarchy, formalization barriers, and procedural barriers), cultural barriers (social influence, expectations, and pressures to conform due to social or institutional norms), and resource barriers (including lack of people, money, time, supplies, or information needed for creative thinking or implementing creative ideas).

TOOLS FOR ENCOURAGING CREATIVITY IN A VIRTUAL TEAM

So, how can team creativity be encouraged? Various tools and techniques, used by individuals and groups and mostly focused on generating ideas, proved useful in a variety of creativity problem-solving situations. Until now, however, no serious research was conducted into which creativity techniques are the most suitable in a virtual environment. In this section, we will propose and describe some of the methods that can help to make a virtual team more creative.

Our experience shows that three variables must be considered when selecting a technique: the effectiveness of the method in finding innovative solutions, the technological context or support system through which the technique can be implemented, and the level of interaction that the technique requires.

The following techniques proved useful from a practical point of view. We selected them to illustrate how to achieve effective team creativity and how to adapt to a virtual environment with a nonverbal type of interaction between team members.

Diverging versus Converging

As stated before, the creative process is a model that is used to deal with ill-defined problems. This model is usually presented as a series of steps that guide the process. A unique feature of the model is that each step first involves a divergent thinking phase in which one generates a lot of ideas, and second, it involves a convergent phase in which only the most promising ideas are selected for further exploration.

In this section, we will differentiate between diverging and converging techniques. Because in the creative process diverging is more difficult than converging, we will emphasize the first type of technique.

Diverging Techniques

Diverging techniques can be classified according to their primary use of related or unrelated problem stimuli (VanGundy, 1992). If the method of stimulation is changed, people can be encouraged to change their paradigm (McFadzean, 1998, 2000). From McFadzean's point of view, idea generation techniques can be divided into paradigm preserving (brainstorming, brainwriting, 5W + H, force field analysis, and the Word Diamond are some of the examples developed by VanGundy, 1992), paradigm stretching (such as object stimulation, metaphors, rolestorming, attribute listing, or assumption reversal), and paradigm breaking (for example, rich pictures, picture stimulation, and collages).

Paradigm-preserving techniques develop ideas using related stimuli and combining words and ideas. These techniques are useful when a high level of innovation is not required. They are not uncomfortable to use, so groups with little virtual experience can use them. Comfort is a key variable during the creative process. McFadzean, Somersall, and Coker (1999) found that participants who were uncomfortable with the process were less effective during creative sessions. Paradigm-stretching techniques use forced association and unrelated stimuli to encourage participants to develop creative ideas. Finally, paradigm-breaking techniques help participants to overcome long-standing patterns of thinking. One way of achieving this is to think visually instead of using words. Both paradigm-stretching and paradigm-breaking techniques require more developed and experienced teams (McFadzean, 2000).

For our purposes, we selected three diverging techniques for use in a virtual environment. These were electronic brainwriting, synectics, and attribute listing. We selected these because they are useful for a wide range of situations, including helping virtual teams to find a balance between creativity and comfort (McFadzean, 2000), between creativity and the level of imaginative thinking required, and between creativity and the technological context. Knowing how each of these techniques works will help the reader gain further insight into these relationships.

Electronic brainwriting

Brainstorming is no longer an unknown word. Many teams all over the world successfully tried this technique, which is based on four uncomplicated ground rules: (a) defer judgement (i.e., avoid criticism and evaluation); (b) welcome freewheeling (because the wilder the idea the better); (c) look for quantity; and (d) seek combination and improvement of ideas.

When electronic means are used, a traditional brainstorming session is not possible, because simultaneous participation is required. However, a variation of this technique may be useful when a virtual team wants to try a brainstorming process: this is called electronic brainwriting. This new technique combines the concept of brainwriting with modern electronics.

Brainwriting is a quieter version of brainstorming that capitalizes on the idea of hitchhiking. As Davis (1998) explained:

> ...members of a small group are instructed to write down an idea or problem solution, then pass the paper to the person on the right. The next person may:
>
> 1. Use the idea to stimulate another idea, and write the new idea on the paper.
> 2. Modify the idea and write down the modification.
> 3. Write down a completely new idea.

The process continues until the sheets circulate back to the original owner. Ideas are discussed further. (p. 176)

In an electronic brainwriting session, the idea or problem solution can be posted onto an Internet bulletin board or on a company intranet, and responses can be registered there. E-mail can also be used. The advantage of these two electronic methods is that they do not require simultaneous participation of members in a single location. In Siau's (1995) words, electronic brainwriting "transcends the time and space constraints that burden groups who meet face-to-face; namely, that all of their members must be at the same place at the same time" (p. 211).

Davis (1998) noted that some of the disadvantages of conventional brainstorming groups disappear with electronic brainwriting. These are as follows:

1. Production blocking (because the ideas are available for consideration at each member's convenience)
2. Evaluation apprehension (due to the fact that there is no F2F interaction)
3. Social loafing (in a way, it is compulsory for everyone to participate)
4. Group size (because many individuals can be linked across space and time, while in a conventional brainstorming session, the number of participants must be limited to 10 or 12)

If people were available simultaneously, other communication technologies, such as synchronous video systems, team chats, telephone conferences, and interactive computer conferences, could be used in order to allow team members at diverse locations to participate in a virtual brainstorming session. If this happened, brainwriting would no longer be necessary, and the new version of the technique could be called electronic brainstorming.

Synectics

Synectics is the "joining together of different and apparently irrelevant elements" (Gordon & Poze, 1980a, 1980b). It is a method that uses analogies and metaphors (unrelated stimulus) in order to analyze a problem and develop possible solutions. It does so through two different mechanisms. The first aims to make strange things look familiar and is designed to help the user better understand the problem. The second aims to make familiar things look strange in order to provide a better perspective of the problem and so encourage more creative solutions.

There are four different types of analogies (Davis, 1998):

1. **Direct analogy:** With this technique, the problem solver is asked to think of ways in which related problems were solved. The objective is to compare the problem with analogous facts, information, or technology.

2. **Personal analogy:** This mechanism emphasizes the use of emotions and feelings in order to develop an idea of purely technological problems. That is, with this method, the thinker achieves new perspectives on a problem by imaginatively becoming part of that problem.
3. **Fantasy analogy:** With this Freudian approach, the problem solver thinks of fantastic and ideal solutions that can lead to creative yet practical ideas.
4. **Symbolic analogy:** This technique uses objective and personal visual images in order to describe a problem.

The synectic process goes as follows (Gascó & Torres, 2002):

1. An assertion about the problem under consideration is read to the whole team.
2. The team members work on making the strange look familiar.
3. The rigid and superficial solutions are eliminated. At the end of this stage, there is a common understanding of the problem to be solved.
4. One part of the problem is selected. Each team member describes how he or she sees the situation, using metaphors or analogies. The leader collects everybody's point of view. One of these perspectives is then selected to be further analyzed.
5. At this stage, the operative mechanisms are used. The leader poses questions that require answers that use analogies. The leader selects one of these answers for deeper analysis.
6. The last analogy, used in Phase 5, and the problem as it is understood, are related, and a practical application is developed.
7. A new perspective (i.e., a new point of view) for solving the problem is born.

Because simultaneity is not needed when a synectic process is carried out (the team members can take their time when analyzing the problem and finding analogies), it is easy to develop it in an asynchronous virtual context. Also, because individuals have to work alone for a while during the process, interpersonal distractions, particularly in Phase 2, must be reduced, because they may interfere with logical, fantasy, and analytical capabilities. Duarte and Snyder (1999) showed that when these requirements are in place, less social presence may work better.

Finally, cartoons, drawings, pictures, collages, and other types of images are said to be an important source of analogies (specifically of symbolic analogies). Some of the more popular Internet search engines, such as Google™ include the possibility of finding images that can be used to start the synectic process with a rich variety of ideas.

The characteristics of the synectic process may mean that it takes longer than a brainstorming session. For this reason, communication technologies that allow for simultaneous interaction may not be suitable with this technique. A combination of e-mail and an electronic bulletin board or an intranet is more suitable when a virtual team wants to use the synectic process. The leader would be the only one allowed to use e-mail, which is more appropriate when unidirectional communication is required (for example, when giving information about the problem or when posing questions). The rest of the team must use the second type of electronic devices, because this ensures that the information and the ideas the team members have are shared among all the participants. Only at the final stage, or when a little debate is required, may a simultaneous or synchronous virtual interaction take place. In such cases, the videoconference works best.

Because of the time an individual needs to work on his or her own, and the role of the leader, synectics has an important disadvantage for virtual teams. It can lead to a feeling of detachment from the group, particularly if the process lasts longer than expected. This is why it is fundamental to set a deadline for which to finish the exercise.

Attribute listing

As Davis (1998) said, "brainstorming is a general thinking strategy that mainly requires creative attitudes and a creative atmosphere. Attribute listing is a more specific technique for generating new ideas" (p. 178). There are two forms of attribute listing: attribute modifying and attribute transferring. With attribute modifying the thinker lists the main attributes (characteristics, dimensions, parts) of the problem object or process and then thinks of ideas for improving each attribute. Two brainstorming processes are then required. Therefore, the same arguments for using electronic brainwriting when working with a virtual team also apply when referring to this technique. Moreover, the same electronic means suggested for electronic brainwriting are suitable for attribute modifying.

Attribute transferring is another name for what we called "analogical thinking" or "synectics." Instead of carrying out a single synectic process, the team must start with a brainstorming session to decide attributes on which to focus. After that, the steps we explained earlier are followed.

The main disadvantage of this method is the amount of time required. As stated earlier, both attribute-listing variations include two different processes that may take longer when they are developed virtually than when they are developed F2F. There may be two consequences of this. The first is detachment. The second is free-riding, which is the tendency to invest less effort in group projects, because members can sit back and leave the work to others. This is mainly due to boredom and lack of interest in the creative process.

Converging Techniques

Training in creative problem solving always emphasizes divergent techniques. This is because we are already used to converging (i.e., to bringing together possibilities, choosing alternatives, strengthening, refining, and improving ideas, and reaching a conclusion).[7] We do not intend to expand on this topic, because divergent thinking is only effective when convergent thinking skills and techniques balance it, but we must say a few words about the use of convergent methods by virtual teams.

First, using converging techniques in a virtual environment is not time-consuming. Although the problem solver needs some time to analyze the different ideas brought about by the divergent process, he or she usually does so quickly. This is why communication technologies that gather team members together at a certain time (such as video conferences or audioconferences) can be suitable for a convergent process, as long as all the participants have the required information for converging before the session begins.

Second, convergent methods are simple and often require only a single action by each participant. This allows the virtual team to use popular electronic means, such as e-mail or even telephones. In these cases, the only requirement is to appoint a leader to collect the messages from the team members and inform them about the results. A simple voting system (for example, voting for the two to three ideas each participant likes the best, then selecting the two to three ideas with the highest number of votes) can easily be carried out in this way.

Finally, because at an evaluation stage a lot of information is needed about the previous creative process steps, the Internet, the electronic bulletin board, and the group intranet are suitable tools for displaying the data required for making a decision. Each participant will view the same information, at the same time, for the same amount of time, and in the same physical format, thus allowing the team members to make their decisions given the same contextual factors.

Although it may be easy to virtually converge, this technique is more complicated than simple voting, because, like the evaluation matrix technique, it involves applying other methods. In the example, brainstorming is needed in order to select the criteria according to the value at which each idea will be rated; also, participants need to debate in order to reach agreement on how to rate each idea. Time constraints and the need to be available simultaneously will again become serious obstacles for the convergence process. For this reason, easy-to-use converging techniques are recommended in a virtual context.[8]

CONCLUSION

In this chapter, we analyzed the relationship between creativity and team performance and some of the variables that enhance creativity in a virtual team. We also explored several creative tools that can play important roles in the creative processes of teams. Our two main conclusions are that creativity can help virtual teams to become more effective, and that not all the methods that foster creativity in a F2F context are appropriate in the virtual environment.

However, several questions remain unanswered, and more research is needed. In particular, three important issues need further development. First, the relationship between creativity and virtual team performance needs to be thoroughly explored. Successful studies will determine how structural and environmental factors influence team creativity. Second, although virtual teams are already using idea-generation techniques (as we showed), their strengths and weaknesses need to be carefully and academically explored. Finally, it is important to consider the effects of technology on both individual and team creativity. Technology has risks that can sometimes outweigh its benefits. When applying creative techniques, people need to focus on the creative process and not on the technology being used. Technology must be easy to use, and it must be effortless and unsophisticated — the simpler the technology the better.

Theoretical and empirical research into creativity and virtual teams will be challenging. This is particularly true because, in our experience, virtual teams are still searching for creativity.

REFERENCES

Aleinikov, A. G. (1999). Human creativity. In M. A. Runco, & S. R. Pritzker (Eds.), *Encyclopedia of creativity* (Vol. 1, pp. 837–844). New York: Academic Press.

Amabile, T. (1983). *The social psychology of creativity*. New York: Springer-Verlag.

Amabile, T. (1988). A model of creativity and innovation in organizations. In B. M. Straw, & L. L. Cummings (Eds.), *Research in organizational behaviour* (Vol. 10, pp. 123–167). Greenwich, CT: JAI Press.

Amabile, T. (1998). How to kill creativity. *Harvard Business Review*, September/October, 77–87.

Amabile, T., & Gryskiewicz, S. S. (1987). *Creativity in the R&D laboratory. Technical Report 30*. Greenboro, NC: Center for Creative Leadership.

Amabile, T. M. (1996). *Creativity in context*. Boulder, CO: Westview Press.

Amabile, T. M., & Conti, R. (1999). Changes in the work environment for creativity during downsizing. *Academy of Management Journal, 42*(6), 630–640.

Andriopoulos, C., & Lowe, A. (2000). Enhancing organisational creativity: The process of perpetual challenging. *Management Decision, 38*(10), 834–840.

Baker, N. R., Winkofsky, E., Langmeyer, L., & Sweeney, D. J. (1976). *Idea generation: A procrustean bed of variables, hypotheses and implications.* Cincinnati: College of Business Administration, University of Cincinnati.

Bal, J., & Teo, P. K. (2001). Implementing virtual teamworking: Part 2 — a literature review. *Logistics Information Management, 14*(3), 208–222.

Basadur, M. (1994). *A flight to creativity* (1st ed.). Buffalo, NY: The Creative Education Foundation Press.

Belbin, R. M. (1993). *Team roles at work.* Oxford: Butterworth-Heinemann.

Bleedorn, B. (1998). *The creativity force in education, business and beyond. An urgent message.* Lakeville, MI: Galde Press, Inc.

Brynteson, R., Wiger, J., & Hardt, P. (1998, August). Virtual teams and creativity: What Dorothy learned on her way home. *Ibiz Magazine.* Retrieved from the World Wide Web : http://www.ibiz.net/aug98/teams.htm

Bunderson, J. S., & Sutcliffe, K. M. (2002). Comparing alternative conceptualizations of functional diversity in management teams: Process and performance effects. *Academy of Management Journal, 45*(5), 875–893.

Davis, G. (1998). *Creativity is forever.* Dubuque, IA: Kendall/Hunt Publishing Company.

Dobbins, R., & Pettman, B. O. (1997). Self-development: The nine basic skills for business success. *The Journal of Management Development, 16*(8), 521–667.

Duarte, D. L., & Snyder, N. T. (1999). *Mastering virtual teams.* San Francisco, CA: Jossey-Bass.

Feurer, R., Chaharbaghi, K., & Wargin, J. (1996). Developing creative teams for operational excellence. *International Journal of Operations & Production Management, 16*(1), 5–18.

Firestien, R. L. (1996). *Leading on the creative edge.* Colorado Springs, CO: Pinon Press.

Gascó, M., & Torres, T. (2002). *Recupera tu creatividad. Ideas y sugerencias para fomentar el espíritu creativo.* Oviedo, España: Septem Ediciones.

George, J. (1996, November). Virtual best practice: How to successfully introduce virtual team-working. *Teams,* 38–45.

Gibson, C. B. (1999). Do they do what they believe they can? Group efficacy and group effectiveness across tasks and cultures. *Academy of Management Journal, 42*(2), 127–137.

Gordon, W. J., & Poze (1980a). SES synectics and gifted education today. *Gifted Child Quarterly, 24,* 147–151.

Gordon, W. J., & Poze (1980b). *The new art of the possible.* Cambridge, MA: Porpoise Books.

Hackman, R. 1983. *A normative model of work team effectiveness. Technical report No. 2*. New Haven, CT: Yale School of Organization and Management.

Harrison, D. A., Price, K. H., & Bell, M. P. (1998). Beyond relational demography: Time and the effects of surface and deep-level diversity on work group cohesion. *Academy of Management Journal, 41*, 96–107.

Henry, J. E., & Hartzler, M. (1998). *Tools for virtual teams*. Milwaukee, WI: ASQC Quality Press.

Hinds, P., & Bailey, D. (2000). Virtual teams: Anticipating the impact of virtuality on team process and performance. *Academy of Management Proceedings 2000 OCIS*.

Kossler, M., & Prestridge, S. (1996). Geographically dispersed teams. *Issues and Observations, 16*(2/3), 9–11.

Lester, S. W., Meglino, B. M., & Korsgaard, M. A. (2002). The antecedents and consequences of group potency: A longitudinal investigation of newly formed work groups. *The Academy of Management Journal, 45*(2): 352–368.

Lipnack, J., & Stamps, J. (1997). *Virtual teams: Reaching across space, time and organizations with technology*. New York: John Wiley & Sons.

Marks, M. A., Mathieu, J. E., & Zaccaro, S. J. (2001). A temporal framework and taxonomy of team processes. *Academy of Management Review, 26*(3), 356–376.

McFadzean, E. S. (1998). Enhancing creative thinking within organizations. *Management Decision, 36*(5), 309–315.

McFadzean, E. S. (2000). Techniques to enhance creative thinking. *Team Performance Management: An International Journal, 6*(3/4), 62–72.

McFadzean, E. S., Somersall, L., & Coker, A. (1999). A framework for facilitating group processes. *Strategic Change, 8*(7), 421–431.

Mohram, S. A., Cohen, S. G., & Mohrman, A. M. (1995). Designing team based organizations. New York: Jossey-Bass.

Nemiro, J., & Runco, M. A. (1996). *Creativity and innovation in small groups*. Unpublished manuscript. Claremont, CA: The Claremont Graduate School.

Nemiro, J. E. (2001). Connection in creative virtual teams. *The Journal of Behavioral and Applied Management, 2*(2), 92.

O'Hara-Devereaux, M., & Johansen, R. (1994). *Global work: Bridging distance, culture, and time*. San Francisco, CA: Jossey-Bass.

Puccio, G. (1994). An overview of creativity assessment. In S. Isaksen, R. Firesteint, G. Puccio, & D. Treffinger (Eds.), *The assessment of creativity. Creativity based information resources project* (pp. 5–27). Buffalo, NY: The Center for Studies in Creativity.

Richards, R. (1999). Four Ps of creativity. In M. Runco, & S. Pritzker (Eds.), *Encyclopedia of creativity* (pp. 733–742). New York: Academic Press.

Roffe, I. (1999). Innovation and creativity in organisations: A review of the implications for training and development. *Journal of European Industrial Training, 23*(4/5), 224–237.

Runco, M. A. (1994). Creativity and its discontents. *ETC: A Review of General Semantics, 11*, 249–260.

Schein, E. H. (1993). On dialogue, culture and organizational learning. *Organizational Dynamics, 22*(2), 40–51.

Siau, K. L. (1995). Group creativity and technology. *Journal of Creative Behavior, 29*, 201–216.

Smolensky, E. D., & Kleiner, B. H. (1995). How to train people to think more. *Management Development Review, 8*(6), 28–33.

Stewart, G. L., & Barrick, M. R. (2000). Team structure and performance: Assessing the mediating role of intrateam process and the moderating role of task type. *Academy of Management Journal, 43*(2), 135–148.

Taggar, S. (2002). Individual creativity and group ability to utilize individual creative resources: A multilevel model. *Academy of Management Journal, 45*(2), 315–330.

Torrance, E. P., & Goff, K. (1992). A quiet revolution. In S. J. Parnes (Ed.), *Source book for creative problem solving* (pp. 78–84). Buffalo, NY: The Creative Education Foundation Press.

Treffinger, D. J., Isaksen, S. G., & Dorval, K. B. (1994). Creative problem solving: An overview. In M. A. Runco (Ed.), *Problem finding, problem solving, and creativity.* Norwood, NJ: Ablex.

Van der Smagt, T. (2000). Enhancing virtual teams: Social relations v. communication technology. *Industrial Management & Data Systems, 100*(4), 148–156.

VanGundy, A. B. (1992). *Idea power.* New York: AMACOM.

Waller, M. J. (1999). The timing of adaptative group responses to nonroutine events. *Academy of Management Journal, 42*(2), 127–137.

ENDNOTES

[1]   Excerpt from "Perspectives: The science of creativity." *Management Development Review, 10*(6/7), 203–304, 1997.

[2]   Other variables could be explored, but two reasons led us to consider these dimensions in particular. First, the few existing studies of virtual teams focused on the variables considered in this section, so only those elements further studied in the research works analyzed are listed here. Second, as we stated in the "Creativity and team performance" section, these are the more important factors to consider when looking for creative, productive,

and effective teams. This is why we previously referred to, among others, the works of the following:

(a) Stewart & Barrick (2000), who showed that the clarity of tasks and responsibilities is related to team performance

(b) Waller (1999), who considered that information collection and communication activities have a positive association with team performance

(c) Amabile (several studies), who stated that effective work teams are made up of individuals who trust and communicate well with each other

[3] For our purposes, affective conflict is defined as conflict that is characterized by anger or hostility, and task conflict is defined as disagreement that is focused on work content.

[4] Also, Lipnack and Stamps (1997) said that because of the dynamic nature of virtual teams, the roles played by team members must be multiple and flexible.

[5] For the purpose of this chapter, communication, to be effective, has to flow in two ways.

[6] As stated before, the variables considered are the main ones, although other authors may have emphasized different or complementary ones.

[7] Some people would also say that we are used to evaluating and criticizing.

[8] Videoconferences or computer chats may be considered a solution when debate is needed. This will be true as long as all the team members share the same time borders.

Chapter XIII

Virtual Teams in an Executive Education Training Program

Martha Reeves, Duke University, USA

Stacie Furst, Louisiana State University, USA

ABSTRACT

The purpose of this chapter is to explore the experiences of 15 different teams from two Fortune 500 companies: a food distribution company and a financial services company. The objectives of the virtual teams for these two companies were twofold: first, to learn how to work in virtual teams, and second, to complete a business project critical to their respective companies. We begin this chapter with a brief explanation of how the teams were organized and for what purpose. Then, the focus is more specifically on the factors that made some teams more successful than others, including the impact of geography, the problem of free-riding, top-level support, and gender differences.

INTRODUCTION

In response to criticism that management education and executive training programs lack relevance to the "real-world" corporate experience, more companies are demanding that their training and development dollars produce tangible results. As a result, companies are turning to "blended training designs,"[1] such as action learning, that combine traditional classroom experiences with other methods. Action learning involves "a small group of people solving real problems while at the same time focusing on what they are learning and how their learning can benefit each group member and the organization as a whole" (Marquardt, 1999). As companies become more geographically dispersed, action learning programs are being used to increase knowledge sharing and cross-functional teamwork through the development of virtual teams.

The integration of virtual-team-based activities into action learning programs appears to be necessary and appropriate for an increasingly global and technology-driven workplace. Virtual teams allow organizations to maximize efficiency and effectiveness by tapping the knowledge, skills, and expertise of employees around the globe and increasing opportunities for information or knowledge exchange through expanded social networks (Majchrzak, Rice, King Malhotra, & Ba, 2000). Yet, experts suggest that more virtual teams fail than succeed. The failure of many virtual teams to realize their potential is often attributed to the inability of team members and team leaders to communicate and coordinate team work processes across time and space boundaries. Action learning designs in an executive education setting represent one way to arm team members and team leaders with the skills and knowledge needed to perform effectively in a virtual environment and to provide an opportunity to apply those lessons in solving real business issues. The objective of these programs is to develop competent virtual team members, reinforce team work, transfer learning across geographic boundaries, and promote innovation and creative problem solving.

Unfortunately, managers and educators are only beginning to understand what makes virtual teams effective. The majority of what we know about virtual teams comes from case studies and anecdotal descriptions of virtual team experiences or from laboratory experiments involving students in controlled, unnatural work environments. Hence, prescriptions for effective virtual team performance may be based on untested findings or from student experiences that do not reflect the realities of the workplace. These ill-conceived prescriptions may threaten the ability of management educators to develop and administer action learning programs that create effective virtual team practices for participants and participating companies. More research is needed to study virtual teams in their natural working environments. By studying virtual teams during an action learning program, we can better assess the factors that contribute to or hinder team performance and identify how action learning programs can be designed to facilitate the development of effective virtual teams.

The purpose of this chapter is to accomplish the latter two objectives by describing the experiences of 15 virtual teams organized into action learning teams in an executive education setting. Each of these teams was assigned the task of analyzing a business problem facing their organizations and generating solutions to the problems. Nine of the 15 teams were from a Fortune 500 financial services company with global operations, and six teams were from a major food distribution company operating in several regions across the United States. These teams' experiences and effectiveness varied widely, providing an opportunity to assess the conditions associated with effective team performance. To identify the factors that influenced team performance and how various elements of the educational program facilitated effective teamwork, we gathered data from both of the executive education programs in which these companies participated, through the use of surveys, participant interviews, and direct observation. In this chapter, we discuss our findings and how they may be used to design action learning programs that promote effective virtual teamwork in the corporate setting.

The chapter is organized as follows. First, we review research relating to virtual teams and computer-mediated communication (CMC) that suggests why virtual team dynamics may differ from those of colocated or face-to-face (F2F) teams. Next, we describe the virtual project teams that we studied, their organizations, and their action learning projects. We then compare the performances of these teams and discuss the factors that influenced team effectiveness, including company culture, the impact of geography, the use of technology, the importance of senior sponsorship, and the quality of teams' work processes. We conclude with observations regarding the differences between colocated and virtual work teams and the implications of these differences for managers and educators charged with developing effective virtual teams.

BACKGROUND

Decades of research and practice on work teams suggest that teams are more likely to be effective when team members work toward a common goal, have the knowledge and skills to reach that goal, and adopt reasonable strategies for achieving those goals (Hackman, 1987). This research, however, implicitly assumes that team members are colocated and therefore fails to consider the unique challenges associated with communicating and coordinating work across time and space boundaries. In this section, we discuss some of the inherent differences between colocated and virtual teams and highlight the key challenges that these differences present for establishing a shared goal, developing the skills necessary to work virtually, and creating and adopting effective work processes.

Commitment to a Common, Shared Goal

For virtual team members, it may be more difficult to establish a common goal than it is for members of colocated teams for several reasons. First, goal setting and consensus building typically require that team members recognize their similarities, shared values, and expectations. Physical proximity enables these perceptions to develop and reinforces these perceptions by providing team members with greater opportunities to monitor others' behaviors, to exchange relevant nonverbal information (e.g., visual cues), and to engage in the informal "water cooler" conversations that build social ties (Finholt & Sproull, 1990). Without the opportunities for exchanging important social information, virtual team members may find it difficult to establish a shared sense of meaning and purpose around their work.

Second, contextual differences between virtual team members' local work units may also make the establishment of a common goal more difficult. Because colocated team members work in the same location, they should share many of the same work experiences, such as the same work climate, physical surroundings, and access to technology. Contextual factors influence how team members communicate to one another and provide important information about the types of goals that are reasonable and attainable (Cramton, 2001). In virtual teams, many contextual factors may vary across work units. For instance, some virtual team members may work in technology-driven or "paperless" offices, where most work — including collaborative work — is accomplished electronically. In contrast, team members in other locations may work in more traditional offices, where most work is accomplished through formal and informal F2F meetings. Team members from these different units may have different ideas about what can be accomplished in a virtual team environment, making it more difficult to establish goals that each team member can agree upon.

Third, it may be more difficult for virtual team members to direct their work efforts toward the shared virtual team goal, because they must balance their virtual team responsibilities with competing local demands. Said differently, virtual team members will likely have expectations and goals at their "home units" that they must fulfill in addition to their responsibilities on the virtual team. Team members may weigh the importance of their local demands more heavily than their virtual demands, because the local work is more immediate and visible to coworkers and supervisors. Moreover, because virtual team members cannot monitor one another's behaviors in "real time," they may find it easier to reduce the effort they afford to their virtual team, believing that those reduced efforts may go undetected (Shapiro, Furst, Spreitzer, & Von Glinow, 2002). Weeks or months may go by before team members talk to one another, and team members may easily manufacture excuses for not doing their fair share of the work.

Knowledge and Skills

Effective virtual teaming also requires specialized skills, knowledge, and technical capabilities. For example, team members must understand how to communicate using various technologies, ranging from simple, lean technologies, like telephones and e-mail, to more complex innovations, such as decision support systems or specialized collaborative software packages (e.g., Lotus Notes®).

Effective communication requires more than simply knowing how to use different technologies. It also requires that team members transmit content and meaning using these technologies. In the absence of visual cues (e.g., body language) or verbal cues (e.g., intonation), team members must supply contextual information that transmits meaning in nontraditional ways. E-mail users attempt to provide the emotional context of messages through symbols such as happy faces :) or via capital letters to indicate outrage, emphasis, or aggression, but these symbols can only convey rudimentary feelings. Moreover, electronic media rarely provide feedback that allows the message sender to confirm whether the meaning of a message was received and interpreted as intended.

Virtual team members must also understand the importance of matching their assigned tasks with the use of appropriate technologies. Research suggests that higher-performing virtual teams not only use information technologies more than low-performing teams, but they also have a better understanding of which technologies are best suited for a given task (Hollingshead & McGrath, 1995). Achieving the fit between task and technology helps virtual teams ensure that the appropriate task and non-task-related information is conveyed across geographic boundaries. For instance, routine tasks that do not require a lot of contextual information or complex communication may be performed efficiently using a lean technology, such as e-mail. More complex tasks, such as consensus building, require richer technologies that also convey body language or verbal cues.

Finally, virtual team members must be able to demonstrate trustworthiness and possess the propensity to trust (Jarvenpaa, Knoll, & Leidner, 1998). To be successful, virtual team members must be able to trust that teamwork is being carried out in each other's absence. Virtual team members often do not see one another and cannot observe one another's behavior all of the time. Hence, they must work under the assumption that team members are fulfilling their expected responsibilities. The propensity to trust is particularly important to help a team get off the ground initially. Trust enables members to take action at the team's onset, which helps the team maintain trust and deal with uncertainty, ambiguity, and vulnerability associated with dispersed work, until team members have time to demonstrate that they are, in fact, trustworthy (Jarvenpaa et al., 1998). Over time, team members learn who performs well, who fulfills their responsibilities, and who helps out others.

Team Processes and Strategies

The process of identifying and implementing effective team work processes may also be more challenging for virtual teams. Virtual team members often work in different time zones, so most of their work must be accomplished asynchronously, that is, during different times and on separate occasions. Also, technological breakdowns may impede team communication and information flow. The disjointed workflow can create scheduling and coordination problems that teams must manage in order to maintain forward progress. Therefore, teams must develop procedures for maintaining workflow and for handling communication breakdowns, such as lost e-mails, attachments that cannot be opened, and conference calls that go awry.

Virtual teams may be especially vulnerable to communication miscues because of their reliance on electronic rather than F2F communication and because team members may speak different languages or come from different cultural backgrounds, where communication styles vary. Hence, the development of communication norms may be especially important for preventing misunderstandings and maintaining work flow. For instance, what some team members may consider acceptable behavior is likely to vary from country to country and even from the East to the West coast of the United States. For instance, in some cultures, silence may signal agreement with another team member's idea, while in others, it may signal respectful deference. Subtle differences in language and meaning may be hard to detect when team members cannot observe verbal and nonverbal behaviors. Team members must also develop backup procedures for lost e-mails, attachments that cannot be opened, and conference calls that go awry. Thus, virtual teams need to establish specific communication norms, such as when and how to criticize each other's work, who should be copied on e-mails, and how to edit documents.

Summary and Implications for Action Learning Using Virtual Teams

Cumulatively, research and practice provide substantial information on the unique challenges associated with virtual teams. However, much of this information is based on anecdotal evidence or on laboratory studies involving students. For managers and educators charged with developing virtual teams, a need exists to study virtual work teams in a natural work setting to identify the factors that influence team effectiveness and how action learning programs may be designed to create and support effective teams. The teams we studied from two executive education programs provided such an opportunity. For both teams, we were able to observe and collect information regarding a number of work process and task-related variables to identify what factors internal to these teams were associated with stronger team performance. Additionally, in her role as program director for both executive education programs, the first author was able to plan and implement many aspects of the action learning programs used by the participating companies. As a result, we were able to examine how factors external to the team (e.g., specific elements of the training intervention and senior management support) can contribute to team performance.

In the section that follows, we describe the 15 teams that participated in the two executive education programs and the nature of their action learning projects. We then highlight performance differences between the teams and offer our insights as to which factors, both internal and external to the teams, differentiated the more successful from the less successful teams. We conclude by discussing the implications of our findings on virtual team development programs used in management education.

THE TEAMS AND
EXECUTIVE EDUCATION CONTEXT

The virtual teams we studied represented a financial services company (FINSERV) and a food distribution company (FDIST). FINSERV provides investment banking services and financial services for high-net-worth residential and institutional customers. FDIST manufactures a limited number of products and distributes a large selection of food products to institutions, such as schools and hospitals, and to fast-food chains and individually owned and operated restaurants. For FINSERV and FDIST, participation in the executive program was selective. Participants were already in positions of substantial responsibility, were nominated to participate in the program by someone more senior than themselves, and were considered to have potential beyond their current levels of responsibility. Neither of the teams from the financial services or the food distribution company had prior experience working on a virtual team. In fact, one of the stated goals for both the FINSERV and FDIST programs was to develop relationships across business units within the United States and, for the FINSERV teams, internationally.

During the first meeting of each executive education program, individuals were assigned to project teams, each of which was charged with completing a challenging business project over several months. Specifically, team members were expected to research a critical business issue or problem currently affecting their organization and to make recommendations for solving or improving it. Although their assignments were similar, the FINSERV and FDIST teams differed along several dimensions, including the degree to which their projects were structured, how they were evaluated, and how much instructional support was provided from program administrators. We summarize these differences in Table 1.

Financial Services Teams (FINSERV)

The FINSERV teams were organized as part of a women's leadership program, an executive education experience provided by the Kenan-Flagler Business School in Chapel Hill, North Carolina, and the Center For Creative Leadership (CCL) in Greensboro, North Carolina. Senior-level women attended a leadership program at two separate time intervals. At Time 1, the women

Table 1: Team descriptions.

	Financial Services (FINSERV)	Food Distribution (FDIST)
Purpose of program	Organized as part of a women's leadership program	Organized as part of an executive management training program
Objective of team assignments	Move the company forward on issues of importance to participants in the program	Move the company forward on a variety of critical issues identified by corporate leaders
Participants	45 senior-level women from a variety of functional areas (e.g., human resources, marketing, investment banking, finance)	29 mid- and senior-level men and women from a variety of functional areas (e.g., operations, human resources, sales management)
Location of team members	Globally distributed	Distributed within the United States
Project assignments	Selected by the team members	Assigned by executive education staff and company senior managers
Duration of project	3 months	8 months
Key dates	Time 1: Team members participated in a 5-day training program in Phase I; teams allowed time to discuss projects. Time 2: Presented projects with recommendations 3 months later	Time 1: Three-day residential training Time 2: Three-day residential training Time 3: Three-day residential training Time 4: Three-day residential training to include project presentations to senior management and faculty

participated in a five-day training program emphasizing issues of globalization, managing change, technology, communication skills, and specific challenges in the financial services industry. At Time 2, approximately three months later, the training program emphasized individual leadership skills, personal style, and individual assessment of strengths and weaknesses. Between Times 1 and 2, the participants were expected to complete action learning projects in virtual teams.

The teams typically included five or six women who differed in terms of geography, age, cultural background, and job function. For example, some teams included members working in London, Hong Kong, or Europe, and in functions such as human resources, marketing, investment banking, and finance. Of the 45 women participating in the program, six were from London; one from Los Angeles; one from Canada; two from Jacksonville, Florida; one from Paris; one from Little Rock, Arkansas; two from Hong Kong; one from South Africa; one from Stamford, Connecticut; 10 from various offices in New Jersey; and 18 from several offices in the New York City area. All teams had representatives from multiple countries and locations within the United States, such that each team had to deal with time-zone differences. All business was conducted in English. Although each participant spoke English, the women from Hong Kong struggled with English idioms. During the first five-day residential executive education program (Time 1), the teams selected topics for their action learning assignment, which included the projects summarized in Table 2.

During Time 1, team members spent a minimal amount of time at the end of each day discussing and planning their projects. Program instructors provided teams with written directions for the projects, project expectations, and recommendations for working with a senior sponsor. However, instructors provided no information about how to work effectively in a virtual environment.

Most of the work on the projects was conducted in team members' natural work environments in the interval between Time 1 and Time 2 of the program. In the early stages of the project, the groups set up conference calls in order for all team members to exchange information. All groups found it difficult to communicate synchronously because of large time-zone differences and other work commitments that appeared to take precedence over attending the

Table 2: FINSERV project teams.

Team	Project Description
1	To create a portal of choice for select global platinum clients
2	To determine the operational "financial" benefits of implementing Web-based collaboration tools
3	To build and foster a diverse cross-enterprise network of leaders
4	To develop a trial mentor program
5	To develop a new Web-based employee orientation
6	To identify methods for retaining talent and becoming the employer of choice
7	Research best-practices for recruitment and retention
8	To formulate a manager — and leader — selection process
9	Research job rotation experiences across business units and regions

conference calls. Although conference call times were agreed to well in advance by individuals on the teams, it was common for one or two members of the team to be absent during a call.

As the projects proceeded, the project teams were more likely to share documents and individual work asynchronously. Despite the availability of Web-conferencing software, such as WebEx™ and Microsoft®'s PlaceWare, teams relied on more rudimentary forms of information sharing, such as sending e-mails with attachments. One participant, whose team members included women from London and various offices in the United States, said:

We didn't use web conferencing software for several reasons. Different parts of the organization use different technologies. What is used in the U.S. may not be used in the U.K. Also it just seemed easier to conference call and send each other attachments.

At the FINSERV organization, Web-conferencing is used routinely for formal presentations by executives and for training financial advisors but is generally not used for informal conversations between or among individuals. As one participant noted, the technology produces a detectable transmission delay, which makes it less than ideal for communication. Moreover, for teams with members from different time zones, synchronous methods of communication may be inconvenient. For example, to communicate with Japan from the United States, individuals in the United States would be calling their Japanese colleagues in the middle of the night and vice versa.

At Time 2, each FINSERV team presented its project to two other teams, a Kenan-Flagler faculty member or a CCL consultant, and, in some cases, a senior manager of the FINSERV organization. All teams made recommendations for further action to be taken by the company. Although the teams evaluated the executive education program, their projects were not evaluated by senior managers or external experts.

Food Distribution Company Teams (FDIST)

FDIST, which is headquartered in the Eastern United States, includes a number of operating divisions across the United States but does not have international operations. The FDIST teams were organized as part of a leadership development program provided by the Kenan-Flagler Business School at the UNC–Chapel Hill. The program was designed to align organizational learning with strategic business needs, to establish cross-organizational networks that encourage best practice, to prepare managers for expanded organizational roles, and to act as a vehicle for change. The program was conducted over an eight-month period, during which participants attended four residencies in Chapel Hill (approximately two months apart) covering topics such as financial manage-

Table 3: FDIST project teams.

Team	Project Objective
1	To develop an integration strategy for acquisitions
2	To determine how to efficiently transfer information technology from one subsidiary company to other parts of the firm
3	To determine how to transfer best practices from one division of the company to another
4	To streamline the accounts payable process
5	To conduct a corporate communications audit
6	To develop career paths for specific jobs

ment, communication skills, marketing, and leadership. Participants included 29 senior- or mid-level managers, 27 of whom were men and two were women.

Program administrators introduced the action learning projects during the first executive education residency (Time 1). Like the FINSERV teams, FDIST team members were assigned to cross-functional and geographically dispersed teams. Unlike the FINSERV teams that chose their own projects, the FDIST team topics were chosen by the CEO and his closest managers. These are summarized in Table 3.

During Time 1, the Executive Education Project Director outlined expectations for the action learning projects, provided detailed instructions about how sponsors should work with teams, and highlighted the typical obstacles and frustrations that virtual teams might encounter. In addition, the Project Director conducted an exercise to simulate a virtual team interaction. During this exercise, team members were sent to their respective hotel rooms, where they convened their first conference call, with the objective of reaching agreement about work and behavioral norms. One team experienced difficulties connecting all members for their call; so, during the debriefing session for this exercise, all groups had the opportunity to discuss contingencies for communication break-downs.

At subsequent residencies, the virtual teams were provided with additional time (ranging from 3 to 6 hours) to work on their projects. This was unstructured time available to participants before and after the dinner hour. However, the expectation was that the majority of the project teams' work would be completed virtually, when managers returned to their home offices. Like the FINSERV teams, the FDIST teams relied almost exclusively on e-mail, telephone, conference calls, and document sharing via e-mail attachments. Although teams varied with respect to the amount of time they devoted to the project while between residencies, most indicated that they convened as a team only once or twice during these periods, usually via conference calls, to exchange and update information. Hence, it was during the residencies, when team members met F2F, that team members discussed work processes, timelines, and commitment levels. At the end of the project, many of the managers commented that they wished they had done more communicating throughout the process to set expectations of deadlines, to maintain enthusiasm and focus, and to communicate responsibilities.

During the final session of the executive education program, senior managers from the company and Kenan-Flagler faculty observed the action learning presentations and evaluated each on the basis of the quality and content of the team's report and the quality of the presentation.

Outcomes of the FINSERV and FDIST Team Projects

The performances of the 15 teams varied widely, as illustrated by comments of participants, by the range of scores FDIST teams received for their final project evaluations, and by the degree to which team projects were implemented and followed-up on after program completion. In general, the FDIST teams' performances were stronger than those of the FINSERV teams, although differences between teams from each company also emerged. Data collected from four surveys of FDIST team members from January 2002 through August 2002 and interviews with team members from both FINSERV and FDIST provided some insights into why some of these disparities exist. In particular, performance differences reflected differences in program design, in the operating cultures of the participating companies, and in the work processes developed by the various teams. Next, we discuss these differences and the lessons learned.

LESSONS LEARNED FROM THE VIRTUAL TEAMS

Corporate Culture Matters

The disparate results achieved by the FINSERV and FDIST teams suggests that for virtual teams operating in the "real world," the climate for virtual teamwork and the underlying corporate culture can greatly impact performance. For instance, the teams from FINSERV did not have sufficient time to devote to their projects, the commitment to work on them outside of their normal work duties, or the overt support of senior management. Not surprisingly, attendance from Time 1 to Time 2 of the FINSERV program dropped from 45 to 41 women because of more pressing business engagements.

The data from these two companies also suggest that organizational culture may impact the degree to which virtual teams will be successful. The company culture of the FINSERV organization is based primarily on transactions rather than on processes and on individual "deal-making" rather than on team contributions. The investment banking culture is one in which senior-level employees are judged on how quickly and successfully they can close lucrative financial transactions. Approximately half of the FINSERV participants worked in investment banking, private-client groups, or institutional-client groups, as opposed to human resources, legal services, marketing, corporate services, or other support functions. In this environment, asking individuals to take time to work on a project unrelated to constructing "a deal" interfered with their commitment to the team project. Many said they wanted to work harder on the action learning teams but knew they would not be rewarded for their efforts. Some even indicated that their personal production would suffer as a result of spending time on the action learning team project, and that this distraction from personal production would ultimately impact their compensation. Their comments may be best summarized by the chief organizer of the Executive Education program from FINSERV, who remarked:

> The culture doesn't fully support the process of virtual teams. People aren't use to working this way and the organization is driven by transactions that are completed by individuals. What is most important is developing business relationships that will help generate business and close deals. Even senior managers who wanted to be there for the project presentations couldn't make it at the last moment. Something more urgent always comes up and they typically have no-one to backfill in their absence. (Personal Interview, November 12, 2002)

The culture of FDIST, on the other hand, is less transactional and more process- and operations-focused. Compared to the experience of individuals in the FINSERV teams, individuals in this environment did not seem as pressed for time or as driven by production goals. As a result, the FDIST team members reported more favorable experiences with the virtual team exercise and found the projects more worthwhile than members of the FINSERV teams. Members of the food distribution teams took the project seriously, at least in part, because the culture supported working in this way. In recent years, FDIST acquired, on average, three companies per year. In response, senior executives repeatedly emphasized the importance of teamwork in the integration of these acquisitions. The difference between these two organizations and their responses to virtual teamwork strongly suggest that some companies and businesses are better suited to virtual teamwork than others because of their underlying cultures.

Importance of Face Time

Although all the teams worked virtually, those that took advantage of F2F meetings had fewer interpersonal conflicts and produced better results. At the end of their projects, the FINSERV teams realized that they had not taken advantage of F2F time (before working virtually) to determine how their team would work together and to define the project assignment. Some F2F meetings are essential for developing trust and individual accountabilities. One participant commented, "We didn't have enough time in phase one to develop the learning teams enough. It [the project concept] was rushed in phase 1 and we needed more time and a better game plan." The problem with lack of face-time seemed to be magnified by the multicultural aspect of the FINSERV teams. Some team members, especially those from Hong Kong, had difficulty communicating with team members, because English was not their first language. For these individuals, conference calls were difficult, because they lacked visual clues to interpret what was being said, and because they did not understand English idioms well. Conversely, the FDIST teams had the opportunity to meet F2F three times during the residential training program. Many realized that having occasional F2F meetings greatly improved their ability to function virtually. During these F2F meetings, the project assignment was refined, expectations of one another were discussed, and responsibilities were assigned. Virtual meetings were reserved for sharing documents, commenting on work, and determining next steps.

Importance of a Good Start

Survey data from the FDIST teams suggest that, at the beginning of the projects, little difference existed among the teams in terms of their perceptions of working virtually. All were optimistic about completing their projects successfully, and all were upbeat about their teammates' capabilities and commitment to the project. However, less than eight weeks later, differences began to emerge. One important difference reflected the extent to which teams clarified their missions and purposes before delving into the work. Misapprehensions about the purpose of the project are harder to correct once people are distanced by geography. For example, Team 5 reported the highest levels of coordination of activities, clarity of mission, and trust. From the early stages of the project in January through March of 2002, Team 5 set specific monthly goals that were used to keep the team focused while they were apart. In addition, this team created an early "win" by conducting a communications survey that was distributed to company employees. The data from the survey provided them with information for recommendations to senior management and clear momentum to continue working. In contrast, teams that floundered experienced a slow start, with coordination problems, ambiguity about the purposes of the projects, and apparent lack of commitment by some members. As one member of Team 2 remarked, "Team members' day to day tasks are being used as an excuse to avoid doing the project."

Coordination Difficulties

Coping with time-zone differences and large geographical distances posed greater problems for the FINSERV teams and seemed to affect their overall commitment to the project. Many team participants complained about the difficulty of attending telephone conferences, and it was common for at least one member to call in for a conference in the middle of the night. Individuals whose time zones were furthest away from the others in their team ended up feeling inconvenienced and eventually developed resentment toward the team project. Although the FDIST teams had time-zone changes to contend with, these time differences were not as dramatic and did not fuel interpersonal conflict.

Coordination seemed to reflect the degree to which teams developed a more rigorous process structure. One participant in the FINSERV teams remarked that her team developed a process structure in order to share documents:

We e-mailed documents to one another and we edited them or added our contributions to them. We quickly learned to date-and-time stamp them so we could keep clear which version of the document we were working with. We had to learn our own rules of engagement. We rotated responsibility for editing the document.

The FDIST teams that appeared to perform the best did not wait for a last burst of productivity prior to their August presentations and had a clear, agreed-upon mission from the start.

It is likely that virtual teams procrastinate more than nonvirtual teams, simply because they have the opportunity to do so. Many of the teams registered surprise at how far behind they were — this is likely due to the virtual nature of their communication. Had they more F2F contact, they would have known how they were progressing. Teams with identified leaders began the process earlier and finished well before the deadline, again reinforcing the notion that leaders in virtual teams function as monitors of individual task performance. Teams that struggled the most lacked this process structure. For instance, with a few weeks left before their final presentations to FDIST executives, teams were asked what percentage of their project was completed. Teams 2 and 3, which received some of the lowest performance ratings, progressed the least — with 26% and 42% of their projects completed, respectively. These same teams also were the least confident that senior management would act upon their recommendations.

Opportunities for Free-Riding

Earlier, we noted that in virtual teams, opportunities for some members to free-ride may be enhanced because their (reduced) efforts are more likely to go undetected. Additionally, team members may feel that it is easier to set aside their virtual team work when their local demands take precedent. These processes seemed to occur more frequently in the FINSERV teams. In addition to working in an environment that did not support virtual teamwork, the design of the project teams may have contributed to reduced work efforts. Unlike the FDIST teams, these teams did not have interim F2F meetings before their final project was due. Moreover, for members of the FINSERV teams, performance on the virtual team did not have implications for their overall job evaluation. In contrast, FDIST members were aware that their efforts would be evaluated by senior managers, and their performance during the leadership program could provide opportunities for future advancement. In one FINSERV team, free-riding produced such frustration and resentment that three members of a team voted two noncontributors "off the island." For both companies' teams, commitment was identified by members as a critical success factor. One member of the food distribution teams put it this way, "Commitment from all members of the group is critical to its [the project's] success."

Virtual Team Leadership

Identification of a team leader early in a team's process appears to impact virtual team performance. Leaderless teams recognized that they were handicapped by not having a dominant player who would keep people on task, monitor work, and discharge responsibilities. Those teams that did not identify a leader floundered early on and spent more time debating and negotiating roles and responsibilities than those with leaders. Recent research confirmed that the communication among virtual team members is almost entirely task-oriented, thus making it difficult to develop trust (Dalton, Leslie, Ernst, & Deal, 2002). In these F2F meetings, a leader should emerge to take on the responsibility of monitoring the team's progress and holding people accountable for tasks they agree to do. Not surprisingly, we found that teams with leaders reported more commitment and the absence of free-riders, because the leader played the role of managing individual performance of individual team members.

The Use of Technology

One would expect virtual teams to take advantage of new technologies, such as Web-conferencing, for communication; however, participants in these teams relied on technologies that were most familiar to them, such as e-mail, one-to-one telephone calls, and teleconferencing. Even though the FINSERV teams had access to Web-conferencing software, none of them used it. One FINSERV participant suggested that e-mailing documents that her team could all respond to in their own time was more efficient than using Web-conferencing software, "People in the company at this level are use to working at odd hours. It worked for me to have dinner, put my kids to bed and then go to the computer to work on the project or respond to a version of a document." Similarly, although the FDIST executives publicly stated that individuals should improve their technology skills through working virtually, none of the FDIST teams did. Although some members had familiarity with these more sophisticated technologies, unless everyone on the team was conversant with them, it was apparently burdensome to use them. In short, the teams did not want the extra responsibility of teaching their teammates how to employ these technologies.

The behaviors of the FINSERV and FDIST teams suggest that managers and educators should include some technology training or experiential learning in the virtual team development process. Asking groups to use new technology without providing them support to do so does not produce the desired results. Even though these groups were encouraged to use sophisticated technologies to enhance their virtual work, they found this burdensome and reverted to more familiar technologies, such as e-mail and conference calls. If new technologies are to be employed, training on their use needs to be built into the curriculum of the executive education program so that all team members feel confident using them.

External Support

An outside facilitator had an impact on the success of the teams and the attitude of individuals toward working virtually. Little facilitation to orient the FINSERV teams to working virtually was provided before the teams began their work. The team members complained about complicated instructions and confusion about expectations and project assignments. This initial confusion created a negative climate around the entire virtual team exercise. Conversely, there was a facilitator for the FDIST teams who explained the potential benefits of working virtually and gave clear, simple directions for the action learning project. For example, at Time 1, the facilitator asked the teams to define their norms for working virtually, had them practice a conference call, and discussed their projects in detail. The facilitator also gave a brief presentation about the pros and cons of working virtually and identified obstacles the teams might encounter. The early discussions about how to work together provided the teams with a baseline for discussing team conflicts as they arose.

Besides providing direction on the business assignment, it is critical to provide guidance on the process of working in a virtual team environment. This guidance needs to be reiterated several times and perhaps in a variety of formats. The executive educational or management development professional can provide guidance by e-mail, participate in periodic conference calls as an observer and provider of feedback to the teams, and can check-in with senior sponsors to encourage them to stay involved with their teams. Program directors can also include structured "learning dialogues" throughout the process to ensure that groups are aware of their progress, are dealing with conflicts when they arise, are learning from working virtually, and are on-track to complete their projects. Through the guidance of these development professionals, individuals should be prepared to deal with some of the frustrations of working virtually and the obstacles presented by working virtually. If documented, these dialogues also can become part of the organization's learning, should virtual teams be employed in the future.

Senior Sponsor Support and Salience of the Project

Senior sponsorship of the team projects and senior involvement were also key factors in team success. Participants of the FDIST teams took their virtual team assignments seriously, at least in part because senior management identified the action learning topics and were involved in them. Evaluation data showed that the perceived importance of the work by team members and the meaningfulness they attributed to their projects were related to team members' satisfaction with working virtually and to their confidence that their teams would be successful. In contrast, the FINSERV teams chose their own projects, and several participants suggested that they did not seem crucial to the organization. As one FINSERV participant expressed, "Assignments were less valuable because they weren't necessary mission critical for the organization."

Each FDIST team was assigned a senior sponsor who either had an interest in the topic or had resources that would be helpful to the team. Interestingly, the lack of active involvement of the senior sponsor did not affect the team's perception of its effectiveness, satisfaction with working virtually, productivity, or commitment. What seemed to matter was that senior managers sanctioned the project and attended the project presentations. Seven managers, including the CEO and President, attended the final program, where the teams presented their projects. The involvement of senior managers in the financial services teams was more haphazard in that the topics were not chosen by senior managers, only a few teams had engaged a senior sponsor, and only three senior managers attended the final action learning presentations. The lack of involvement by senior managers seemed to negatively influence the degree of commitment individuals had to their team and to their project assignment.

The stakes were higher for the FDIST team members, because they presented their projects to all of the other teams, senior managers, and four Kenan-Flagler faculty members, whereas the FINSERV teams presented to only two other teams and either one Kenan-Flagler faculty member or one consultant from the Center for Creative Leadership. Most teams did not have an audience of corporate senior managers.

Our findings suggest that if senior sponsors are to be part of the program, they need to be apprised of the type of support they are expected to provide.

Senior management support is particularly important to the team's perception of the importance of their project to the company, and thus affects their commitment to the work. Senior sponsors can show their support by attending the teams' project presentations and by providing meaningful critique. If projects are deemed to be of value, senior sponsors should continue stewardship and provide the necessary resources to implement them.

Ancillary Benefits of Virtual Teaming

An unintended consequence of the action learning teams for the FINSERV teams was the network it provided women, particularly for help with their careers. In financial services organizations, women who reach the top are often isolated from one another. The action learning experience brought women who worked in different parts of the organization together in a supportive environment. One woman explained the positive effect of this network in this way, "It [the virtual team experience] was one of the most valuable parts of the program. These people form the basis of my friendships and overall support. Invaluable advice, counseling, knowledge and help." Another commented, "The team building was a very good experience and deepened ties I felt with the women's leadership program network."

CONCLUSIONS AND IMPLICATIONS FOR MANAGERS AND EDUCATORS

The experiences of the 15 FINSERV and FDIST teams demonstrate that virtual team dynamics mirror those of colocated teams in a number of ways. For instance, teams demonstrated how important it is to establish a clear mission and well-defined and enforced norms for behavior. Clearly, the most effective virtual teams that we observed established clear accountabilities that team members understood and followed. In the absence of this direction, team members seemingly refocused their energies away from the virtual team demands. Both virtual and nonvirtual teams require F2F contact to establish norms, trust, and comfort in working together. F2F communication builds a platform for trust, where people naturally engage in conversation that strays away from the work setting. Without F2F interaction, team communication becomes more task-oriented. On conference calls, teams forego social "chit-chat" and focus immediately on discussing the business at hand. Social dialogue and the visual cues that accompany it build a sense of community.

In contrast to the similarities between these virtual teams and colocated teams, the FINSERV and FDIST teams also demonstrate that some significant differences exist between virtual and nonvirtual teams. Because of the lack of visual communication cues and information that team members gather from day-to-day observation and interaction with one another, virtual teams struggle with several issues. In the intervening months between March and August with the FDIST teams, the trust level of members deteriorated, and the perception that it was acceptable (or psychologically safe) to disagree with the group declined. Open-ended responses from individuals indicted that little work was actually being done in the early phases, and as individuals became actively involved and aware of their lack of progress, this most likely led to a lack of trust in fellow team members. Free-riding is more easily accomplished in virtual teams, because no one is monitoring activity on a day-to-day basis. Over the intervening months between executive education sessions, the perception that it was safe to disagree with the group declined; time was running out, and suggesting alternative ways of completing the project would only put groups further behind and add to the stress they were already experiencing. Identifying a leader in virtual teams is important, because communication about roles and responsibilities needs to be managed more actively than in nonvirtual environments.

In conclusion, our findings regarding the development of virtual teams in an executive education setting provide important new insights for managers and educators charged with developing high-performing virtual teams. Notably, by studying virtual teams in their natural working environments, we were able to demonstrate how factors characteristic of those environments (e.g., culture and reward systems) may contribute to or hinder virtual team performance. We were also able to identify a number of methods that executive education program directors can use to maximize team learning experiences. For instance, we observed that some focus should be paid to using technology and giving team members hands-on experience using more sophisticated technologies to communicate and streamline workflow. Teams that are challenged by the dispersion of geographical time zones should employ asynchronous technologies, such as Web sites, Web-casts, and Internet file transmission, as well as lean methods, such as e-mail.

Our findings demonstrate the importance of involving senior sponsors and communicating senior managers' support for virtual teaming. As we observed, senior management support helps communicate to team members the importance of these projects and may help lessen the tendency for team members to free-ride, if they know they are going to be evaluated on their performance. Finally, our results highlight the importance of structuring the development process. For example, the human resource professional or executive education program administrator should build in initial F2F team interactions, organize technology training before the team begins to work virtually, and encourage teams to choose a leader whose responsibilities would include assigning tasks and monitoring individual participation and team progress.

REFERENCES

Cramton, C. D. (2001). The mutual knowledge problem and its consequences for dispersed collaboration. *Organization Science, 12,* 346–371.

Dalton, M., Leslie, J., Ernst, C., & Deal, J. (2002). *Success for the new global manager: How to work across distances, countries and cultures.* San Francisco: Jossey-Bass.

Finholt, T., & Sproull, L. S. (1990). Electronic groups at work. *Organization Science, 1,* 41–61.

Hackman, J. R. (1987). The design of work teams. In J. W. Lorsch (Ed.), *Handbook of organizational behavior* (pp. 315–342). Englewood Cliffs, NJ: Prentice Hall.

Hollingshead, A., & McGrath, J. (1995). Computer-assisted groups: A critical review of the empirical research. In R. Guzzo, & E. Salas (Eds.), *Team effectiveness and decision-making in organizations* (pp. 46–78). San Francisco: Jossey-Bass.

Jarvenpaa, S. L., Knoll, K., & Leidner, D. E. (1998). Is anybody out there? Antecedents of trust in global virtual teams. *Journal of Management Information Systems, 14,* 29–64.

Majchrzak, A., Rice, R. E., King, N., Malhotra, A., & Ba, S. (2000). Computer-mediated inter-organizational knowledge-sharing: Insights from a virtual team innovating using a collaborative tool. *Information Resources Management Journal, 13,* 44–53.

Marquardt, M. (1999). Action learning in action. Paolo Alto: Davies-Black Publishing.

Shapiro, D. L., Furst, S. A., Von Glinow, M. A., & Spreitzer, G. (2002). Transnational teams in the electronic age: Are team identity and high performance at risk? *Journal of Organizational Behavior, 23,* 455–467.

ENDNOTES

[1] Blended training design is a term used by many management development professionals to suggest blending traditional classroom training methods with other methods, such as distance learning via the World Wide Web or action learning assignments.

Chapter XIV

Motivational Antecedents, Constituents, and Consequents of Virtual Community Identity

Utpal M. Dholakia, Rice University, USA

Richard P. Bagozzi, Rice University, USA

ABSTRACT

In understanding the influence of virtual communities on its members, examined in this chapter is the role of identity — *the member's conscious knowledge of belonging and the emotional and evaluative significance attached to the membership. Drawing from research and analyses across different disciplines, we present an integrative framework considering and elaborating on the motivational antecedents, constituents, and consequents of virtual community identity. We also discuss its implications for virtual community organizers and highlight promising research opportunities in this area.*

INTRODUCTION

The rising research interest in virtual group interactions corresponds to the overall acceptance and growth of the Internet as an influential social forum, and has spanned many disciplines in the last few years, including sociology (e.g.,

Wellman & Gulia, 1999), social psychology (e.g., McKenna & Bargh, 1998), communications (e.g., Postmes, Spears, & Lea, 2000), and marketing (e.g., Bagozzi & Dholakia, 2002; Dholakia, Klein, & Bagozzi, 2003).

While such interactions may be analyzed using many different theoretical perspectives and lenses, as the chapters in this book illustrate, our focus is on a particular type of virtual group: the network-based virtual community. We define such a virtual community to be "a specialized, geographically dispersed group, interacting together in an online forum, and characterized by a structured, relatively sparse, and dynamic network of relationships among participants who share a common focus" (Dholakia, Klein, & Bagozzi, 2003). Current examples of such virtual communities include the slashdot Web site community of software enthusiasts, the alt.games.sony-playstation newsgroup on Usenet, and the Internet Bonsai Club.

Although collaborative, researchers acknowledged that interactions between members in such virtual communities are often focused, initially driven by self-interest, and generally narrow in scope (Wellman & Gulia, 1999). Many such interactions also tend to be unplanned, often motivated by a functional goal (for example, wanting information regarding available products prior to a purchase) or a situational happenstance (e.g., logging into the chat room at the same time as another member). Moreover, the frequency and extent of participation by members is driven entirely by volitional choice, in that one can sever ties with the virtual community relatively effortlessly (simply by not returning to the venue).

In spite of their seemingly tenuous hold on members for all these reasons, marketers have been struck at how influential such virtual communities can be — from influencing purchase decisions and choices of their members, to rapidly disseminating knowledge and perceptions regarding new products (called "buzz" by marketers) and influencing their success, to strengthening company–customer relationships (Dholakia & Bagozzi, 2001). This influence only seems to be growing in range and extent as more people come to join and participate regularly in these virtual groups.

Because of this, researchers studying virtual communities have become interested in understanding why virtual communities are so influential for their members. In seeking to answer this question, one theoretical perspective that offers a useful starting point is that of social identity theory (SIT) (Tajfel, 1972; Turner, 1985), which posits that a crucial basis of the group's influence on its individual members arises from the individual's identification with the group (i.e., his or her conscious knowledge of belonging to the social group) and the emotional and evaluative value attached to this membership. Belonging to the group is a psychological state that is distinct from being a unique and separate individual and confers social identity (i.e., a shared or collective representation of who one is and how one should behave) (Hogg & Abrams, 1988).

Drawing from the SIT and organizational research (e.g., Bergami & Bagozzi, 2000; Dutton, Dukerich, & Harquail, 1994), in previous work, we showed virtual community identity (defined in cognitive, affective, and evaluative terms) to be an important predictor of the member's desire to participate in such virtual groups (Bagozzi & Dholakia, 2002; Bagozzi, Dholakia, & Klein, 2003).

In this chapter, we build on these findings and consider the construct of virtual community identity in greater detail. Specifically, we consider three aspects of virtual community identity here: (a) its motivational antecedents, (b) its constituents, and (c) its consequences, as they pertain to its individual members. Through this analysis, we not only hope to develop a better understanding of this important basis of virtual community influence but also seek to raise some interesting questions to stimulate future research. Our framework, summarizing the key constructs covered here, is provided in Figure 1. The discussion is organized in three sections, corresponding to each of the antecedents, constituents, and consequents of virtual community identity, in order.

Figure 1: A framework of motivational antecedents, constituents, and consequents of virtual community identity.

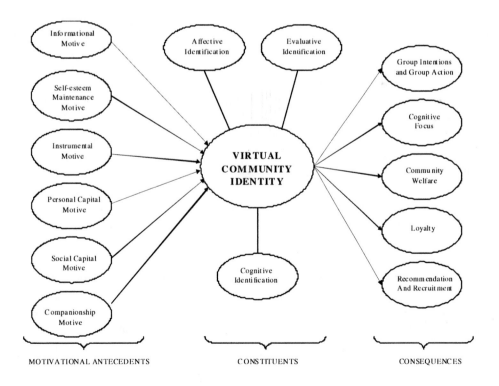

ANTECEDENTS OF
VIRTUAL COMMUNITY IDENTITY

What turns a diverse group of far-flung individuals, who have never seen each other in person, and usually with only a few shared characteristics or interests, into a virtual community of members who identify with it and are influenced by it? SIT researchers posit that identification with social groups is, first and foremost, derived from their functionality — they are influential and identified with, to the extent that they fulfill important individual and social needs of participants (Hogg & Abrams, 1988). This functional view of virtual groups follows from a long tradition of social psychological research that holds that people who depend on each other to satisfy one or more of their needs, and who achieve or expect to achieve positive outcomes from their interactions together, tend to develop feelings of mutual attraction and support and become a cohesive group (Deutsch, 1973; Sherif & Sherif, 1969; Turner, Hogg, Oakes, Reicher, & Wetherall, 1987).

It follows that participants' motivations, which are closely associated with specific perceptions that the virtual community offers value, are crucial antecedents to developing virtual community identity. Consistent with this reasoning, in a recent study, we found that specific value perceptions from participation were significant predictors of emotional attachment to the virtual community (Dholakia, Klein, & Bagozzi, 2003). Several different participant motivations are noteworthy in this regard (e.g., Bickart & Schindler, 2001; Dholakia, Klein, & Bagozzi, 2003; Flanagin & Metzger, 2001) and are considered in detail next.

Informational Motive

An important reason given by many members for participating in virtual communities is to receive and share information, to keep up-to-date regarding a topic, to know what others think, and then to use this information in decision making (Bickart & Schindler, 2001). As an example, a consumer buying a new computer may visit different chat rooms to learn about available choices and the prevailing tenor of opinions regarding different brands. A good current instance of a commercial virtual community built around participants' informational motives is Epinions.com, where the primary content is comprised of member-generated opinions regarding a variety of products. While those seeking information find a wealth of detailed reviews provided by (presumably) disinterested members, reviewers can earn money if their reviews are deemed to be useful by other members. Not surprisingly, Bickart and Schindler (2001) found that such Internet forums are more influential than marketer-generated sources of information, such as advertisements and Web sites, for many consumers.

Self-Esteem Maintenance Motive

SIT researchers noted that the maintenance and enhancement of one's self-esteem is one of the most important motives for group identification (Abrams & Hogg, 1988; Hogg & Abrams, 1990; but see Brewer, 1993, for a different view). Enhancement of self-esteem may occur in one of two ways on account of the virtual community. First, participants may be able to positively compare themselves to other group members and thereby feel better about their own capabilities, qualifications, and attributes. In virtual communities, this could occur either through passive "lurking," as when others' responses are evaluated negatively relative to one's own knowledge, or through active participation, when receiving affirmation from other members for the quality of one's contributions. This personal distinctiveness outcome or motive may be more of a factor in independent-based cultures than in interdependent-based cultures (e.g., Markus & Kitayama, 1991).

Second, self-esteem enhancement may occur for many members through a positive social distinctiveness of the ingroup from other salient outgroups, or nonmembers in general. Thus, belonging to a particular exclusive virtual community might enhance the member's self-esteem from the consideration of others not belonging to it. Marketers commonly use these means of self-esteem enhancement to motivate consumers, such as when offering "Platinum Clubs," "Valued Customer Rewards," etc., for their profitable customers; virtual community organizers have similar opportunities by raising the difficulty of obtaining and retaining membership in the community, and increasing identification as a result.

Instrumental Motive

Many members participate to achieve specific objectives, such as to solve a problem, to generate an idea for a project, to collaborate with a team, to influence others regarding some favored issue or product, and to buy or sell products. All such motives are instrumental in the sense that they are specific to achieving a subsequent end and are well defined by the member, prior to participation. Marketers recognized that gauging and facilitating instrumental motives of participants are important building blocks of commercial virtual communities and provide an opportunity to build a successful business. Many of the most robust and financially successful online business models at present, such as eBay, Amazon.com, etc., are built around the nurturance of instrumentally oriented virtual communities.

Personal Capital Motive

Social psychologists noted that many interpersonal interactions are driven by a motive for self-enhancement, which involves the discovery and expansion of aspects about the self from interacting with others. More formally, this motive was defined as the striving to achieve one's potential efficacy through increasing social resources, perspectives, and identities that facilitate the attainment of future goals (Aron, Aron, & Norman, 2001; McKenna & Bargh, 1998). In a practical sense, specific instances of this motive may involve elements of networking for professional advancement or an interest in gaining expertise in a chosen topic or in honing new skills or interests. For many members, virtual communities are particularly useful for these types of self-enhancement, because they offer the opportunity to interact with, learn from, and form ties with people who would otherwise be difficult to get access to (e.g., Flap, Bulder, & Volker, 1998). The personal capital motive may also be purely expressive or creative.

Social Capital Motive

In addition to increasing one's personal capital, participation in the virtual community also involves aspects of gaining acceptance and approval from other members, prestige within the group, and enhancement of one's social identity as a result. Social capital was studied in formal organizations but seems possible in virtual communities as well (e.g., Nahapiet & Ghoshal, 1998). This may be especially relevant in professional or work-based virtual communities, where participation yields rewards not only from enhanced reputation and status but also through positive instrumental gains, such as financial rewards.

Companionship Motive

Interestingly, among the early studies of virtual communities, researchers first noted the prevalence of those seeking companionship through participation. For many members, virtual communities provide an opportunity to establish and maintain contact with other people, dispelling loneliness and satisfying the "need to belong," recognized as a primary motive by social psychologists (Baumeister & Leary, 1995). Many participants use virtual communities for a range of social support, such as help and advice regarding an affliction or difficulty, sharing personal views and accomplishments, finding romantic partners, as well as for entertainment and fun (McKenna & Bargh, 1998).

Differentiating Between Participants' Symbolic and Pragmatic Motives

In studying participants' antecedent motivations, it is important to make a distinction between motives that are pragmatic and those that are symbolic, from the member's perspective (Brown, 1969). Whereas symbolic motives refer to those that implicate ego involvement and intrinsic motivation, pragmatic motives

(Brown, 1969) refer to the drive to correct "a state of deficiency where the result rather than the activity performed is valuable to the member" (p. 347). Brown (1969) suggests that only symbolic motives have relevance to social identity; pragmatic motives may link the individual to the group in the short-term but generally without engaging the psychological processes of identification or its consequences (e.g., without creating a sense of community or responsibility to group members). Relatively little research examined the distribution, incidence, or evolution of symbolic and pragmatic motives among members in virtual communities thus far, offering a promising opportunity.

It is also useful to note here that the classification of motives as pragmatic or symbolic is more appropriate from the member's rather than from the virtual community organizer's perspective. For instance, with respect to the informational motive, one member may view his or her need to obtain information as strictly pragmatic, not engaging in identification with the community, even though valuable information was obtained therein. In contrast, another member may view his or her information acquisition in the larger context of sharing resources with like-minded others and, thereby, implicate processes of identification. Much remains to be known regarding the process by which members come to view their participation motives as symbolic or factors contributing to this classification.

Understanding the Complementarity of Participants' Motives

Many participants' motives, especially those having informational or instrumental foci, tend to complement other members' motives in virtual communities. For instance, some members may look to the virtual community primarily for seeking information, while others may only have the giving of information as their primary motive. To the first type, the virtual community is only useful to the extent that useful information is received. To the second type, the virtual community's value is almost entirely derived from having questions to answer. In such cases, one way to view the virtual community is as a "motive-matching market," where complementary motives of participants are paired and matched efficiently. To the extent that such a matching is achieved, community identification among its members may be expected to increase. From a practical standpoint, this complementarity of members' motives has important implications for organizers, regarding issues such as recruiting new members, rewarding participation, influencing the roles played in the interaction, and so on (see Dholakia, Klein, & Bagozzi, 2003, for a detailed discussion).

Having analyzed the antecedent motives, we now turn to studying the identification construct in greater depth.

CONSTITUENTS OF
VIRTUAL COMMUNITY IDENTITY

Following from SIT, social identity refers to the member's conception of oneself in terms of the defining features of the social category, in our case, the virtual community, rendering the self stereotypically interchangeable with other community members and stereotypically distinct from nonmembers (Hogg, 1992). Consistent with other researchers, we view virtual community identity to be an active, selective, and volitional act, resulting from the fulfillment of one or more motives described above (Bhattacharya & Sen, 2003; Dutton, Dukerich, & Harquail, 1994). Identity defined this way implies a set of individual- and group-referent cognitions, emotional expressions, and evaluations, enabling the maintenance of a positive self-defining relationship with the virtual community.

In understanding the constituents of social identity, Tajfel (1978) suggested that a person achieves a social identity through a conscious self-awareness of one's membership in the group and the emotional and evaluative significance associated with this membership. Building on these early insights, Ellemers, Kortekaas, and Ouwerkerk (1999) proposed that three components comprise one's social identity:

> ...a cognitive component (a cognitive awareness of one's membership in a social group — self-categorization), an emotional component (a sense of emotional involvement with the group — affective commitment), and an evaluative component (a positive and negative value connotation attached to this group membership — group-based self-esteem). (p. 372, emphasis added)

(For more information, see also Bagozzi & Bergami, 2002; Bagozzi, Dholakia, & Klein, 2003; and Bergami & Bagozzi, 2000.) Each of these components is crucial to understanding virtual community identity and is discussed in greater detail next.

Cognitive Identification

The cognitive aspect of identification postulates a cognitive categorization process, whereby similarities between the self and group members are recognized, elaborated upon, and accentuated, as are dissimilarities with nonmembers, and the individual self is perceptually and behaviorally depersonalized in terms of the relevant group prototype (Hogg, 1992). The definition of organizational identification provided by Dutton, Dukerich, and Harquail (1994) is succinct and insightful: "identification is the degree to which a member defines him- or herself by the same attributes that he or she believes define the (virtual community)" (p. 242). Research in marketing and organization psychology suggests that cognitive identification may implicate knowledge structures of the member regarding the virtual community, including attributes that identify the community's core values, objectives, venue, and member characteristics (Bhattacharya & Sen, 2003). It is also likely to involve a general understanding, and acceptance, of the community's goals. Communication researchers showed that such a cognitive self-categorization process operates effectively in the case of communicators in online environments (Spears & Lea, 1994).

Emotional Identification

The emotional meaning of group membership is central to the social identification process (Tajfel, 1978). Drawing from organizational research (e.g., Allen & Meyer, 1996; Bergami & Bagozzi, 2000), in earlier work, we referred to this emotional component of virtual community identification as affective commitment (Bagozzi & Dholakia, 2002) and characterized it in a manner similar to Allen and Meyer (1996), who define affective commitment as "identification with, involvement in, and emotional attachment to" (p. 253) the virtual group. Given the volitional membership and the value of symbolic motivations discussed before, we expect that emotional identification may be the most influential of the three constituents for many virtual communities, but further research is necessary to verify this.

Evaluative Identification

The evaluative component of social identity — *group-based self-esteem* — was defined as the positive or negative value connotation attached to group membership (Ellemers, Kortekaas, & Ouwerkerk et al., 1999, p. 372), and it arises from evaluations of self-worth derived from membership. In a sense, this component of identification is closely tied to, and follows from, the personal capital motive of members described above.

Alternative Construals of Self in Virtual Community Identity

In identifying with the virtual community as described above, it is also useful to consider how the member construes self in relation to the virtual community, and the implications thereof. Brewer and Gardner (1996) made an interesting distinction between two alternative self-construals in this regard. The first possibility is that the virtual community member's self-construal occurs at the interpersonal level, called the interdependent or relational self, and is defined as the self-concept derived from connections and role relationships with significant others within the group. This construal would imply that the individual identifies with a few significant other members within the virtual community (e.g., the friends that one regularly chats with, or the most prominent contributors).

An alternative possibility is that the member's self-construal occurs at the group level, called the collective self. In this case, one's identity is defined in the context of the entire group, and the identification would be with the broad, more abstract category of the entire virtual community, rather than with particular members within it. Brewer and Gardner (1996) identified interesting differences between the alternative self-construals that have implications for two important consequences of virtual community identity: (a) what members focus on, and (b) how they behave, in the two cases. We examine these in detail in the next section.

CONSEQUENCES OF VIRTUAL COMMUNITY IDENTITY

Identification with the virtual community results in cognitive, motivational, and behavioral responses that have practical relevance for the community's organizers. Motivationally speaking, identification musters a commitment on the member's part to the achievement of the community's objectives, causing the member to participate more, as well as to invest more voluntary effort on its behalf. It also makes the member more amenable to engaging in greater varieties and degrees of cooperation with other members (Bhattacharya & Sen, 2003). We consider five different types of consequences of virtual community identity in greater detail here: group intentions and action, the participant's cognitive focus, an interpersonal welfare motive, promotion and recruitment, and loyalty to the virtual community.

Group Intentions and Group Action

The distinction between personal identity and social identity made earlier brings into focus the corresponding differences between personal and group intentions to act, and subsequent behavior of virtual community members. Usually, social psychologists tend to define intentions in personal terms, i.e., as a "person's motivation in the sense of his or her conscious plan to exert effort to carry out a behavior" (Eagly & Chaiken, 1993). But for virtual communities, the relevant participation intentions of identifying members more appropriately pertain to the plural target of the group, e.g., "I intend to chat together with my community members."

In philosophical terms, such joint activity entails shared intentionality by its participants. Philosopher Gilbert (1992) pointed out that action in relation to such plural subjects requires different conceptual schemes than the more common theme of personal action (see Bagozzi, 2000, for a detailed explication). Philosophers have given a great deal of attention to group intentions, using such labels as "we-intentions" (Tuomela, 1995) and "shared-intentions" (Bratman, 1999) to characterize such intentions. For instance, Bratman (1999) defined a "shared intention" as having the form "I intend that we act." In a similar vein, Tuomela (1995) defined a "we-intention" as a "commitment of an individual to participate in joint action, and involves an implicit or explicit agreement between the participants to engage in that joint action" (p. 2).

Bratman (1999) suggested that shared intentional activity is explainable by a shared intention between group members, along with associated forms of mutual responsiveness — implying that identification may serve as the basis for activity to be defined and enacted in this way by virtual community members. Interestingly, in analyzing intentions for joint action, philosophers make the further subtle distinction between shared intentions (Bratman, 1999), which pertain to the intention of the group, as a whole, to engage in joint activity, and we-intentions (Tuomela, 1995), which are not shared, per se, but are the intentions of the individual concerning his or her contribution to a group activity (see Bratman, 1999, for a detailed discussion).

Social psychologists have given little attention to this issue, but from a practical standpoint, the distinction is useful, because shared intentions may be more predictive of group behaviors in virtual communities than we-intentions (and I-intentions; see Bagozzi & Lee, 2002). Much also remains to be done in examining the role of the member's self-construal and group identification in formulating these different types of intentions and acting on them.

Cognitive Focus

In addition to joint action, the process of virtual community identity involves a self-construal either at the interpersonal or at the collective level, as noted earlier (Brewer & Gardner, 1996). These alternative possibilities result in interesting differences in the cognitive focus of participants, as a result. Because the relational self is defined in terms of relationships with significant others in specific contexts, self-worth in this case is typically derived from appropriate role behavior. A virtual community member construing him- or herself relationally may therefore accord great importance to the value of his or her responses or contributions to the group's goals, as perceived by other group members. As a result, the focus of such an identifying member would be inward, toward the reactions of the community.

In contrast, the collective self is determined by assimilation to the prototypic representation of the in-group, with self-worth derived from the status of the in-group in intergroup comparisons (Brewer & Gardner, 1996). Virtual community members construing themselves as a collective may therefore be expected to have an outward focus, toward gauging competitive communities and establishing differences between their own and other communities. These differences in focus in the two self-construals imply that the dynamics of interaction as well as effective organization guidelines may be different in the two cases. Little research has examined these issues.

Community Welfare Motive

Further, in spite of the seemingly self-interested motivations of many members, both interpersonal and collective self-construals implicate a change in the basic goals of social interaction for members. In both types, the individual's personal self-interest is augmented by a concern for the interests of others. The relational self-construal is characterized by a mutual concern for the interests and outcomes of the significant others. In the collective self-construal, the welfare of the group, as a whole, may become an end in itself, with members willing to restrict individual gain to preserve a collective good (Brewer & Gardner, 1996). Both of these outcomes accord importance to the identification process in broadening the emphasis of the member from selfish, functional gain, to the interests of the larger virtual community, and in fostering relationships among group members having stronger, more lasting ties with the virtual community.

Loyalty to the Community

Organization researchers also showed that social identity implies stronger commitment, manifesting itself in a stronger attitudinal and behavioral bond to the group (Bagozzi & Bergami, 2002). Whereas emotional attachment is a state of identification, loyalty as defined here pertains to its attitudinal and behavioral responses to this state — encapsulating the multivaried ways in which the member expresses commitment. In specific terms, this may be observed through more (quantity-wise and frequency-wise) and regular participation, a greater resistance to interacting in competitive virtual community venues, and resilience to negative experiences when interacting within the community.

Loyalty has long been deemed a powerful measure by which to gauge success by marketers because of its direct links to profitability. In virtual communities, we may expect it to be a similarly effective measure. Anecdotal and proprietary research hints at this (e.g., PeopleLink, 2000), but more systematic research is needed.

Recommendation and Recruitment

In addition to engaging in increasing, and more spirited forms of, participation, social identity also implies that the member has a vested interest in the success and welfare of the virtual community (Bhattacharya & Sen, 2003). It follows that the identifying member will be more likely to, and interested in, recommending the community to others, with the end of recruiting new members. The member may play an active role in new member recruitment for another reason as well. Bhattacharya and Sen (2003) pointed out that the heightened perception of in-group and out-group membership and differences among identifying members may result in a drive to strengthen the in-group by recruiting other like-minded candidates. The resulting larger grouping will also likely contribute to further legitimizing and reaffirming the member's social identity.

The exploding growth of many virtual communities, unsupported by traditional, commercial forms of promotion, may be explained, at least in part, by this consequence of virtual community identity, with systematic research needed to gauge the extent of this relationship.

CONCLUDING THOUGHTS

It is our thesis that the virtual community identity construct offers significant explanatory power in helping understand why these virtual groups are so influential for their members, and their success. Researchers have only just begun to examine and understand the processes by which identification occurs, its constituents, and its consequences in virtual communities. In this chapter, we drew from existing research and analyses across different disciplines and provided an integrative framework to help readers think about identification with virtual communities.

While we highlighted opportunities for future research throughout the chapter, in closing, it is appropriate to point out one practical issue. This pertains to the role and the ability of organizers in increasing member identification with their virtual community. In a recent analysis of corporate identity, Bhattacharya and Sen (2003) suggested that companies can actively influence the identification process through appropriate forms of communication. They suggest that traditional communications (such as advertisements, logos, annual reports, etc.) as well as indirect means (such as types of products offered, corporate social initiatives, company-sponsored forums, etc.) are useful in this regard. When compared to managers of companies, virtual community organizers may have fewer alternatives available to communicate the group's identity. But the different attributes of the virtual community venue — its appearance, the availability of real-time communication technologies, the organization of member-generated and organizer-created content, the different tools and applications available to members when interacting, the role played by the community's moderator — all offer useful opportunities for such identity building and dissemination.

Further, Bhattacharya and Sen (2003) noted that communication processes are influential in fostering identification only to the extent that the identity inferred by the member from this information is deemed to be trustworthy, prestigious, and coherent. Virtual community organizers may have to put in an effort to understand their members well and then use the venue attributes appropriately in designing impactful identity-building programs.

In conclusion, it is important to underscore the value of virtual communities as a promising research area by pointing out that not only are these virtual groups well-established as contemporary arenas of social interactions, but also their adoption, acceptance, and range of use is sure to grow as new technologies remove existing constraints of wired networks and lower bandwidths in the coming years. Virtual communities deserve attention from social science researchers and practitioners.

REFERENCES

Abrams, D., & Hogg, M. A. (1988). Comments on the motivational status of self-esteem in social identity and intergroup discrimination. *European Journal of Social Psychology, 18,* 317–334.

Allen, N. J., & Meyer, J. P. (1996). Affective, continuance, and normative commitment in the organization: An examination of construct validity. *Journal of Vocational Behavior, 49,* 252–276.

Aron, A., Aron, E. N., & Norman, C. (2001). Self-expansion model of motivation and cognition in close relationships and beyond. In G. J. O. Fletcher, & M. S. Clark (Eds.), *Blackwell handbook of social psychology: Interpersonal processes* (pp. 478–502). London: Blackwell.

Bagozzi, R. P. (2000). On the concept of intentional social action in consumer behavior. *Journal of Consumer Research, 27*(3), 388–396.

Bagozzi, R. P., & Bergami, M. (2002). Antecedents and consequences of organizational identification and the nomological validity of the Bergami-Bagozzi scale. Working paper, Rice University.

Bagozzi, R. P., & Dholakia, U. M. (2002). Intentional social action in virtual communities. *Journal of Interactive Marketing, 16*(2), 2–21.

Bagozzi, R. P., & Lee, K. -H. (2002). Multiple routes for social influence: The role of compliance, internalization, and social identity. *Social Psychology Quarterly, 65*(3), 226–247.

Bagozzi, R. P., Dholakia, U. M., and Klein, L. (2003). Antecedents and consequences of online social interactions. Working paper, Rice University.

Baumeister, R. F., & Leary, M. R. (1995). The need to belong: Desire for interpersonal attachments as a fundamental human motivation. *Psychological Bulletin, 117,* 497–529.

Bergami, M., & Bagozzi, R. P. (2000). Self-categorization, affective commitment, and group self-esteem as distinct aspects of social identity in the organization. *British Journal of Social Psychology, 39,* 555–577.

Bhattarcharya, C. B., & Sen, S. (2003). Consumer-company identification: A framework for understanding consumers' relationships with companies. *Journal of Marketing,* forthcoming.

Bickart, B., & Schindler, R. M. (2001). Internet forums as influential sources of consumer information. *Journal of Interactive Marketing, 15*, 3, 31–40.

Bratman, M. E. (1999). *Faces of intention: Selected essays on intention and agency.* Cambridge, UK: Cambridge University Press.

Brewer, M. B. (1993). The role of distinctiveness in social identity and group behaviour. In M. A. Hogg, & D. Abrams (Eds.), *Group motivation: Social psychological perspectives* (pp. 1–16). London: Prentice-Hall.

Brewer, M. B., & Gardner, W. (1996). Who is this "We"? Levels of collective identity and self representations. *Journal of Personality and Social Psychology, 71*(1), 83–93.

Brown, M. E. (1969). Identification and some conditions of organizational involvement. *Administrative Science Quarterly, 14*(3), 346–355.

Deutsch, M. (1973). *The resolution of conflict.* New Haven, CT: Yale University Press.

Dholakia, U. M., & Bagozzi, R. P. (2001). Consumer behavior in digital environments. In J. Wind, & V. Mahajan (Eds.), *Digital marketing: Global strategies from the world's leading experts* (pp. 163–200). New York: Wiley.

Dholakia, U. M., Klein, L. R., & Bagozzi, R. P. (2003). On the value of virtual communities for marketing. Manuscript submitted for publication.

Dutton, J. E., Dukerich, J. M., & Harquail, C. V. (1994). Organizational images and member identification. *Administrative Science Quarterly, 39*, 4, 239–263.

Eagly, A. H., & Chaiken, S. (1993). *The psychology of attitudes.* Fort Worth, TX: Harcourt Brace Jovanovich.

Ellemers, N., Kortekaas, P., & Ouwerkerk, J. W. (1999). Self-categorization, commitment to the group, and group self-esteem as related but distinct aspects of social identity. *European Journal of Social Psychology, 29*, 371–389.

Flanagin, A. J., & Metzger, M. J. (2001). Internet use in the contemporary media environment. *Human Communication Research, 27*(1), 153–181.

Flap, H., Bulder, B., & Volker, B. (1998). Intra-organizational networks and performance: A review. *Computational and Mathematical Organization Theory, 2*, 109–147.

Gilbert, M. (1992). *On social facts.* Princeton, NJ: Princeton University Press.

Hogg, M. A. (1992). *The social psychology of group cohesiveness: From attraction to social identity.* New York: New York University Press.

Hogg, M. A., & Abrams, D. (1988). *Social identifications: A social psychology of intergroup relations and group processes.* London: Routledge.

Hogg, M. A., & Abrams, D. (1990). Social motivation, self-esteem and social identity. In D. Abrams, & M. A. Hogg (Eds.), *Social identity theory: Constructive and critical advances* (pp. 28–47). New York: Springer-Verlag.

Markus, H. R., & Kitayama, S. (1991). Culture and self: Implications for cognition, emotion, and motivation. *Psychological Review, 98,* 224–253.

McKenna, K. Y. A., & Bargh, J. A. (1998). Coming out in the age of the internet: Identity "demarginalization" through virtual group participation. *Journal of Personality and Social Psychology, 75*(3), 681–694.

Nahapiet, J. E., & Ghoshal, C. (1998). Social capital, intellectual capital, and the organizational advantage. *Academy of Management Review, 23,* 242–266.

PeopleLink. (2000). What's the value of eCommunity? Understanding the return on investment of eCommunities. White Paper.

Postmes, T., Spears, R., & Lea, M. (2000). The formation of group norms in computer-mediated communication. *Human Communication Research, 26*(3), 341–371.

Sherif, M., & Sherif, C. W. (1969). *Social psychology.* New York: Harper & Row.

Spears, R., & Lea, M. (1994). Panacea or panapticon? The hidden power in computer-mediated communication. *Communication Research, 21*(4), 427–459.

Tajfel, H. (1972). Some developments in European social psychology. *European Journal of Social Psychology, 2,* 307–322.

Tajfel, H. (1978). Social categorization, social identity and social comparison. In H. Tajfel (Ed.), *Differentiation between social groups: Studies in the psychology of intergroup relations* (pp. 61–76). London: Academic Press.

Tuomela, R. (1995). *The importance of us: A philosophical study of basic notions.* Stanford, CA: Stanford University Press.

Turner, J. C. (1985). Social categorization and the self-concept: A social cognitive theory of group behavior. In E. J. Lawler (Ed.), *Advances in group processes: Theory and research* (Vol. 2). Greenwich, CT: JAI Press.

Wellman, B., & Gulia, M. (1999). Net-surfers don't ride alone: Virtual communities as communities. In B. Wellman (Ed.), *Networks in the global village* (pp. 331–366). Boulder, CO: Westview Press.

Chapter XV

A Model for the Analysis of Virtual Teams

J. H. Erik Andriessen, Delft University of Technology, The Netherlands

Robert M. Verburg, Delft University of Technology, The Netherlands

ABSTRACT

Presented in this chapter is a model for the analysis of virtual teams. The model is a helpful tool for mapping the different aspects of effective virtual teams and will be explained through several examples from practice. Before the model is introduced, an overview of the main challenges of virtual teams in performing their tasks is presented. There are hardly any technical obstacles for communication and collaboration across geographic boundaries, as these processes are being supported by high-tech collaboration solutions, such as groupware and other collaborative applications. However, these new types of groups create major organizational challenges for both managers and employees. It is the aim of this chapter to give insight into the design and performance of effective (global) virtual teams.

INTRODUCTION

The developments in globally distributed commerce and science and the availability of communication technology encouraged the growth of virtual geographically distributed teams (see, e.g., the special issue of *Communications of the ACM* on global virtual teams and collaborative technologies, December 2001).

Virtual teams may be defined as groups of geographically and culturally dispersed coworkers using a combination of communication and information technologies to accomplish an organizational task (Townsend, DeMarie, & Hendrickson, 1999; Jarvenpaa, Knoll, & Leidner, 1998). Hutchinson (1999) distinguished three types of virtual teams: intraorganizational teams, interorganizational teams, and interorganizational distributed teams. The intraorganizational teams consist of geographically distributed members. Interorganizational distributed (project) teams cooperate, over a certain period, toward reaching a common goal, e.g., freelance or organization-bound experts who work together to provide a certain service. In interorganizational teams, the cooperation is sequential, and each participating organization is responsible for particular tasks (such as in "round the globe" design teams). In this chapter, we will have mostly all three types in mind when discussing our approach.

Virtual teams perform a variety of tasks and come in many different forms. As a worldwide supplier of fast-moving consumer goods, Unilever provides an example of an organization that utilizes traditional and virtual teams. The company uses virtual teams to connect specialists who work in comparable areas (for instance, personal care products, foods) but are geographically distributed across different offices in cities in Europe and the rest of the world. Unilever also uses virtual teams to build task forces of various specialists for building new products. Other examples are British Petroleum's virtual team network that enables employees to connect, communicate, and share knowledge on oil exploration across borders (Prokesch, 1997), or the growing number of student teams with members from universities across the globe who work together on various group assignments.

Being "virtual" is a matter of degree, and refers, according to various authors, to dimensions such as spatial distance, time, cultural diversity, temporality, and mode of interaction (Mowshowitz, 1997; Jarvenpaa & Leidner, 1998; DeSanctis, Staudenmayer, & Wong, 1999; Vartiainen, 2002). "Virtuality" refers, according to these authors, to the extent to which a group is geographically distributed, is organizationally and culturally diverse, has different time frames for work, and communicates electronically (mode of interaction). The more of the above, the more a team is considered to be a virtual group. Jarvenpaa and Leidner (1998) added the dimension of temporality of the group and considered virtual teams to be temporary by definition. In our opinion, however, permanent groups can also be virtual.

In our conceptualization, the dimensions of organizational or cultural diversity and temporality are important and related concepts. Nevertheless, we consider the dimensions of *mode of interaction* and *space and time distance* as crucial elements of virtuality. Virtuality is the highest in globally dispersed teams that communicate exclusively via electronic means. However, a team that works in the same building and organization that has exactly the same working hours may also have a certain level of virtuality if the members often interact via e-mail, telephone, or video. A team is also virtual to some degree when members work individually at a relatively large distance from each other, in diverse time zones, and if their interaction is mainly limited to a weekly meeting in a restaurant at the airport.

The reason for not including organizational and cultural distribution or temporality in our definition of "virtual teams" is that traditional teams can also differ in these aspects. Moreover, there are several other dimensions that may make interaction in virtual teams more difficult, such as formality of leadership, rules and roles, clarity of purpose, and legal context. But again, these dimensions have the same effects in traditional teams. Including such aspects in a definition of virtuality makes the concept of "virtual" identical to "difficult to manage," which is not the intention.

Mode of interaction is another wide-ranging dimension. Some teams meet regularly but also have some e-mail-based interaction, while other teams interact intensively and almost exclusively via various media and sophisticated groupware tools. Geographical distance and different time frames are important reasons for groups to communicate electronically.

The Internet as the almost universal medium for interaction across boundaries created an infrastructure that enables many organizations to launch virtual teams. Hardly any technical obstacles for communication and collaboration across geographic boundaries remain, as these processes are supported by high-tech collaboration solutions, such as groupware and other collaborative applications (e.g., videoconferencing, electronic blackboards). Nevertheless, in practice, the infrastructure and the groupware applications often do not provide the support that is expected. Even if the technology is reliable, these new types of collaboration create major challenges for managers and employees. So far, the development of virtual teams has mostly been technology driven, almost neglecting other aspects of work, such as knowledge sharing, combining expertise, and dividing tasks. As a consequence, the performances of many virtual teams are far below their potentials, thus producing poor business results (see, e.g., Jarvenpaa & Leidner, 1998).

In order to provide systematic insight into the design and performance of effective (global) virtual teams, it is desirable to have comprehensive concepts and tools. We will present a model for the analysis of virtual teams, which is a helpful tool for analyzing team activities in general. In this chapter, it will be applied to the special case of virtual teams. Before we present the model, we will highlight the main challenges of virtual teams in performing their tasks.

CHALLENGES OF VIRTUAL TEAMS IN GETTING THE WORK DONE

Virtual teams are, to a large extent, comparable to colocated teams. They have the same responsibilities of adequately performing the basic processes of groups, such as information sharing, cooperation, coordination, and team building (see next section). They also have to mobilize the necessary resources and need to develop a cohesive team with clear goals. However, virtual teams have to care for these processes under conditions of less than optimal communicative channels, of higher distance in time, space, and culture than those of face-to-face (F2F) teams. Inadequate information and communication technology (ICT) tools or infrastructures and the incompatibility of technology will result in barriers for cooperation. In the aforementioned virtual team network at British Petroleum, the corporation had to spend millions of dollars on behavioral science consultants, who helped to prepare employees to work effectively in a virtual team environment (Prakesch, 1997).

Other problems may include missing nonverbal cues in communication and lacking unplanned social encounters, resulting in problems with "awareness" of availability and the state of others, of progress of the work, or of the setting in which others work (see, e.g., Steinfield, 2002). These barriers may result in a lack of trust and cohesion, which often may lead to lower performance levels. Jarvenpaa and Leidner (1998) confirmed that global virtual teams might start with a form of "swift trust" (Meyerson, Weick, & Kramer, 1996) but that such trust appears to be fragile and temporal. Cramton (1997) illustrated, for instance, the multiple interpretations members of virtual teams may give to the meaning of silence of their distant team members.

On the other hand, being virtual may also have advantages over being on traditional teams. Virtual teams require certain tools in the area of ICT to support interaction. Some modern tools have sophisticated functionalities that provide such teams with opportunities that traditional teams do not have. One of the major effects of the introduction of collaboration technology has been that certain types of meetings can now be held with a large number of participants. Moreover, some tools allow for easy storage and retrieval of information and for collaborative editing of documents.

Global virtual teams have to deal with the additional issues of communicating across different time zones, using different languages, and encountering different cultures (e.g., Dubé & Paré, 2001; Montoya-Weiss, 2001). Nevertheless, these teams may have opportunities that colocated teams do not have, such as opportunities involving specific expertise or different cultural viewpoints. Businesses are no longer tied to a single time zone and are, for example, able to develop software around the clock. International Business Systems (IBS) is such a global software developer, with over 2,000 employees located in 90 offices in 20 countries. Although the company is headquartered in Stockholm, Sweden, its advanced systems enable a global approach to collaborative software development. Teams located in different countries are able to work on the same product's code around the clock (see www.ibsus.com, for more information).

MODEL FOR THE ANALYSIS OF VIRTUAL TEAMS

It is clear that virtual teams may face substantial barriers for effective cooperation, and that the probability of failure is ever present. The model we present below can help to analyze the reasons for failure and can support the design of virtual groups. The model is based on a general model of group functioning, called the Dynamic Group Interaction model (DGIn model), which is honed through application in several case studies (Andriessen, 2002). The purpose of this model is not to limit the analysis of collaborative activities to specific aspects but to structure the analysis by providing ideas and insights that have proven their value in other contexts.

Figure 1: Adapted from the Dynamic Group Interaction model (DGIn model) (Andriessen, 2002).

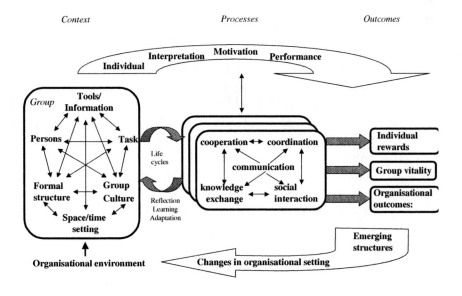

In this model, elements of several theories are brought together. Three levels of behavior are taken into account, i.e., individual goal-directed behavior and cognitive processes (based on action theory, activity theory, media richness theory), interpersonal and group processes (activity theory, adaptive structuration theory, social information theory, coordination theory), and a macrosocial perspective (structuration theory). The various notions are brought together in an heuristic model concerning group processes, related to traditional input–process–output schemas (see, e.g., McGrath, 1984; Hackman, 1987; Kraemer & Pinsonneault, 1990; McGrath & Hollingshead, 1994). However, they are enriched with interpretative and structurational notions and feedback cycles (see Figure 1).

The model has the following basic principles:

1. Effectiveness of groups can be analyzed in terms of three outcome categories, namely, organizational outcomes, such as the quantity or quality of the products; group vitality and continuity; and individual rewards, such as satisfaction, growth, and money.
2. The effectiveness of a group depends on the quality of the group processes. Six basic group processes are distinguished: first, *communication*, and second, the processes that exist on the basis of communication, i.e., task-oriented *cooperation, coordination, learning, reflection,* and group-maintenance-oriented *team building*. These processes need to be aligned to one another.
3. The quality of group processes depends on characteristics of the context. Six groups of characteristics are distinguished: the task of the team, tools, member characteristics (knowledge, skills, attitudes), team structure (such as role division and meeting type), culture (norms, trust, cohesion, cognitive distance), and time–space setting (e.g., geographic distribution). The context characteristics need to match in order to optimally support the group processes.
4. Where the matching of group processes to the context characteristics is not adequate, groups develop, and tools become adopted and adapted to, through interpretation and interaction processes and feedback, by which the original context-of-use factors are changed. Groups build cohesion and trust (or distrust), shared knowledge, and new task definitions through interaction. Tools will be appropriated and adapted. New ways of interaction will be developed. This feedback takes place directly as a result of the interaction processes, or indirectly via the route of outcomes and their effects on organizational processes. These changes can emerge unplanned, develop slowly in daily practice, or can be the result of explicit reflection of the group on its functioning, and of explicit change.

APPLYING THE MODEL

Below, the principles of the DGIn model are applied to virtual teams.

1. **Effectiveness on three levels.** Some virtual groups cooperate only once, so in those cases, vitality and continuity of the group as the outcomes (basic Tenet 1) may not be that interesting for the members. In case of traditional (project) teams, however, it is not enough to come up with clear results and with rewards for members. It is also necessary to cater to group vitality and continuity in order to be effective. Virtual teams do not differ from traditional teams in this respect. However, developing vitality is more difficult in virtual teams than in colocated groups. The specific problems are related to the other principles of the model.

2. **The quality of group processes.** Six basic group processes were distinguished: communication and the five other processes that can only exist on the basis of communication (cooperation, coordination, learning, reflection, and team building). These processes need to be aligned. The type of communication (mediated to a smaller or larger extent) constitutes the core dimension for the concept of "virtuality." In the case of virtual groups, the model implies that collaboration, coordination, knowledge exchange, social interaction, and reflection need to be adjusted to the degree of mediation of communication. This is reflected, among other things, in the fact that remote cooperation and social interaction in mediated meetings need to be more explicitly structured than F2F meetings in order to be effective. The already mentioned lack of nonverbal cues in communication, resulting in problems with awareness of availability and the states of others, makes it difficult to interact. Overall, F2F meetings allow for more flexibility during meetings and do not need to be as structured as mediated meetings. It is important to provide minutes of virtual meetings, as these help to assure that all members understand the same conclusions. In the case of virtual student teams, Cramton (1997) showed that team members have difficulty in extracting information about the context in which their distant partners operate, while members often fail to provide important information about their contexts. Globally distributed teams should give sufficient time and attention to group members who are less assertive than most members from Western countries. Leadership and coordination of virtual teams play critical roles in facilitating the work and organization of virtual teams (see Bell & Kozlowski, 2002). In general, the activities of virtual teams appear to need more preparation and explicit coordination than those of colocated teams.

3. **The quality and match of the context characteristics.** The task of the team, the tools and information, the member characteristics, the team structure, and the team culture need to be adjusted to the time–space

setting. In other words, they need to be adjusted to the geographical, organizational, and possibly cultural distribution.

ICT support. *The technical tools and their usage should be adjusted to the virtuality of the group. The following suggestions can be made:*

- Virtual groups require information storage and exchange tools.
- Virtual groups may benefit from a database with information on background and expertise of the group members (*"yellow pages"*).
- Virtual groups with intensive and nonroutine interaction may benefit from tools for synchronous communication: chat features and, where possible, video links.
- Virtual groups with complex and time-sensitive tasks require workflow management tools for providing information regarding the progress of the project and activities of group members.
- The tools have to be easy to use and equally accessible to all members.
- Group members should be sufficiently trained in remote interaction and in using the technology.
- Global virtual teams should be careful in choosing and using the right tools. Research suggests that people from individualistic cultures (the European Union, the United States) prefer direct expression of ideas (Trompenaars, 1993). They, therefore, generally prefer synchronous communication and online tools, such as telephone, video, and chat. People from collectivist cultures, such as in many countries in Asia, however, are sensitive to nonverbal cues and group relations and prefer asynchronous communication in order to be able to express themselves more carefully. Attention to such matters is important.

Storage of information. Special attention should be given to information (document) exchange and storage. Effective virtual teams rely heavily on information exchange. Systems and procedures that allow for swift information exchange are prerequisites. Such systems need to be usable and accepted by all members of the team. In multicultural teams, such systems are not always easy to obtain. Differences in preferred practices of communication and storage of information will limit the choice of an equally usable tool.

Cultural diversity may be large in virtual teams. In order to avoid conflicts and facilitate a smooth work process, group members should be trained to understand the potentially disturbing effect of cultural diversity. The next step is to learn about each other's backgrounds, so that differences in solving problems and in ways of working will not form a source of major misunderstandings. As soon as members respect and trust distant team members, virtual teams will be able to benefit from the diversity of their members.

4. **Development and adaptation: team building.** Groups develop and tools are adopted and adapted through interpretation, interaction processes, and feedback. One of the processes through which this development and adaptation can be explicitly structured is team building. Team building proves to be a critical aspect of team performance and acts as the foundation for the development of necessary levels of trust, cohesion, and cognitive closeness among team members. In many cases, team building in virtual teams can benefit strongly from a F2F kickoff meeting (see Gould, 2000; Maznevski & Chudoba, 2001, for overviews). Coordinators should organize such meetings whenever needed or possible.

CONCLUSION

Virtual teams offer great opportunities for collaboration across boundaries. This has encouraged many companies to form such teams in order to benefit their organizations. We discussed the challenges and potential pitfalls of virtual teams and presented the DGIn model for team analysis. On the basis of our analysis, we recommend that virtual teams should more explicitly pay attention to issues of team building, awareness, preparation, and information storage in order to work and collaborate effectively. Virtual teams should also benefit from the use of specialized groupware tools, if applied properly.

REFERENCES

Andriessen, J. H. E. (2002). *Group work and groupware: Understanding and evaluating computer supported interaction.* London: Springer Verlag.

Bell, B. S., & Kozlowski, S. W. J. (2002). A typology of virtual teams: Implications for effective leadership. *Group & Organization Management, 27*(1), 14–49.

Cramton, C. D. (1997). Information problems in dispersed teams. *Academy of Management Best Paper Proceedings* 1997 (pp. 298–302).

DeSanctis, G., Staudenmayer, N., & Wong, S. -S. (1999). Interdependence in virtual organizations. In C. Cooper, & D. Rousseau (Eds.), *Trends in organizational behavior.* New York: John Wiley & Sons.

Dubé, L., & Paré, G. (2001). Global virtual teams. *Communications of the ACM, 44*(12), 71–73.

Hackman, J. R. (1987). The design of work teams. In J. W. Lorsch (Ed.), *Handbook of organizational behavior* (pp. 315–342). Englewood Cliffs, NJ: Prentice Hall.

Hutchinson, C. (1999). Virtual teams. In R. Stewart (Ed.), *Handbook of team working*. Aldershot, Hampshire, UK: Gower.

Jarvenpaa, S., Knoll, K., & Leidner, D. (1998). Is anybody out there? Antecedents of trust in global virtual teams. *Journal of Management Information Systems*, *14*(4), 29–64.

Jarvenpaa, S. L., & Leidner, D. E. (1998). Communication and trust in global virtual teams. *Journal of Computer-Mediated Communication*, *3*(4).

Kraemer, K. L., & Pinsonneault, A. (1990). Technology and groups: Assessment of the empirical research. In J. Galegher, R. E. Kraut, & C. Egido (Eds.), *Intellectual teamwork: Social and technological foundations of cooperative work*. Hillsdale, NJ: Lawrence Erlbaum.

Maznevski, M. L., & Chudoba, K. M. (2001). Bridging space over time: Global virtual team dynamics and effectiveness. *Organization Science*, *11*(5), 473–492.

McGrath, J. E. (1984). *Groups: Interaction and performance*. Englewood Cliffs, NJ: Prentice Hall.

McGrath, J. E., & Hollingshead, A. B. (1994). *Groups interacting with technology: Ideas, evidence, issues and an agenda*. London: Sage.

Meyerson, D., Weick, K. E., & Kramer, R. M. (1996). Swift trust and temporary groups. In R. M. Kramer, & T. R. Tyler (Eds.), *Trust in organizations: Frontiers of theory and research* (pp. 166–195). Thousand Oaks, CA: Sage.

Montoya-Weiss, M. M. (2001). Getting it together: Temporal coordination and conflict management in global virtual teams. *Academy of Management Journal*, *44*(6), 1251–1263.

Mowshowitz, A. (1997). Virtual organization. *Communications of the ACM*, *40*(9), 30–37.

Prokesch, S. (1997). Unleashing the power of learning: An interview with British Petroleum's John Browne. *Harvard Business Review*, *75*(5), 147–168.

Qureshi, S., & Zigurs, I. (2001). Paradoxes and prerogatives in global virtual collaboration. *Communications of the ACM, 44*(12), 85–88.

Steinfield, C. (2002). Realizing the benefits of virtual teams. *IEEE Computer*, *35*(3), 104–106.

Townsend, A., DeMarie, S., & Hendrickson, A. (1998). Virtual teams: Technology and the workplace of the future. *Academy of Management Executive, 12*(3), 17–29.

Trompenaars, F. (1993). *Riding the waves of culture: Understanding cultural diversity in business*. London: Nicholas Brealey.

Vartiainen, M. (2002). The functionality of virtual organisations. Unpublished manuscript. Helsinki University of Technology.

About the Authors

Susan H. Godar is associate professor and chairperson in the Department of Marketing & Management Sciences at the Christos M. Cotsakos College of Business, William Paterson University, USA. Her research, primarily on virtual groups, the ethics of mobile commerce, and marketing practices, appeared in such journals as *Journal of International Management*, *Industrial Marketing Management*, *Services Marketing Quarterly*, and *Teaching Business Ethics*. She is currently the section editor ("e-Marketing") for *Marketing Education Review Electronic Teaching Resources*. Dr. Godar served as a consultant to numerous companies and organizations in the aviation industry, and has been a member of the National Academy of Sciences Transportation Research Board. Prior to joining academe, she marketed helicopters and light airplanes. She holds a B.A. in Sociology from Creighton University, an M.B.A. from the University of Iowa, and a Ph.D. in International Business from Temple University.

Sharmila Pixy Ferris (Ph.D., the Pennsylvania State University, 1995) is associate professor and graduate program director in the Department of Communication at William Paterson University, USA. With an M.A. in English and a B.A. in Psychology, Dr. Ferris brings an interdisciplinary focus to her research in computer-mediated communication. This relatively new field builds on an investigation of the potentials and innovations introduced to the field of communication by new computer technologies. Within the broader area of computer-mediated communication, Dr. Ferris studies gender, small groups, orality and literacy, and adoption patterns. She is an experienced consultant who has worked with regional, national, and multinational corporations to conduct diversity training as well as workshops in communication skills, leadership, and teamwork. Dr. Ferris has a recent book in the area of faculty development, titled *Beyond Survival in the Academy* (May 2003, Hampton Press). She has published in a variety of journals, including *Qualitative Research Reports, The New Jersey Journal of Communication, The Electronic Journal of Communication, Interpersonal Computing and Technology,* and *The Journal of Electronic Publishing* and *Computer-Mediated Communication Magazine.*

* * *

J. H. Erik Andriessen is professor of Work and Organizational Psychology at Delft University of Technology, The Netherlands. His research concerns new forms of work and organization related to telematics and telework; human–computer interaction; innovation processes; computer-supported cooperative work (CSCW); and knowledge management. He is the author of the book *Group Work and Groupware: Understanding and Evaluating Computer-Supported Interaction* (Springer, 2002).

Richard P. Bagozzi is the J. Hugh Liedtke professor of Management in the Jesse H. Jones Graduate School of Management and professor of Psychology in the Department of Psychology, Rice University, USA. Dr. Bagozzi's research interests are primarily in action theory and the psychological and social aspects of decision making. He also does research concerning methodology, particularly structural equation modeling and its philosophical and operational foundations.

Pierre Balthazard is associate professor of Information Systems in the School of Management at Arizona State University West, USA. He received a bachelor's degree in Mathematics and Computer Science from McGill University, and an MSIS and Ph.D. in IS and Systems and Industrial Engineering from the University of Arizona. His current research interests include the design and investigation of collaborative and decision technologies to support teamwork across time and distance. His past research appeared in publications such as *Journal of Management Information Systems, Group Decision and Negotiation, Journal of End User Computing, International Journal of Quality and Reliability Management,* and *Data Base.* He was awarded a grant from the National Science Foundation to study influence allocation in decision groups. Dr. Balthazard is also founder and president of Knowledge Instruments, a Phoenix, Arizona-based consultancy specializing in organizational development for conventional and virtual organizations.

Clint A. Bowers is an associate professor of Psychology at the University of Central Florida (USA) and assistant dean of Research for the College of Arts and Sciences. He is also director of the Team Performance Laboratory and lead scientist of the FAA/UCF/NAWCTSD Partnership for Aviation Team Training. Dr. Bowers received his Ph.D. (1987) in Clinical Psychology from the University of South Florida and a B.S. from the University of South Carolina. Dr. Bowers is a past president of the American Psychological Association's Division of Applied Experimental and Engineering Psychology and a fellow of the American Psychological Association.

Wray E. Bradley is assistant professor of Accounting in The University of Tulsa School of Accounting, USA. He is the program advisor for the school's nationally recognized online Master of Taxation program (http://bus.cba.utulsa.edu/mtax). Students in this program are located across the United States. The program is entirely administered using information and communication technology systems. Dr. Bradley published articles in accounting, information systems, and management journals. He actively conducts research related to various aspects of virtual teams.

Ann Frances Cameron is a Ph.D. student of MIS and Organizational Behavior at Queen's University, Kingston, Canada. Previous degrees include a Master of Science in Management (Queen's University), and a Bachelor of Information Systems (St. Francis Xavier University, Nova Scotia, Canada). Ann Frances also spent some time in practice, working as an application analyst. Working for Imperial Oil Ltd. at various Canadian sites, her responsibilities included on-site training and coordinating of global distribution of an in-house developed application. Currently, her main areas of research are the use of technology in virtual teams, as well as the unintended and unexpected consequences of emerging communication technologies. She published in the Administrative Sciences Association of Canada Conference Proceedings and presented her work at the Academy of Management Conference.

Stacey L. Connaughton (Ph.D., The University of Texas at Austin) is an assistant professor in the Department of Communication at Rutgers University, USA. Her research interests include "organizational identity" and fostering stakeholders' identification with organizations, particularly virtual organizations and political parties. One of Dr. Connaughton's current projects examines how leaders of global organizations successfully lead across time and space, probing issues of trust, identification, motivation, and isolation. Another project employs focus groups, survey methods, and in-depth interviews to investigate long-distance leadership in municipal government during a period of new technology implementation. She is also collecting longitudinal data on young voting age Americans' perceptions of politics.

Janel Anderson Crider is assistant professor of Rhetoric and Scientific and Technical Communication at the University of Minnesota, USA. She earned her Ph.D. in Communication from Purdue University (2001). Her research interests include virtual collaboration in international contexts, communication technology, and distance education.

Haydee M. Cuevas is a doctoral candidate in the Applied Experimental and Human Factors Psychology program at the University of Central Florida and is employed as a research assistant in the Team Performance Laboratory, USA. Her research interests involve knowledge acquisition of complex systems, including such factors as knowledge structure development (e.g., mental models), the use of metacognitive strategies in learning, and the role of individual differences. She was recognized as Student Member with Honors (2002) by the Human Factors and Ergonomic Society.

John A. Daly (Ph.D., Purdue) is Liddell professor in the College of Communication, University Distinguished Teaching Professor, Texas Commerce Banc Shares Professor of Management, and professor of Pharmacy, The University of Texas at Austin, USA. His research focuses on practical ways of bolstering the communication skills of individuals. He examined topics such as shyness, personality difference in communication, communication difficulties people experience in their personal and professional relationships, and issues involved in assessing communication competency, publishing more than 90 scholarly articles. He edited two academic journals and completed five academic books. In addition, he has served as president of the National Communication Association and on the board of directors of the International Communication Association and the International Customer Service Association.

Utpal M. Dholakia is an assistant professor of Management at the Jesse H. Jones Graduate School of Management at Rice University (USA). Dr. Dholakia's research interests lie in the study of motivational aspects of consumer behavior and marketing issues pertaining to digital environments.

Stephen M. Fiore is director of the Consortium for Research in Adaptive Distributed Learning Environments at the University of Central Florida (USA), Institute for Simulation and Training and Team Performance Laboratory. He earned his Ph.D. in Cognitive Psychology from the University of Pittsburgh, Learning Research and Development Center (2000). Dr. Fiore maintains a multidisciplinary research interest that incorporates aspects of cognitive, social, and organizational psychology, and he has published in the area of learning, memory, and problem solving at the individual and the team levels.

Stacie Furst is an assistant professor/instructor of management in the Ourso College of Business at Louisiana State University, USA. She is completing her Ph.D. in Management from the University of North Carolina at Chapel Hill. Her research interests include virtual teams, organizational change, and interpersonal influence processes.

Shiv Ganesh is assistant professor of Communication Studies at the University of Montana, USA. He obtained his Ph.D. in Communication from Purdue University (2000). His research interests include nongovernment organizations, nonprofit organizations, and globalization and technology. His research was published in *Management Communication Quarterly, Organization-Communication: Emerging Perspectives,* and the *Journal of Communication Inquiry.* He is coauthor of *Organizational Communication in an Era of Globalization: Issues, Reflections and Practices* (forthcoming in 2003, Waveland Press).

Mila Gascó-Hernández (Bachelor and Master in Management; Ph.D. in Public Management) is a senior analyst in the International Institute on Governance, where she is in charge of the Information Society Project. She is a professor in the Universitat Oberta de Catalunya and one of the Spanish associates of the Center for Research in Applied Creativity (Canada). She is co-author of the book, *Retrieve Your Creativity* and co-editor of the book *Changing the Way You Teach: Creative Tools for Management Education* (both published by Septem Ediciones, Spain). She has also written several articles on public management and creativity.

Michele Jackson (Ph.D., Minnesota, 1994) is assistant professor in the Department of Communication at the University of Colorado, Boulder, USA. She teaches, consults, and advises in areas of the organizational implications of new communication technologies. A general theme in her work is the contribution of communication to technical areas, including the development of collaboration skills in engineering professions and the design and use of technologies to support group work. She is a past Charles Babbage Institute Tomash fellow for the History of Information Processing and a past research fellow with the Poynter Institute for Media Studies. Her research appeared in the *Journal of Computer Mediated Communication, Information, Communication, and Society, Communication Theory,* and the *Journal of Organizational Change Management.*

William H. A. Johnson is currently an assistant professor in the Management Department at Bentley College, USA. His award-winning research and teaching involves areas of process management, with a particular focus on the management of knowledge and its creation during technological innovation. He published papers in a number of journals, including *International Journal of Technology Management, Engineering Management Journal, International Journal of Innovation Management*, and *Journal of Intellectual Capital and Entrepreneurship: Theory and Practice*. He has also acted as a consultant for Merck Frosst, York Consulting Group, and the Royal Bank of Canada. To contact: wjohnson@bentley.edu

Gary F. Kohut is a professor of Management at the University of North Carolina at Charlotte, USA. He received his Ph.D. from Southern Illinois University at Carbondale. His research focuses on corporate communication strategy, leadership and management development, applied technology in business communication, and strategies for teaching improvement. Dr. Kohut has published in such journals as the *Journal of Management Studies*, the *Journal of Managerial Psychology*, the *Journal of Business Communication*, and the *Journal of Business and Technical Communication*. He is also the co-author of three textbooks. Dr. Kohut is the 2002 recipient of the Bank of America Award for Teaching Excellence, the university's most prestigious teaching honor.

Olivia Kyriakidou is interested in studying the social psychological and identity dynamics of organizational change, development, and innovation. In particular, she is interested in understanding processes of construction and development of organizational and individual identities in temporal organizational systems, such as networks, virtual organizations, as well as processes of construction of superordinate identities in mergers and acquisitions. Moreover, her research interests include investigating the social psychological and cognitive processes of emerging organizational forms. She is particularly interested in the construction of psychological contracts and the interplay between social representations and identities in cases of organizational change. Her consultancy program to date pursues a long-term interest in the application of psychology to organizational issues, with a particular interest to the management of change, corporate identity and its management, the psychological contract at work, virtual teams, and the creation of virtual working environments, as well as measures of team effectiveness.

Paul M. Leonardi (M.A., University of Colorado) is a doctoral student at the Center for Work, Technology and Organization in the Department of Management Science and Engineering at Stanford University, USA. His research interests include the impact of new technologies on work practices, the organization of technical work, and the relationship between technologies and organizational culture. His recent research appeared in *Critical Studies in Media*

Communication, Qualitative Research Reports in Communication, and the *Journal of Organizational Change Management*. Additionally, he has served as a consultant to technical work groups in the areas of teamwork and collaboration skills.

Shawn D. Long (Ph.D., University of Kentucky) is an assistant professor of Communication Studies at the University of North Carolina at Charlotte, USA. His teaching and research interests include organizational communication, organizational dialogue, critical theory, and interpretive methods associated with the study of organizational culture and symbolism and diversity communication. He is presently coinvestigator on a grant to study organ donation communication between African-Americans and their families. He has consulted for several local, regional, and national organizations on communication culture, diversity, and structure.

Natalie Marsh is a doctoral student at the University of Colorado at Boulder, USA. Her master's thesis focused upon the professional identity of telecommunications workers in the New Economy. Currently, she is interested in organizational communication, information technology, and law, policy, and standards setting in the telecommunications industry.

Lynne J. Millward (Ph.D., University of Kent, CPsychol, AFBPsS) is a senior lecturer in the Department of Psychology at the University of Surrey, UK. Her research interests include psychological contract in organizational settings, organizational and corporate identity; group and leadership processes, and possible selves in a career context. Her articles were published in the *British Journal of Management*, *Journal of Applied Social Psychology*, and the *European Journal of Social Psychology*. Three research questions she recently addressed are as follows: Do contractors necessarily hold transactional (instrument, calculative, self-oriented) psychological contracts? Do male and female differ in the psychological contracts they form in organizational settings? Why are nurses leaving the NHS? For this last project, she developed a psychological contact model, i.e., training and retention.

Maureen C. Minielli (M.A., The Pennsylvania State University, 1991) is a doctoral candidate in Communication Arts and Sciences at The Pennsylvania State University and a lecturer at Indiana University–Purdue University at Indianapolis, in Indianapolis, Indiana (USA). Her academic interests include rhetorical theory and criticism, political communication, American public address, and educational technology. To contact: mminiell@iupui.edu

Gaelle Picherit-Duthler (Ph.D., University of Kentucky) is an assistant professor of Communication Studies at the University of North Carolina at

Charlotte, USA. Dr. Picherit-Duthler's teaching and research interests include computer-mediated communication, issues of communication technologies in organizations, and intercultural and international communication in various contexts such as education and organizations. She has participated in numerous national and international conferences on these topics. Before coming to UNC Charlotte, Dr. Picherit-Duthler taught at the University of Kentucky. She also worked for several years in Paris. In addition to her research, she has consulted for several for-profit and nonprofit organizations on organizational culture and benefits communication.

Richard Potter is assistant professor of Information and Decision Sciences in the College of Business Administration at the University of Illinois at Chicago (USA). He received a bachelor's degree in Psychology from California State University–Hayward, and an M.S. in Management and Ph.D. in Management and Management Information Systems from the University of Arizona. Dr. Potter was a postdoctoral fellow at the University of Michigan's School of Public Health, and visiting scholar and adjunct professor of MIS at the University of Arizona's Keller School of Management. He also served Mexico's ITESM system as director of research and doctoral programs at their Mexico City Graduate School of Business. His current research focuses on cognition and behavior in the electronic environment, with emphases on performance assessment and intervention with virtual teams. He has published in a number of scientific journals on organizational psychology and on management and information systems, coauthored a leading IT textbook, and presented his work in conferences around the world. Dr. Potter is also a consultant and research associate of Knowledge Instruments, a Phoenix, Arizona-based consultancy specializing in organizational development for conventional and virtual organizations.

Martha Reeves (visiting assistant professor, Duke University, USA) served as a program director in Executive Education at the University of North Carolina at Chapel Hill's Kenan-Flagler Business School. Dr. Reeves has had corporate experience in both the United Kingdom and the United States. She continues to consult with businesses, local government, and social services organizations on a number of issues and projects, including women's development and gender issues in the workplace, needs analysis, evaluation, leadership development, mentoring, management assessment centers, sales management and sales strategy, and organizational culture and team building. Dr. Reeves received her Ph.D. in Human Resources Management and industrial relations from the University of Keele (UK). She has published articles on reward management and appraisal systems and authored a book about women in business, focusing on the mechanisms of gender discrimination at work.

Eduardo Salas is a professor of Psychology at the University of Central Florida (USA), where he also holds an appointment as program director for Human Systems Integration Research Department at the Institute for Simulation and Training. He is also the director of UCF's Applied Experimental and Human Factors Psychology Ph.D. program. Previously, he was a senior research psychologist and Head of the Training Technology Development Branch of the Naval Air Warfare Center Training Systems Division for 15 years. Dr. Salas is a fellow of the American Psychological Association, the Human Factors and Ergonomics Society, and a recipient of the Meritorious Civil Service Award from the Department of the Navy. He received his Ph.D. degree (1984) in Industrial and Organizational Psychology from Old Dominion University.

D. Sandy Staples is an associate professor in the School of Business at Queen's University, Kingston, Canada. His research interests include the enabling role of information systems for virtual work and knowledge management and the assessment of the effectiveness of information systems and IS practices. Sandy has published articles in various journals and magazines, including *Organization Science, Information & Management, Journal of Strategic Information Systems, Journal of Management Information Systems, Communications of the Association of Information Systems, International Journal of Management Reviews, Business Quarterly, Journal of End-User Computing, OMEGA,* and *KM Review.* He is currently an associate editor of *MIS Quarterly* and serves on the editorial boards of other journals.

Teresa Torres-Coronas has a Bachelor's in Economics and a Ph.D. in Management. She won first prize in the 2000 edition of EADA-related management research. She is the author of the book *Valuing Brands* (Ediciones Gestión 2000, Spain), co-author of the book *Retrieve Your Creativity* (Septem Ediciones, Spain), co-editor of the book *Changing the Way You Teach: Creative Tools for Management Education* (Septem Ediciones, Spain, in press), and author of many articles about intangible management and creativity. She is professor at the Universitat Rovira i Virgili (Spain), and she is one of the Spanish associates of the Center for Research in Applied Creativity (in Canada).

Robert M. Verburg joined the faculty of Technology Policy and Management at Delft University of Technology (The Netherlands) in 2002 and is currently an assistant professor of Organizational Psychology. He teaches in the areas of human resource management, organizational psychology, and knowledge management. His current research interests include the strategic management of human resources, knowledge management, coordination mechanisms, and mobile work. Specifically, he is interested in the impact of human resource management on knowledge sharing in organizations. He is a member of a consortium of researchers involved in an international comparative study on mobile working life in Europe.

George S. Vozikis is the Davis D. Bovaird Endowed chairholder of Entrepreneurial Studies and Private Enterprise at The University of Tulsa (USA). He is the founding director of the Family-Owned Business Institute and the Tulsa University Innovation Institute. In addition to numerous journal publications, conference papers, and books, he has served as consultant for many organizations, such as Aramco, Goldstar, McDonnell Douglas, GTE, The Medical University of South Carolina, the U.S. Army Missile Command, and the Williams Companies. He is a past chair of the Entrepreneurship Division of the Academy of Management. Dr. Vozikis is an active researcher in the field of virtual teams.

Index